Barbara Gittings: Gay Pioneer

By Tracy Baim

Foreword by Lillian Faderman
Photos by Kay Lahusen

Prairie Avenue Productions / Chicago

Unless otherwise indicated, photos are from the Barbara Gittings and Kay Tobin Lahusen gay history papers and photographs. Copyright Manuscripts and Archives Division, The New York Public Library.
Cover photo by Lahusen, of Gittings in a Philadelphia Reminder Day protest, mid-1960s.

Prairie Avenue Productions
Chicago, Illinois
Contact: editor@windycitymediagroup.com

This book is available in black-and-white through Amazon, color and black-and-white through CreateSpace.com, and color on Kindle.
Black-and-white edition:
ISBN-13: 13:978-1512019742
ISBN-10: 10:1512019747
Color edition:
ISBN-13: 13:978-1512019780
ISBN-10: 10:151201978X

To all our pioneers:
Thank you for paving the road.

And for William B. Kelley.
Irreplaceable.

Tracy Baim is publisher and executive editor at Windy City Media Group, which produces *Windy City Times, Nightspots*, and other gay media in Chicago. She co-founded *Windy City Times* in 1985 and *Outlines* newspaper in 1987. She has won numerous gay community and journalism honors, including the Community Media Workshop's Studs Terkel Award in 2005 and several Peter Lisagor journalism awards. She started in Chicago gay journalism in 1984 at *GayLife* newspaper, one month after graduating with a news-editorial degree from Drake University.

In 2014, Baim received the Chicago Headline Club Lifetime Achievement Award for her 30 years in journalism. The same year, she was inducted into the National Lesbian and Gay Journalists Association Hall of Fame.

Baim is the editor and co-author of *Gay Press, Gay Power: The Growth of LGBT Community Newspapers in America* (2012), a finalist for a Lambda Literary Award and a Top 10 selection from the American Library Association GLBT Round Table.

She is the author of *Obama and the Gays: A Political Marriage* (2010). She is also the co-author and editor of *Out and Proud in Chicago: An Overview of the City's Gay Community* (2008), the first comprehensive book on Chicago's gay history (the companion website is ChicagoGayHistory.org), and she wrote *Where the World Meets*, a book about Gay Games VII in Chicago (held in 2007, and for which Baim served as co-vice chair of the Gay Games board). Her other recent books include a novel, *The Half Life of Sgt. Jen Hunter*, about lesbians in the military prior to Don't Ask, Don't Tell (a novelization of her stage play *Half Life*, 2005), and the biographies *Leatherman: The Legend of Chuck Renslow*, *Jim Flint: The Boy From Peoria* and *Vernita Gray: From Woodstock to the White House*, all written with Owen Keehnen. She also co-wrote *The Fight for Marriage Equality in the Land of Lincoln* with Kate Sosin in 2014.

Baim was executive producer of the lesbian feature film *Hannah Free*, starring Sharon Gless (2008), and the film *Scrooge & Marley*, a gay *Christmas Carol* (2012). She was inducted into the Chicago Gay and Lesbian Hall of Fame in 1994 and was named a *Crain's Chicago Business* 40 Under 40 leader in 1995. She has received numerous other awards, including one from the international Astraea Lesbian Foundation for Justice.

She is also creator of That's So Gay!, a 2,400-question LGBT history trivia game.

Lillian Faderman is a retired professor and author of numerous books, including her latest, *The Gay Revolution: The Story of the Struggle* (Simon and Schuster, 2015). She was a professor of English at California State University, Fresno, and a visiting professor at UCLA.

Her other books include *Surpassing the Love of Men: Romantic Friendship and Love Between Women from the Renaissance to the Present* (1981); *Scotch Verdict: Miss Pirie and Miss Woods v. Dame Cumming Gordon* (1983); *Odd Girls and Twilight Lovers: A History of Lesbian Life in Twentieth-Century America* (1991); *Chloe Plus Olivia: An Anthology of Lesbian Literature from the 17th Century to the Present* (1994); *To Believe in Women: What Lesbians Have Done for America—A History* (1999); *Naked in the Promised Land: A Memoir* (2003); *Gay L.A.: A History of Sexual Outlaws, Power Politics, and Lipstick Lesbians* (2006); and *My Mother's Wars* (2013).

Faderman's numerous awards include Yale University's James Robert Brudner Memorial Prize for exemplary scholarship on lesbian/gay studies, a Paul Monette award, the Publishing Triangle's Bill Whitehead Award for Lifetime Achievement and Judy Grahn Award for Lesbian Nonfiction, and several Lambda Literary and Stonewall Book awards.

Table of Contents

Acknowledgments

I want to thank Kay Lahusen for allowing me to provide an overview of the life of her amazing partner of 46 years, Barbara Gittings. Kay initially envisioned this to be primarily a photo book, because the many photographs in her collection tell the story of their lives as activists and partners. I thank the New York Public Library for allowing the use of the Lahusen images from its archives, as well as Lahusen and her friends for additional photos for this book.

Many people shared their stories and images with me for this project. Not everything could make it in, but thank you to those who gave of their time, including Patsy Lynch, Karen Ocamb, Randy Wicker and Mark Meinke.

I want to extend my gratitude to the authors, historians, academics and journalists who interviewed Gittings over the years. Their work was especially important in doing this posthumous book. Especially critical were books by Jonathan Ned Katz, Eric Marcus, the Reverend Troy Perry, Thomas Swicegood, Robert Ridinger, Marcia Gallo, and Lahusen herself, for her own book *The Gay Crusaders* as well as her chapter on Gittings for Vern Bullough's book. I also want to acknowledge the work of historian Marc Stein. I recommend two of his books for further details about Gittings' life: *City of Sisterly and Brotherly Loves: Lesbian and Gay Philadelphia, 1945-1972*, and *Rethinking the Gay and Lesbian Movement*.

Thank you also to this book's editors Jorjet Harper and William B. Kelley. Sadly, Kelley died May 17, just as we were finishing this book. His contributions to our community were immense, and I am forever in his debt for his assistance and friendship.

Our book designer was Kirk Williamson, and I had research support from Sarah Zimmerman. Thank you to Judith Armstrong, Lahusen's friend, for providing guidance on this project, and Carole Smith for help in reviewing pages with Lahusen.

Finally, I'd like to acknowledge my appreciation to Marie J. Kuda, a Chicago-area gay historian, who has helped provide support and documents for so many of my LGBT history projects. She, too, is an important gay pioneer. Thanks, Marie, for the historical clues you unearthed that led me to new discoveries in our movement's past.

— *Tracy Baim*

Foreword

Barbara Gittings, who came of age in the conformist 1950s, who wore floral blouses and modest skirts when she paraded in homophile demonstrations in the 1960s, didn't look like a revolutionary. But she was one. She is a crucial figure for anyone interested in the history of the LGBT civil-rights movement—and in *Barbara Gittings: Gay Pioneer*, Tracy Baim lovingly and thoroughly shows why that is so.

Baim's book, the first full-length biography of Barbara Gittings, demonstrates why Frank Kameny, who earned the right to be considered a father of the gay civil-rights movement, so aptly deemed Gittings its mother. As Baim shows, more than any lesbian leader of the 20th century, Gittings kept her eyes sharply focused on the prize of civil rights for gay people. She was undistracted even by the feminist movement that raged in the '70s and '80s. "Where does it hurt the most?" Gittings had asked herself; it was the question that would determine where she put her political energies. She concluded that it wasn't as a female that she'd suffered the most from bigotry and bias; it was as a homosexual. She devoted her life to making that hurt go away not just for herself but for those she called "my people"—the huge community that has come to be dubbed "LGBT."

A few highlights—which *Barbara Gittings: Gay Pioneer* develops in detail, illustrated by Kay Tobin Lahusen's remarkable photographs of Gittings and the early movement:

Gittings' first foray into the homophile movement came in 1956, when she discovered the nascent Daughters of Bilitis that had been founded by Del Martin and Phyllis Lyon the year before. But from the beginning, Gittings was bothered by Daughters of Bilitis' conservative goal to "educate" the lesbian to "adjust" to society, as though the lesbian were an unruly child who needed correction—"a scolding-teacher approach," she thought. Much more to the point, Gittings insisted, was to find a way to educate society—to confront its unreasoning prejudices about homosexuals with intelligent argument and dogged persistence.

In 1963, when Gittings became editor of DOB's magazine, *The Ladder,* she began taking on the "experts"—the psychiatrists whose pronouncements about homosexuality as a sickness had seldom been questioned. They were largely responsible for the prejudices against homosexuals, she believed. Gittings boldly declared of a 1964 New York Academy of Medicine report characterizing homosexuality as a preventable and treatable illness, "It's a reminder of the sly, desperate trend to enforce conformity by a 'sick' label for anything deviant." On Daughters of Bilitis stationery, she sent the Academy of Medicine a letter, reprinted in *The Ladder*, calling the revered "experts" to task. This was one of the first times such a challenge to psychiatric wisdom had been made in print—anywhere.

Gittings' revolutionary fervor was emboldened by Frank Kameny, a brilliant strategist—indeed, the Bayard Rustin of the movement for LGBT civil rights—whom she met shortly after taking over the editorship of *The Ladder*. Gittings opened the pages of *The Ladder* to Kameny's call for homosexuals to stop being "gentlemanly and ladylike." Homosexuals must move from "endless talk to firm, vigorous action," Gittings and Kameny agreed. They urged homosexuals to join them in picketing the White House, the Civil Service Commission, the Department of Defense, the United Nations, Independence Hall: It was time for homosexual American citizens to *demand* of the federal government redress for their grievances, they said.

The Daughters of Bilitis' leadership was never comfortable with Gittings' militancy and her calls for direct action. She was informed by the leadership that DOB would never engage in picketing unless "there were support and involvement from the larger community"—that is, from heterosexuals. Gittings was too bold and revolutionary for DOB. The relationship between her and the organization's leaders became irreparable. Despite the growth in circulation and distribution of the magazine under Gittings, they axed her just after the August 1966 issue went to press.

But that meant that now she had more time to team with Frank Kameny and take on the Defense Department by acting as co-counsel for people such as Benning Wentworth, a civilian worker who'd lost his Defense Department-issued security clearance when it was discovered he was homosexual.

In 1967, Gittings and Kameny invited all the press services, all the major newspaper columnists and national magazines of importance, and the radio and TV networks, too, to attend Wentworth's Defense Department hearing and to report and broadcast freely about the injustices of the department's policy. Homosexuality would be dragged out of the shadows and into the light of day, because homosexuals had nothing to be ashamed of. Barbara Gittings, wearing a big "Equality for Homosexuals" button on the collar of her neat dress, told the reporters—appropriating the rhetoric that had always been used against homosexuals and applying it to Wentworth's accusers: "We consider the very existence of this case to be part of the government's *improper, unethical,* and *immoral* effort to enter into the field of private morality."

A major argument that the Defense Department used to bar homosexuals from security clearance was that they were considered emotionally unstable individuals whose sexuality was a manifestation of their severe neurosis. Defense Department attorneys at the Wentworth hearing called as an "expert" witness Dr. Charles Socarides, a Freudian psychoanalyst who had made a considerable reputation by "curing" homosexuals. Socarides coolly confirmed that homosexuality was a sick adaptation to an unfortunate family constellation, that homosexuals were mentally unsound and unpredictable, that he'd never encountered a healthy homosexual, and that by their very nature homosexuals were poor security risks. But Kameny and Gittings had their turn with Dr. Socarides in cross-examination. During the three hours of their questioning, Socarides' composure morphed to irritation and then agitation as it became clear that Kameny and Gittings were leading him into traps and knocking down his claims. They made his theories look so much like quackery that some weeks later they were formally notified by the Defense Department that Dr. Socarides' name had been taken off the department's list of expert witnesses.

Socarides and his ilk became a major target for Barbara Gittings, who soon decided to take on the entire American Psychiatric Association. She went undercover, became "a sheep in wolf's clothing," as she quipped to Kameny when she infiltrated a 1968 APA meeting in Boston, to see what they were saying about homosexuals. She was outraged by the ubiquitous assumption of the APA members that homosexuality was something to be gotten rid of; and she was horrified by the aversion therapy movies she watched while sitting in an audience of psychiatrists. The top priority of activists needed to be the overturning of the APA's classification of homosexuals as crazies, she and Kameny argued with irrefutable logic. Unless homosexuals were acknowledged to be as mentally sound as the average heterosexual, they'd never be first-class citizens.

After four years of agitation, they managed to get the APA to give them a platform. In 1972, Gittings received a generous grant from the Pennsylvania-based Falk Foundation to pay an architect friend to make a "Gay, Proud and Healthy" booth, which she'd gotten permission to set up in the APA exhibit hall. The booth was constructed of plastic foam so that Gittings could easily transport it from Philadelphia, but it was eye-grabbing. "Gay, Proud, and Healthy: The Homosexual Community Speaks," it announced (to the evident discomfort of those who hurried past but couldn't avoid seeing the message anyway). Never in the history of the APA had there been anything remotely like it: Pictures of happy-looking homosexual couples plastered all over; a whole rack of literature—essays by gays and lesbians on their hurtful experiences with shrinks who tried to cure them; and a display of every bit of important psychiatric writing that challenged the notion that homosexuality was an illness: an article by Dr. Evelyn Hooker on her 1950s study that showed that psychiatric experts could not distinguish between homosexual and heterosexual respondents in blind tests; a study by biologist Frank Beach that concluded that human homosexuality was a reflection of the bisexual character of our mammalian inheritance; an article that had just been published by Dr. Judd Marmor, a vice president of the APA, titled "Homosexuality—Mental Illness or Moral Dilemma?" that strongly refuted the sickness theory.

The word "LOVE," printed in huge white letters on a red background, was the booth's focal point. "The only place at the whole APA convention where that word appears," Gittings pointed out to any psychiatrist who stopped to look at the booth's displays.

But even more remarkable was a panel at the 1972 convention titled "Psychiatry: Friend or Foe to Homosexuals?—A Dialogue," for which Gittings and Kameny had agitated and on which they were invited to participate. They were to be joined by heterosexual psychiatrists Judd Marmor and Robert Seidenberg, who both rejected the pathologizing theories of colleagues such as Charles Socarides. The panel was set at four participants—until Gittings' partner, Kay Tobin Lahusen, came up with a startling suggestion. "You've got two gays who are not psychiatrists and two psychiatrists who are not gay," she said. "What you need now is a gay psychiatrist." Gittings started searching for the fifth panelist.

She knew personally several psychiatrists who were members of a secret gay social group within the APA, who called themselves the GayPA. She was close enough to them that she could joke about being their "fairy godmother." But they refused even to think about participating on the panel because they feared that if their colleagues in the APA knew they were gay they'd never get referrals or respect. They could even lose their licenses. Finally, however, Gittings convinced Dr. John Fryer to agree to do it—in disguise. When Frank Kameny heard of Gittings' offer to disguise Fryer, he was irate. "A masked psychiatrist goes against everything we've been fighting for!" he shouted. He'd find a gay psychiatrist for the panel himself—someone who wouldn't think he had to resort to disguise! But after weeks of trying, with the 1972 conference looming close, Kameny had to concede to Gittings that there was no such animal as an uncloseted psychiatrist.

On the day of the panel, Gittings spirited Fryer into the packed auditorium through a back corridor, so no one would get too close a look at him. He wore a tuxedo that was three sizes too large, a rubber mask of Richard Nixon that went over his head and face and was crimped to look clownlike, and a frizzy fright wig. He was billed as Dr. H. Anonymous. Kameny admitted he'd been wrong about not presenting a gay psychiatrist in disguise: The effect was sensational. But even more important, this was the first time an auditorium packed with psychiatrists heard not only healthy homosexuals talk about homosexuality, and straight psychiatrists talk about healthy homosexuals, but also a homosexual psychiatrist talk about the unscientific prejudices of his colleagues.

The success of the panel that Gittings organized had much to do with the decision the following year by the American Psychiatric Association to take homosexuality out of the *Diagnostic and Statistical Manual of Mental Disorders,* the psychiatrists' bible. The APA had thereby declared that homosexuals were mentally sound. It was a crucial tipping point—a necessary precursor to the many triumphs in LGBT rights that followed over the next 40 years. Gittings' role in struggles such as this one, so well documented by Tracy Baim in *Barbara Gittings: Gay Pioneer*, leaves little doubt that Gittings was, as Frank Kameny called her, "the mother of the gay civil-rights movement."

— Lillian Faderman

Introduction

Her smile was perhaps her biggest asset.

Barbara Gittings countered the vitriol of homophobes by using any tactic at her disposal. Sometimes that was verbal debate. Or wearing a flowery dress, smiling, and carrying a protest sign. Or creative activism with a kissing booth. But mainly, Gittings used her persistence and boundless energy to wear down her enemies, winning victory after victory for the LGBTQ community over the course of her nearly five decades of activism.

Gittings and her colleague Frank Kameny are often viewed as the two most significant and longest-serving activists on behalf of the gay-rights movement, before it even used the term "gay" in a defining way.

Born in 1932, by the mid-1950s Gittings was on her way to a life of activism, launching the New York chapter of the Daughters of Bilitis in 1958, two years after meeting DOB's co-founders, Phyllis Lyon and Del Martin, in California.

By her side for almost all of this work was Kay Tobin Lahusen. The women met in 1961 and were together until Gittings' death. Lahusen became a critical documentarian of the movement. She photographed some of the most important moments of the fledgling community, including the couple's own historic activist moments. She also wrote articles for gay newspapers, as well as chapters on Gittings for key movement books.

Gittings' long association with the Daughters of Bilitis included serving as editor of the group's national magazine, *The Ladder*, from 1963 to 1966. Gittings was becoming upset with the status quo of the homophile movement and soon pushed *The Ladder* in new directions, including using Lahusen's photos of actual lesbians on the cover, replacing the line drawings that had until then dominated the magazine.

As *The Ladder* addressed more controversial issues, including advocacy for more activism, Gittings also started to take to the streets in picket lines and rallies.

Once she had a taste of organizing, Gittings never slowed down, fighting for equality until her death in 2007 at age 74.

In 1965, she joined the pioneers who participated in the first wave of public gay pickets at the White House, at the Pentagon and at Independence Hall in Philadelphia. In subsequent years, Gittings continued attending public protests, especially the Annual Reminders in Philadelphia, where she lived for most of her life.

But she also joined Kameny in efforts to fight against institutional homophobia in a wide variety of places, from the Defense Department to the media.

Two of the biggest institutions she helped to take on were the American Psychiatric Association and the American Library Association. Her groundbreaking efforts to change those two national organizations are among her most important achievements.

Summarizing the life of any one activist can be difficult, but because of the expanse of her work, it is nearly impossible when it comes to the work of Barbara Gittings. This book will provide an overview of her life and work, especially as seen through the eyes of Kay Lahusen and her iconic images of Gittings.

Despite years of work advocating for change against great resistance, Gittings remained an optimist. Her love of music is perhaps what carried her through all the battles.

She was ferocious, tenacious and committed beyond almost anyone else in the movement. And her accomplishments were garnished with that big, charming smile.

— *Tracy Baim*

Kay Lahusen's favorite photo that she took of her partner, Barbara Gittings.
Copyright Manuscripts and Archives Division, The New York Public Library

Chapter 1
Early Years and Family Life

Barbara Brooks Gittings was born to Elizabeth "Mimi" Brooks and John Sterett Gittings on July 31, 1932, in Vienna, Austria, while her father was a diplomat in the U.S. Foreign Service.

Elizabeth was born in New Albany, Indiana, in 1901 or 1902. Her passport application and other records show 1902, but her father's consular registration certificate says 1901. Her sister Katharine was born there in 1896 according to her father's consular registration certificate, but about 1898 by calculation from a census record. The certificate, from the Buenos Aires embassy, says that their father Richards Turner Brooks arrived in Buenos Aires in 1909 to represent the National Paper & Type Company, of New York.

Elizabeth and Katharine (also known as Tante Kay) grew up in Argentina and attended a Swiss finishing school. Barbara, in a family history she produced in the early 1990s, wrote: "Hence at an early age my mother spoke English and Spanish along with French and Italian and German. Despite having little formal education, she became a woman of some sophistication, with fine artistic talent as well."

John's father was a prominent Marylander who at one point was state treasurer. He headed John S. Gittings & Son, then the second-oldest private bank in the South, which had been founded by his grandfather.

Elizabeth was 18 when she married John, 31, and they moved back to the U.S., "then lived in Europe with many moves from capital to capital," where her father worked at various U.S. embassies, Barbara wrote. Barbara's sister Eleanor was born in 1925 in Riga, Latvia; John Jr. was born in 1929 in Prague, Czechoslovakia. In the 1930 census, Elizabeth and John, with children Eleanor and John, were living in Helsinki (known as Helsingfors), Finland. Barbara was born in Austria two years later. A later passport application by Elizabeth is stamped with the notation that her husband was assigned to Berlin in 1935.

Barbara wrote that her father "suffered a nervous breakdown and left the diplomatic service in the mid-1930s … . He became ever more engrossed in his religiosity (Catholicism) and he came to lead a rather somber and anti-social life."

Elizabeth, who had "no special religious orientation of her own," according to Barbara, had declined to "turn Catholic" upon marrying John. But she agreed to raise the children Catholic, as a condition of her marriage. "This promise had profound effects on her life and her family," Barbara wrote. She and her siblings attended an academically demanding Catholic boarding school in Montreal, Canada. "We were withdrawn and brought back to the States when the U.S. entered World War II," Barbara wrote. The family moved to Wilmington, Delaware, where Barbara went to Catholic school and later to public junior and senior high schools.

"My life was so steeped in bilingual Catholicism that for a time I wanted to become a nun," Barbara told Kay Lahusen for Kay's book *The Gay Crusaders*.

Barbara also felt resentment for her brother John Jr., as he was favored by her mother. He experienced a trauma, having been molested by a priest at around age 9. His father insisted it be dealt with by another priest, though his mom and others had wanted him to see a psychiatrist. Barbara wrote that her mother felt the incident "shattered him," and that later in life Elizabeth begged her son for forgiveness. He died in 1988, preceding his mother's 1995 death. John Sr. had died in 1961.

"Except for Tante Kay and my maternal grandparents, I did not much like the family into which I was born, and I have created my own family," Barbara wrote. "My mother and my sister and I just are not on the same wave-length."

Emotional Changes

Barbara's feelings for other females started in eighth grade.

"I carried the torch for one particular girl all through high school in Wilmington, Delaware, but it was not reciprocated. I got to see a lot of her in extracurricular activities, and we also double-dated," Gittings told author Eric Marcus, for his book *Making History: The Struggle for Gay and Lesbian Equal Rights, 1945–1990.* "I think if I were to look at my high school records today, they would be shot through with comments from my teachers saying, 'This child is homosexual,' or 'This child is becoming queer,' or whatever words they would have used in that day. I think it must have been very obvious to them, but it wasn't obvious to me because I was still pretty naïve.

"A little later in my high school career, one of my teachers tried to warn me that I would have a difficult time ahead in college. I can't remember the context, but she used the word *homosexual* as a label for me. I kind of knew what it meant in a vague intellectual sense, but it didn't seem to apply to me. I didn't really put the two together until I went to college. By the way, I found out later that I had been rejected for a kind of high school honor society that I was otherwise qualified for, on the grounds of character. I think the character problem had something to do with my obvious homosexual leanings."

In 1949, Gittings went west for college, to Northwestern University in Evanston, a northern suburb of Chicago. Gittings' mother left her with a warning to avoid certain kinds of women she might meet, according to Lahusen, who wrote the chapter on Gittings for Vern L. Bullough's book *Before Stonewall: Activists for Gay and Lesbian Rights in Historical Context.* Gittings was "labeled a lesbian because of a close but platonic friendship she had with another student. She was the last to hear of this rumor—from the dormitory director," Lahusen wrote.

Gittings attempted to seek professional help—from a psychiatrist. This would lead to an activist passion for Gittings, to fight against the psychiatric world's treatment of homosexuality as an illness.

The Reverend Troy D. Perry and Thomas L.P. Swicegood detailed Gittings' 1949 psychiatric visit in their book *Profiles in Gay & Lesbian Courage.* An excerpt follows.

The psychiatrist, a woman, was all business—but that suited her seventeen-year-old client, who would pay for the visit out of her allowance. "You're a freshman at Northwestern?" asked the doctor. "Yes."

"And you've had some trouble?"

"No, but they say I'm ... I don't know if I am. My girlfriend at school won't see me anymore—because of what's been said. I want to find out if it's true. And how other students can know, if I don't know myself?"

... "You have to relax," [the doctor] said, "I'll listen, and you will put before me the evidence of your life. When you're done, I'll give you an answer if that is possible." ...

"I had no dislike for boys," Barbara told the psychiatrist, "but in high school, I felt a special kind of interest for girls. After graduation, I wanted to go to California to study drama, but my father said it was too far and would cost too much. So I came to Northwestern instead. I became a friend, just a friend, with one girl I particularly liked. That's when the whispering began. Now my girlfriend is frightened—and keeps her distance from me—as if we'd done something wrong."

... "So tell me," she said, "am I a homosexual or not?"
"You are definitely homosexual," the psychiatrist replied.
There was no equivocation.
Later, a friend declared, "That psychiatrist shouldn't have labeled you."
"On the contrary," replied Barbara, "she did me a favor by giving me the information—and I appreciated it—although I never returned to her office. Sure, she put a tag on me, and proposed to 'cure' me with extensive—and expensive—psychotherapy. But at least the penny dropped. I knew who I was. I was a homosexual. And that was fine. My next step was that I had to find out what being a homosexual meant! Homosexuality was a mystery as far as I was concerned, and solving that mystery became a consuming desire.

"At that time, most newspapers wouldn't print the word homosexual, *much less discuss anything about it of a positive nature. Nor was homosexuality considered subject for polite discussion, even among friends. Television shows wouldn't touch the topic. Visible gay role models didn't exist. So, I very soon discovered, my path toward better understanding was actually leading me into badly charted territory."*

While she did love the glee club, and singing remained a passion throughout her life, Gittings didn't last long at college. It was her love of books that saved her, and contributed to her lifelong commitment to books and libraries—and set her on another of her activist missions.

"I flunked out [of college freshman year] because that was the year I put the homosexual label on myself and tried to come to terms with what it meant to be gay," she told Marcus. "I stopped going to classes and started going to the library and ended up with a lot of incompletes which turned into failures. I haven't returned to college since. But despite the fact that I failed all my classes, I learned a great deal that year. I wanted to know what my life was going to be like. I also started to try to find my people. The first place I found them was in books. Oh, I devoured everything! I looked myself up in the books on abnormal psychology. I tried to find myself in legal books. I tried to find myself in encyclopedias. I found everything I possibly could.

"What I found was puzzling. It was me they were talking about, but it wasn't me at all. It was very clinical; it didn't speak of love; it didn't have very much humanity to it. They were talking about some kind of condition, an alien condition that was a departure from the norm. It was possibly treatable, but possibly not. There was something wrong with people like this—everything I read said that we were deviants. So that's what I thought about myself."

Jonathan Ned Katz, for his book *Gay American History*, interviewed Gittings on July 19, 1974. She recalled her research: "At one extreme I remember a scientific study in which a group of male heterosexuals and a group of male homosexuals were compared for micrometric measurements of their bodies—the diameter of the cranium, the circumference of the neck, the length of the nose, the length of the earlobe, the circumference at the hips—to see if there were significant differences between the two groups. The fact that it was about male homosexuals really didn't bother me that much. Most of the material was on male homosexuals. But I couldn't see that there were significant body differences, so this kind of study puzzled me. And then at the other extreme there'd be pop-level material which said 'the homosexual's favorite color is green.' That upset me, because my favorite color was blue. I actually thought I ought to change my color preference, in order to fit in. I did believe for a while that there were group characteristics that applied to all homosexuals. But then I began to say, 'Well, no, there must be different kinds of homosexuals. They can't all be that much alike.'"

"It was necessary to spend a tremendous amount of time just searching for homosexual topics in print, even though there usually was not much substance," Gittings told Perry and Swicegood. "Nevertheless, every encyclopedia was rifled by me for tidbits of information. And I was not deterred in my quest even by the necessity of looking up homosexuality under such headings as 'abnormal,' 'perverted,' or 'deviate.'"

Eventually, a few books helped her navigate this brave new world. She didn't just stick to the library at school—she went to facilities all over Chicago and the suburbs.

"The closest I got to some sense of gay people with personalities and real lives was in Havelock Ellis' book, of all things, *Studies in the Psychology of Sex*, his famous two-volume work, which was published in the 1930s," she told Marcus. "It was full of good stuff because you could find something to identify with in most of the people Ellis wrote about, even if they sounded very peculiar."

While nonfiction could not fully meet Gittings' needs, novels were another story. "They had their moments of happiness, even if the endings were terrible," she said. "It made me feel better about myself. You could take a novel like the great classic, *The Well of Loneliness*, which was my first big gay novel."

The Well of Loneliness was written by Radclyffe Hall. The book, first published in 1928, was targeted by James Douglas, editor of the *Sunday Express*, who wrote, "I would rather give a healthy boy or a healthy girl a phial of prussic acid than this novel." The book did survive censorship battles in the U.S.

"A tragic story—very overwritten, of course, and a very unhappy ending," Gittings said of the book. "But even though the heroine was a moneyed Englishwoman of good breeding, who had horses, a place in the country, and rich parents, who lived a rich life in Paris, which was nothing like my life, I could feel what she was feeling."

Gittings told Perry and Swicegood that "locating material on homosexuality occupied most of my time. Other studies were just incidental. That showed my priorities. I had no thought other than to solve the riddle of who I was, and the problem of what my life was going to be."

With failing grades, she returned to Wilmington. Her family was not very communicative, so the subject was not discussed. She took a course in abnormal psychology, which gave her access to more books on homosexuality, and led to a short love affair with a young woman in the class.

But her father sent her a letter—while they lived under the same roof—as a way to communicate with her. He wanted to let her know that *The Well of Loneliness* book had been discovered in her bedroom, telling her it was banned immediately from their home.

"We were living in the same house, and he couldn't bring himself to talk to me about it," she told Katz. "He sent me a letter telling me this was an immoral book, that I had no business owning it, and that I should dispose of it. Not by giving it away, where someone else would be contaminated by it; I had to dispose of it by burning. Well, I simply hid it better and told him I had disposed of it. This incident reinforced my sense of taboo about the subject matter."

She had nobody else to talk to about the issue. "So I went looking in the bars. I didn't have much success talking to people in the bars, especially about the literature," she said to Katz. "These were women's bars in New York City. I had great difficulty in finding women who had read the same books I had. It was important to me to meet other lesbians as lesbians, but I still needed more than that. I needed to find lesbians who shared my interests. Once when I went to a bar in New York City I had with me Colette's very first novel, from Philadelphia Free Library, one of the Claudine series, *Claudine à l'école,* and it happened to have illustrations. There was an illustration of Claudine's two female schoolteachers who were having an affair—one sitting on the lap of the other, embracing very ardently. I was fascinated by the novel, and fascinated by the picture, a line drawing. It seemed to me very bold to have a picture like that in a book published early in the twentieth century for the general public. I was in this bar and trying to talk to somebody—and I showed her this book, and this drawing, trying to make her understand why this is such a remarkable illustration, and she says, 'Oh, at home I've got a lot sexier pictures than that.' I didn't understand what she meant; now I do!"

But the letter from her father was a warning sign to Gittings. At age 18 she moved to Philadelphia to make it on her own.

Lahusen wrote in the Bullough book: "She settled in a rooming house, did frugal cooking on a hot plate, got a job clerking in a music store, and found a choral group to sing in. She took up hiking and biking and canoeing. She was making her own life. Even her own father admired her spunk and [six months after she moved out] wrote a formal note 'relieving you of the onus of your disobedience' in running away from home. Despite his moralistic views, she seems to have been his favorite child."

In 1954, Barbara again visited a psychiatrist, at her own choosing. In her files at the New York Public Library, there are letters back and forth between her father and Dr. Paul J. Poinsard—Barbara was complaining about the treatment of her personality problems.

Her father wrote to Poinsard on August 26 that he felt his daughter's problems were "a form of stubbornness, or pride, or inability to accept any suggestions or advice that happen to go contrary to her own position in any given instance." He asked for a treatment outside of psychiatry that might help her.

"We have all heard of people changing by 'falling in love'; doubtless a quaint thing nowadays," John Sterett wrote. "And there is always, of course, the grace of God, in which I, for one, deeply believe. However, the first cannot be produced at will and the second is likewise not readily and invariably available."

On September 9, 1954, Poinsard wrote to John Sterett, in part: "As long as her conscious and unconscious conflicts continue to plague her, there is no effective means that I know of resolving them other than continuing psychiatric treatment. Involuntarily, even this will not have any guarantee of cure." It's not clear what the problem is from these letters, except that Barbara herself was seeking help, for what her father deemed as "stubbornness." The psychiatrist suggests she continue to live away from home, but not alone, perhaps getting a "congenial roommate."

Poinsard went on to write that he felt Barbara was working at a job "beneath her potentialities."

"Underneath [my father] seemed to like my independent spirit," Gittings said about her father, in *Crusaders*. He died in 1961 before becoming aware of Barbara's involvement in the gay-rights movement.

Barbara's first forays into the gay world were not easy. She said in *Gay Crusaders*: "I felt there was no real place for me in the straight culture, but the gay bar culture wasn't the place for me either. It was a painful and confusing time in my life.

"I wore drag because I thought that was a way to show I was gay. It's changed now, but in the early '50s there were basically two types of women in the gay bars, the so-called butch ones in short hair and plain masculine attire and the so-called femme ones in dresses and high heels and makeup. I knew high heels and makeup weren't my personal style, so I thought, well, I must be the other kind! And I dressed accordingly. What a waste of time and energy! I was really a mixed-up kid."

Gittings' first serious relationship was with a Black writer and poet who attended Swarthmore College. When their half-year affair ended, Gittings, in her early 20s at this point, said she "fell apart in a way," but then returned to a job she had at an architectural firm, and continued her search for the gay movement.

It seemed Gittings was already set on the path that would consume the rest of her life. She was homosexual, she loved books, and she wanted to fight against a system that would treat her as if she were sick.

Barbara Gittings as a young child.
Copyright Manuscripts and Archives Division, The New York Public Library

A childhood home of Gittings, in Wilmington, Delaware.
Courtesy of Kay Tobin Lahusen

Right: Barbara (middle) with her siblings John and Eleanor.
Copyright Manuscripts and Archives Division, The New York Public Library

Below: The Gittings family at Rehoboth Beach, Delaware, taken on or about August 31, 1939. Parents Elizabeth "Mimi" Brooks and John Sterett Gittings, with Barbara (front) and her siblings John and Eleanor.
Copyright Manuscripts and Archives Division, The New York Public Library

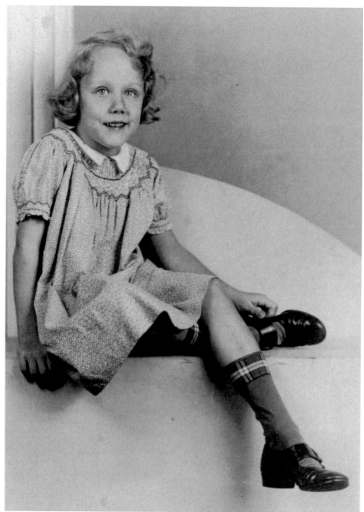

Two photos showing the young Barbara.
Copyright Manuscripts and Archives Division, The New York Public Library

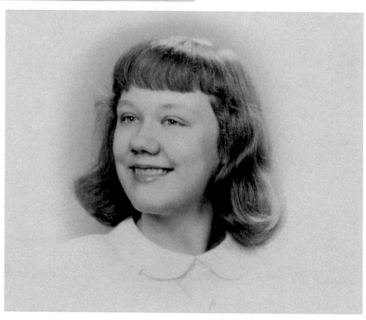

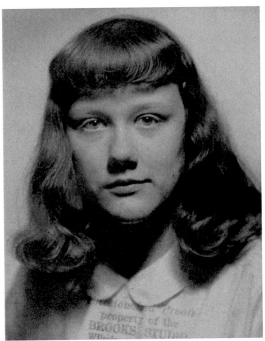 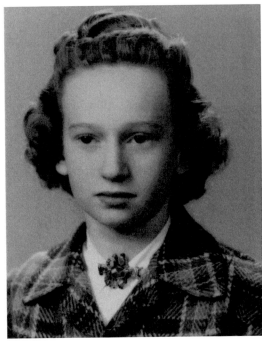

Photos of the young Barbara Gittings and Kay Tobin Lahusen. Below, Barbara shows her free-spirited nature.
Copyright Manuscripts and Archives Division, The New York Public Library

Copy of letter from Barbara's father, John Sterett Gittings, to Dr. Paul J. Poinsard, a psychiatrist to whom Barbara had been referred.

August 26, 1954

Dear Dr. Poinsard:

This is to acknowledge your letter of August 20, received August 23.

It would have taken us completely by surprise, save that Barbara—who was here for that weekend—had inadvertently let something slip. This led to questioning and then it was learned that your letter was on its way.

At our insistence, Barbara then told us what had occurred, giving us, quite naturally, her side of the story; citing verbatim from her letters to you. We are sorry indeed about that sort of pinpointing, but it is only a sample of what has been dished out here, from time to time, over the years!

As I personally see the problem (from a purely lay point of view) Barbara's basic trouble is a form of stubbornness, or pride, or inability to accept any suggestions or advice that happen to go contrary to her own position in any given instance. Naturally psychiatry has a more involved formula and doubtless an explanation.

We would of course be interested in a possible explanation. But what is sorely needed at this juncture—if you feel like giving it—is a suggestion for a practical and inexpensive programme, outside of psychiatric treatment, towards overcoming this trouble.

Would it be possible, therefore, for you to give us a résumé of Barbara's character, temperament, etc., (as observed by you) and a hint or two concerning counter-measures? I am speaking here of measures on a simple non-scientific every-day living-plane.

I do not suggest that future psychiatry in Barbara's case is absolutely ruled out, but one cannot wait for further months, maybe years, of study and trial, with possible additional failures. Some practical programme is needed and needed now.

We have all heard of people changing by "falling in love": doubtless a quaint thing nowadays. And there is always, of course, the grace of God, in which I, for one, deeply believe. However, the first cannot be produced at will and the second is likewise not readily and invariably available.

So, Dr. Poinsard, any ideas you feel like offering will be gratefully received. Again our apologies for the somewhat rough time you have had.

You will, I take it, let me hear about my pending indebtedness.

Cordially yours,

**Barbara and her mother,
Elizabeth Brooks Gittings.**
Courtesy of Kay Tobin Lahusen

**Kay and Barbara with
Gittings' mother (left) and
aunt Katharine Batchelder.**
Courtesy of Kay Tobin Lahusen

Gittings with her Aunt Katharine, also referred to as Tante Kay.
Courtesy of Kay Tobin Lahusen

Gittings reads in front of a portrait of her maternal grandmother.
Courtesy of Kay Tobin Lahusen

Chapter 2
Daughters of Bilitis,
The Ladder, and Love

Barbara Gittings and Kay Tobin Lahusen met at a Rhode Island picnic in 1961. Gittings was 29; Lahusen, 31. As with almost everything in Gittings' life, the circumstance revolved around activism—in this case, a party for *The Ladder*, a national publication of the lesbian group Daughters of Bilitis (DOB).

Five years earlier, in 1956, Gittings discovered DOB through connections to a homosexual organization, the Mattachine Society, which had an affiliate in New York City.

The original Mattachine was organized in 1950, 26 years after the first known U.S. homosexual rights group, the Society for Human Rights, was founded in Illinois by a homosexual postal worker, Henry Gerber. Harry Hay, Mattachine's chief organizer, first thought about starting a homosexual group in 1948, and it took two years to launch Mattachine.

In 1952, members of the group broke off to form ONE, Inc., and started the first long-lasting publication of the homophile movement, *ONE*. The first issue of *ONE* magazine was published in January 1953, produced by W. Dorr Legg (who sometimes used the pseudonym William Lambert), Martin Block, Dale Jennings and Don Slater. Started in Los Angeles, *ONE* soon had a national following. By November 1953, its subhead was "The Homosexual Magazine." The Los Angeles postmaster declared *ONE* "obscene" in October 1954, and it took four years for *ONE* to win its case, which ended in the U.S. Supreme Court.

Members of the Mattachine Society's San Francisco chapter wanted their own publication, the *Mattachine Review*, and it served an important role in documenting the gay movement from its founding in 1955 through 1967. Some of the other Mattachine Society chapters had their own publications.

Meanwhile, DOB, founded in San Francisco in 1955 by Phyllis Lyon and Del Martin with the encouragement of their friend Rose Bamberger, was groundbreaking in its own way. It provided a place for lesbians, because many of them felt uncomfortable in the male-dominated Mattachine Society.

DOB eventually had chapters across the country, and its publication, *The Ladder,* was a critical part of the growing lesbian movement. *The Ladder* started in 1956, when it was edited by Lyon, and ran monthly through 1970 and then every other month through 1972. *The Ladder*'s name was related to an image on the publication's first cover: a line drawing of women moving toward a ladder that ascended into the clouds.

Like some other early alternative newsletters, initially it was typed on a typewriter, mimeographed, stapled and sent through the mails to subscribers. It was distributed in a "brown paper bag." Even gay publications into the 1990s sent their magazines through the mail in envelopes, not free-standing, so as not to out subscribers. In later years, copies of *The Ladder* were sold on newsstands. By the end of the 1950s, there were several hundred subscribers to *The Ladder*.

"I was so glad to find that my people existed, that there was literature about them, and a literature that portrayed them as human beings," Gittings told author Jonathan Ned Katz in 1974. "There was definitely a sense of community, and for history, conveyed by the novels; I really appreciated them enormously—I started collecting. I used to go to the secondhand bookstores and search out the titles, starting with the list in Donald Webster Cory's *The Homosexual in America,* which was remarkable.

"I even wrote to the publisher, and found that Cory lived in New York City. [Cory's real name was Edward Sagarin.] I had two or three meetings with him to discuss the literature. I was keenly interested in seeing what more there was. I must admit I hadn't done any analysis of his book. I was simply interested in compiling a large list of literature, finding out what was available, getting to see it for myself. Cory also told me about the existence of ONE, Inc., and the Mattachine Society out in Los Angeles and San Francisco. In the summer of 1956, I made a trip out there—I guess I made it for that reason. I went to the offices of ONE in Los Angeles, and they told me about the Mattachine Society in San Francisco and about a relatively new organization called the Daughters of Bilitis who, fortuitously, were having a meeting that very evening [at someone's apartment]—and I went. That was my first contact with Daughters of Bilitis. ...

"That was the first time I had sat down with a dozen or 15 lesbians outside of a bar situation. It was very appealing to me, it was something I had been looking for, the chance to be with people of my own kind in a setting other than the bars. ... There were about 15 women discussing the business of putting out a periodical. I had to do a great deal of listening to try to understand. Even then I was pretty assertive, because I sounded off about the name of the organization. Having just heard about it, and having just been invited by these nice people, I said the name was too complicated, too long, too difficult to pronounce, too difficult to spell, and what the hell, Bilitis was a bisexual fictional character anyway, not even a real person, not even truly a homosexual. What were they doing with a name like that? It wasn't very nice of me, but they seemed to take it with reasonably good spirits. They must have already been accustomed to having upstart lesbians coming up out of nowhere and coming to their meetings. So I wasn't anything special. Del Martin and Phyllis Lyon were very much the leaders. They definitely ran the show. They had strong ideas, and they saw to it that they were carried out."

Chance Encounter

Kay Lahusen was born January 5, 1930, in Cincinnati, Ohio. She grew up in a multi-generational household. Kay went to the Cincinnati College Preparatory Schools for first through tenth grade, and then to Withrow High School. She went to the University of Cincinnati for one year, and then completed her college education at Ohio State University.

She remembers crushes on girls in her school and women in the movies, especially Katharine Hepburn.

She told Marcus:

"You can't hide those things—my word, at that age, you don't even think to hide them. Of course, my family was aware of what I was doing, and I remember a couple of disapproving remarks. But I had barely heard the word homosexual at that time, and I had no sense of being one myself. So I didn't realize the implications of what I was doing.

"The summer after I graduated, in 1948, I met a girl who had gone to the same high school I had. We hadn't met before. I fell in love with her. She fell in love with me. She had had a little experience, so we very quickly developed a physical relationship. For a year I thought it was the world's greatest friendship. But after a year together, I finally faced the fact that this was more than friendship. This was desire and sex and lust and love, just like straight people feel. I have to tell you, I had a breakdown over this revelation. I literally had to go to bed and lie down. I was totally weak. It was like a hammer was pounding my head. This went on for two weeks.

"I was raised by my grandparents in a partly Christian Science household, so they arranged for a Christian Science practitioner to come to the house and pray over me. Of course, I wasn't about to tell her what I was agonizing over. And I couldn't turn to my lover because she wasn't the strong one. So I finally brought it to a head within myself, I just decided that I was right and the world was wrong and that there couldn't be anything wrong with this kind of love. I had a quick healing, but I had a hard time convincing my lover that there was nothing wrong with what we were doing. She felt that our love was really not right but, of course, she loved it. You know how it is, forbidden love—this is so wrong, but it feels so good.

"In any case, we had a difficult relationship. She went to Ohio State, so I went there to be with her even though I was supposed to go to a small, wonderful liberal arts school. Her family didn't have the means to send her to one, so I went where she went. We were together in the dormitory. I remember those incidents where somebody opened the door when we were about to embrace and we jumped apart and wondered what they thought. … One time, the dorm mother caught two girls in bed together. That incident in itself was totally shocking, but what put [those] girls beyond the pale was that they were sort of butch-femme, which we weren't. They were even shocking to me because of that. I saw them on the bus one night holding hands and I thought, My God, what a terrible thing to do in public. I was against that kind of display back then. Oh, and to top it all off, one was black and the other was white! Well, they broke every rule.

"When the dorm mother caught these two girls, what did she do, first thing? She turned to my lover and said, 'I found these girls. What should I do? How do I handle this?' I forget what Jane (a pseudonym) said to her, but Jane was all upset and wouldn't touch me for two weeks! It was totally traumatic for us. The other girls were separated. They had to have separate rooms and they were warned that they would be tossed out of school, or out of the dorm, whatever it was, if they were found together again. Of course, we didn't go near them. God forbid—they had been tainted; their cover was blown.

"We were together all through school and for another two years afterward. Jane had always told me that she wanted to get married and have children. She came from a Jewish family where the whole purpose in life was to get married and have children. Not only that, she wanted to be Miss Wonderful in the larger community. She wanted to be looked up to, and she couldn't be if she was a lousy lesbian. Six years we were lovers!

"There are some people who are gay but don't have the strength to go against the crowd. I'm glad to say that it's not so hard to go against the crowd anymore, but back then, it was very hard. Jane finally came to the point where she said to me, 'I agree with you that there isn't anything intrinsically wrong with our loving each other, but we cannot have a good life together because there's no way we can integrate ourselves into the world. We'll always be this separate little twosome off to the side without any friends.'

"Jane met a guy she liked and he liked her, and they got married. … I never spoke to her again. Never! I tore up every photo and threw it all in the garbage. I was devastated. Jane was a very central thing in my life. I tried to find some solace in religion. I tried to find a way to love men, which didn't work because I couldn't just conjure up those feelings. So even though I had a couple of quick liaisons with men, it wasn't true to my nature. There just wasn't any real love there. I liked them. I didn't love them."

Lahusen moved to Boston to work for *The Christian Science Monitor* in the reference library, doing research for the writers and editors. She was there from 1956 to 1961. She told Marcus: "I had worked in the reference library for several years when the light bulb went on, and I said to myself, I'm researching every other damn subject in the world for all these writers and editors, why don't I research what interests me most in this world? So I went to the reference books and looked up homosexuality. *The Christian Science Monitor* filed homosexuality under *vice*. When you looked under the listing for *homosexuality,* it said, 'See Vice.' That got me! I used to argue with some of the other staff about that. Of course, I didn't say that I was gay. I pretended to argue purely as an intellectual exercise. There was hardly any material; you hardly ever even saw the word. Some British spy was found, and he was homosexual. Or an occasional shrink would say something."

Lahusen came out to a Christian Science practitioner who was British. She told Lahusen: "Well, what of it? One of my good friends is in California, and she is homosexual."

"She agreed with me that the church was just very culture bound and that it had the biases of the general culture. She was very reinforcing," Lahusen said.

Lahusen found out about *The Ladder* from a psychiatrist in New York City.

"In doing my research at the *Monitor*, I found a book called *Voyage From Lesbos: The Psychoanalysis of a Female Homosexual,* written by a psychiatrist named Richard Robertiello," she told Marcus. "In the book, Robertiello focused on a lesbian he had treated—and believed—cured. He was a well-known psychoanalyst at the time. So in 1961 I made an appointment with him in New York. I asked him a couple of questions about what made people gay, which I wasn't really interested in. Then I came to the real question, 'How do I meet others?' So he said, 'Oh, if that's what you want, that's easy.' He reached over on his desk and pulled out this old copy of *The Ladder* and gave it to me. He said, 'Here. This is published by the Daughters of Bilitis. They have an office here in New York. You can call them up. Here's the phone number.' Well, I almost fell off the chair. I said, 'That's enough,' and even though I only spent 10 minutes with him, I wrote him my check for $20 for the full hour. I was lifted to the skies, but I was so thrown I couldn't even think of contacting DOB that minute. I had to regroup. I drove back to Boston on a cloud.

"When I got back to Boston, I read my copy of *The Ladder*. I could see they were trying to improve things for lesbians and that they were providing a [kaffeeklatsch] kind of meeting place for lesbians, as well as opportunities to meet by working in the organization. So I said to myself, This is it! I can improve things in the world for gay people and I can meet other women. I will join this group and I will work in it until I find somebody. If I join the New York chapter and don't find anybody, I'll go to Chicago and join the Chicago chapter. If I don't find anybody there, I'll go to San Francisco. I'll do whatever it takes. I didn't see myself going on for years not finding anybody.

"So I wrote to DOB in New York, and who got my letter but Barbara. I wrote that I wanted to come to the next meeting and participate. Barbara was going on a trip to California, but she said I should come to the meeting in New York. So the day of the meeting, I got in my car and drove down to the DOB office. Well, I imagined this big place with a lot of people. When I got there, it was like this postage-stamp office that they shared with the Mattachine Society. The office could accommodate no more than 10 people, but only five came: Marion Glass, Florence Conrad from California, two others, and me. I was very much in the spotlight. Here was this stranger from *The Christian Science Monitor* in Boston! I had driven all that way, and they were all wondering what the hell I was going to look like and be like. I remember I was just in a sweat, and I think my face was red. My heart was probably pounding. …

"As I quickly learned, the purpose of DOB was to get gay people to jack themselves up. If you were a lesbian, you were to put on a skirt and join the human race."

Soon after that meeting, Lahusen met Gittings. Lahusen quickly became immersed in the world of homosexual activism and publishing. "After a brief courtship, we settled into her efficiency apartment in Philadelphia. We've been together in the gay cause ever since," Lahusen wrote in Bullough's book.

East Coast Expansion

In 1958, Gittings had launched the East Coast chapter of DOB, in New York City. She served as the chapter's first president, ending that role in 1961. That same year, she met Lahusen.

"I've always been a joiner," Gittings told Lahusen for *Gay Crusaders*. "Some people just like to get in there and pitch. And at the same time, the idea that there were organizations of the people I identified with most closely was extremely appealing."

From 1963 until the summer of 1966, Gittings edited *The Ladder*, and Lahusen joined her in working on the publication—and contributing photos for its covers.

"I kept the job because I found that I liked being editor. I liked the power," Gittings told Troy Perry and Thomas Swicegood. "Suddenly I had a new way of expressing things. Not that I wrote editorials or articles for the magazine—I wasn't good at that. But I understood how to use the prerogative of an editor—to choose, to deliberately seek what needed to be written. Although Kay's name didn't appear on the masthead, her vision, as much as mine, shaped the magazine for three and a half years. It was Kay who introduced the photographic portraits of real lesbians on the cover of *The Ladder,* a historic breakthrough. … Kay and I believed we could eventually reach tens of thousands of lesbians who had never heard about our movement, lesbians who didn't necessarily want to join us but needed to see themselves in a better light, who needed to know that they were not alone, that something was being done to change things."

Gittings spoke with Katz about her development as a lesbian and the founding and early history of the New York Daughters of Bilitis. There was a Mattachine convention in New York City in 1958, and on Sunday, September 7, there was a meeting called "for all women in the New York area who are interested in forming a chapter of the DOB," according to Katz. Gittings said the meeting was on Sixth Avenue, "a small loft building where the Mattachine had offices. I think only about eight or 10 of us met. A notice had been sent out to DOB's mailing list contacts in the New York area, and I suppose to women who were on the Mattachine mailing list.

"Our motives were pretty hazy. We didn't have any clear sense of what we were going to do. It just seemed enough that lesbians were getting together. Just sheer survival of the group was important at first. Even though we had San Francisco DOB's four-part statement of purpose when we started the New York chapter, the discussions were awfully vague and groping. We kept seeking for ways of making the meetings interesting, without having clearly said to ourselves, 'What exactly are we meeting for?' We continued in a rather chaotic condition for a very long time. Most of the time it was just, 'Well, of course we should continue; when will the next meeting be?' It was taken for granted that it was desirable to continue.

"DOB had its four-part statement of purpose printed inside the front cover of *The Ladder,* and that, supposedly, provided guidelines for us. The Daughters of Bilitis was defined as 'A Women's Organization for the Purpose of Promoting the Integration of the Homosexual Into Society … .' The word 'lesbian' was not used once."

Four purposes were listed:

1. Education of the variant … to enable her to understand herself and make her adjustment to society … this to be accomplished by establishing … a library … on the sex deviant theme; by sponsoring public discussions … to be conducted by leading members of the legal, psychiatric, religious and other professions; by advocating a mode of behavior and dress acceptable to society.

2. Education of the public … leading to an eventual breakdown of erroneous taboos and prejudices …

3. Participation in research projects by duly authorized and responsible psychologists, sociologists, and other such experts directed towards further knowledge of the homosexual.

4. Investigation of the penal code as it pertains to the homosexual, proposal of changes … and promotion of these changes, through the due process of law in the state legislatures.

Gittings commented on these to Katz: "'Education of the variant,' not even the word '*lesbian!*' 'Adjustment' became a major controversy phrase later on. The idea of having gay people speak was totally foreign to us at the time. It never occurred to us in those early days that we could speak for ourselves, that we had the expert knowledge on ourselves. We were the ones explored, but we thought we needed the intervention of experts to do the exploring. Homosexuality had traditionally been the domain of people in law, religion, and the behavioral sciences."

Gittings explained to Katz why *The Ladder* included what might now be called homophobic "experts": "At first we were [so] grateful just to have people—anybody—pay attention to us that we listened to and accepted everything they said, no matter how bad it was. That is how different the consciousness at the time was. But, I must emphasize, it was essential for us to go through this before we could arrive at what we now consider our much more sensible attitudes. You don't just spring full-blown into an advanced consciousness. You do it step by step. Well, this was an important first step. We invited people who were willing to come to our meetings; obviously, it turned out to be those who had a vested interest in having us as penitents, clients, or patients.

"It's hard for you who came in later to understand. Just to be mentioned, no matter what they said, was important at first. It broke the taboo of silence about homosexuality—anything that helped break the silence, no matter how backward, how silly and foolish it may look to us today, was important. The first publications, the first discussion groups and lectures and panels—these carried a lot of weight with us. When somebody with professional credentials came to address your meetings, that legitimized the existence of your organization. And then when you went out and approached other people, you could say that Dr. So and So or the Rev. So and So had addressed you; that made you less pariahlike to these other people whom you needed."

Gittings said this approach changed even prior to the 1969 Stonewall rebellion: "[All] these consciousness changes were definitely fomenting in the '60s, well before Stonewall. The one thing that Stonewall represents, in my view, is a sudden burgeoning of grassroots activity. It doesn't represent a distinctly changed consciousness in the movement. The militancy—the 'we are the experts, not these non-gays'—all that developed well before Stonewall, thanks largely to Frank Kameny; he was the first one who articulated a complete, coherent philosophy for the gay movement."

The Unstoppable Force of Kameny

Kameny and Gittings maintained a similar worldview on how to combat society's approach to homosexuality, and they fought side by side for decades. But in her 1974 interview with Katz, Gittings was already impressed with how far the movement had come since 1961, when Kameny stepped into activism full-force after losing his court battle to keep his job as an astronomer with the U.S. Army's Map Service. He had been fired for being homosexual, and though he lost at the U.S. Supreme Court, his was the first civil-rights claim based on sexual orientation ever to reach the high court. He founded the Mattachine Society of Washington that year, and began to work with others to seek change.

Perry and Swicegood summarized Kameny's case for their book *Profiles in Gay & Lesbian Courage*:

"Dr. Kameny was a brilliant physicist-astronomer who, because federal agents had viciously disrupted his life, boldly transformed himself into a gay activist of major importance. Kameny had been summarily fired from a civil service position in which he made sky surveys for the Army Map Service. His curt dismissal for being homosexual was not related to job performance. Following four years of frustrating legal battles for reinstatement, his self-written brief reached the United States Supreme Court in 1961; but the high court rejected Kameny's appeal. Thereafter, to the considerable chagrin of the holier-than-thou federal busybodies, Frank embarked upon a crusade against his government's pervasive antigay policies in both military and civilian areas of jurisdiction, donating much of his time to the counseling of gay people whom the Department of Defense and the Civil Service Commission were victimizing with impunity. Very often, Kameny, a fast learner, enabled others to win cases similar to those he had not won for himself.

"In his brief for the U.S. Supreme Court, Kameny had written, 'In World War Two, petitioner did not hesitate to fight the Germans, with bullets, in order to help preserve his rights and freedoms and liberties—and those of others. Now it is ironic but necessary that he fight Americans, with words, in order to preserve some of those same rights, freedoms, and liberties for himself and others. ... Our government exists to protect and assist *all* of its citizens, not, as in the case of homosexuals, to harm, to victimize, and to destroy them.'"

" ... Frank was among the first to formulate and verbalize a dynamic challenge to the prejudicial 'sickness' label then in vogue. In the absence of scientific evidence to the contrary, he declared homosexuality is a healthy state fully equal to, and on a par with, heterosexuality."

"It is amazing to us now," Gittings told Katz for his 1974 book, "but again we have to remember that we are wise in hindsight—when he articulated the idea that homosexuality was not a sickness, and had Washington Mattachine, and later New York Mattachine, adopt this view, that was a controversial thing to do in the movement. When Kameny said that in the absence of scientific evidence to the contrary, we are not sick—homosexuality is not a sickness—many movement people disputed him, saying 'We have to leave that up to the experts.' DOB's own research director, Florence Conrad, a woman who lived on the West Coast, opposed Kameny and engaged in a written debate with him which I published in *The Ladder.* She strongly opposed Kameny's ideas; she felt we did not have the credentials or the right to stand up and say this for ourselves. That's how far we've come in 10 years. Now we even have the American Psychiatric Association running scared."

Gittings also had changed her view of herself. She told Katz: "My personal problem, mainly, was one of self-image. I have traveled a long, long way since the days when I thought it was a misfortune to be homosexual, that I should do everything possible to change." She said her initial activism "was more a desire to ameliorate the bad condition of life for gay people, to make the inevitable more bearable—certainly not to insist on a full and equal place in society. In the early years of the movement, in the '50s, the purpose of our organizing was to find out more about the nature and cause of homosexuality, to get information out to the general public, to soften their dislike and hostility, to try and persuade them to grant us some privileges. By the late '60s, we began to see that discussing the cause and the nature of homosexuality would not help us. We began to insist on our rights, to spell them out clearly, to go to court to get them, to demand what was ours. The whole consciousness changed; in the early days, it was much more nebulous. … We felt that if only we knew more about what kind of people we were, and could get this information out, the public would say, 'Oh, well, they're not such bad characters after all.'"

The New York DOB, with Gittings at the helm, usually attracted tens to sometimes as many as 30 or 40 people at their twice-monthly meetings in the space it shared with Mattachine. "I realize now that these women were showing up in order to meet others. It was that simple. Up until the mid-'60s, every single one of the gay organizations flatly denied it acted as any kind of agency for social introductions. The reason for this was simply to avoid flak from the outside society that we might be in the business of 'procuring,' arranging for 'immoral contacts,'" Gittings said to Katz. "[T]here was reason to think we could get into more trouble than we could cope with. That kind of feeling carried over for a very long time. When DOB had its third national convention in '64 in New York City, Donald Webster Cory was one of the speakers."

Cory, the pseudonym of Edward Sagarin, had written one of the most influential early books on homosexuals, *The Homosexual in America: A Subjective Approach*, published in 1951.

"That was the time [Cory] gave his swan song to the gay movement," Gittings told Katz. "In his speech he chided us for not saying openly that it was a legitimate purpose of our organization to provide a social place. After all, he said, under what better auspices can homosexuals meet each other? He was prophetic on that issue of socializing. Because only a few years later everyone was saying, 'Well, of course, what better place for gay people to meet each other but in places sponsored and run by gay people?'"

Personal Risks

Before she took on the editor's role of DOB's national publication, Gittings put out a chapter newsletter for DOB in New York. She used the supplies and machines at an architectural firm where she worked. "One of my mailings got into the hands of my bosses," she told Katz. "Unfortunately, I had used a company envelope with a sticker over the name, with another return address, either mine or DOB's. Somebody received it—I assume someone other than the gay person who was supposed to receive it—and had gone to the trouble of tearing or soaking off the sticker, had uncovered the company name, and had written a letter to the company complaining about this stuff being sent out. And so I was called in. My immediate boss, a woman, got stuck with dealing with me. … I explained it to her with my heart zipping about 10 miles away from me in all directions. I was very scared, I didn't know what was going to happen. Was I going to be fired? Was I going to get a severe talking to? I explained the purposes of the organization, and I did not deny that I was using company time and company materials. All she said was that she knew something about the subject of lesbianism because she had been in the armed service. She was not saying that she was gay, merely that she was acquainted with the existence of lesbianism. … I don't remember exactly what she said, but I wasn't fired. I was simply told to be more careful about this sort of thing."

"Gittings did much of the work herself, including stenciling and mimeographing after hours at her office, then typing and stuffing envelopes to ensure absolute security for those on the mailing list," Lahusen told writer Margaret Rubick for a chapter in the book *Gay Press, Gay Power*. Rubick said Gittings and Lahusen were the first to organize lesbians on the East Coast.

In 1962, Gittings became the "corresponding secretary" of *The Ladder*, Rubick said, noting: "Initially, women authors did not use their own names. Barbara Grier, under the pen name Gene Damon, wrote book reviews, often five or six per issue. 'Lisa Ben' was an anagram disguise for one writer (and Ben had started the first lesbian publication, *Vice Versa*, years before); others adopted their own pseudonyms. They mostly wrote poetry, articles and short stories. That would soon change." Gittings said she never felt the need to use a pseudonym.

One of the long-standing conflicts within the movement was between Grier and Gittings. Grier was perhaps best-known as the co-founder of Naiad Press, which launched in 1973 and ran for decades, publishing the works of known and lesser-known lesbian writers including Anyda Marchant (writing as Sarah Aldridge), Valerie Taylor, Katherine V. Forrest, Jane Rule, Ann Bannon and Gale Wilhelm.

In Paul Cain's book *Leading the Parade: Conversations With America's Most Influential Lesbians and Gay Men*, he said those interviewed would have elected Gittings as their Miss Congeniality of the movement—with the exception of Grier, who said Gittings "is the only person, actually, from the early movement with whom I really did not get along." A September 30, 1974, letter from Grier to Jeannette Foster, author of *Sex Variant Women in Literature*, discussed the reissuing of that groundbreaking 1956 work. In it, Grier warned Foster away from dealing with Gittings: "I categorically do not like nor trust Barbara Gittings. I will not work with her (not that she would with me either)."

Gittings, in a 2005 letter to Chicago activist Marie J. Kuda, said "No doubt much of this was resentment that I was editor of *The Ladder*, *over her*, for 3½ years."

Rubick continued: "Gittings was asked to be interim editor of *The Ladder* in 1963, when her title changed from 'corresponding secretary' to 'corresponding secretary and editor.' She was editor for three years, and, during that time, she and Lahusen built the subscriber base while making stylistic and philosophic changes. Lahusen photographed Gittings at a chalkboard planning future issues. Visible on the board are sections for December 1964 through May 1965. Some of the topics can be read in the photo, which demonstrates the increase in nonfiction reporting: 'Report on Les Crane … Report on Becker … Married Lesbian - Fiction – Masquerade Part II – Lesbiana – Renée Vivien.'

"At the suggestion of her partner, Gittings added the subtitle 'A Lesbian Review' to *The Ladder*. Although not everyone in the DOB was in favor of having these words on the cover, this subtitle slowly grew in size until in 1966 it was the same height as the title, then appeared in dark typeface as **The Ladder | A Lesbian Review**. The subtitle would remain until September 1968.

"Lahusen designed new covers, changing from line drawings to photographs, and 'bird-dogged' [watched over carefully] contributing writers. Her name was added to the credits in March 1966, 'Assistant to the editor; art director—Kay Tobin.' (Lahusen used the pen name Tobin because it was easier, she said, to pronounce and remember. Later, she used Lahusen so that she would not appear closeted.)

"As photographs started replacing drawings on the cover, the content began to change as well. An Indonesian woman, Ger van Braam, had obtained a copy of *The Ladder* from Holland, a clear sign that distribution was expanding." As Lahusen wrote in Bullough's book: "*The Ladder*, for many women of the era, was a lifeline that reminded them that they were not alone, not crazy, and that there was nothing wrong with them. Its circulation grew to be worldwide."

In the documentary film *Before Stonewall*, Gittings points out that skin color identified a recognizable minority, "while lesbians were hidden even from each other." Even the word "gay" was not said in public—"Oh, the word 'gay' was not in such widespread use at all. It was still a code word, a kind of covert word among ourselves," Gittings told Katz.

Ironically, Ger van Braam "was the first woman to be portrayed full-face on the cover of *The Ladder*," in November 1964, according to Marcia Gallo. Previously, women posed partially obscured. This was followed by Lahusen's photos of women from the U.S.

The January 1966 cover model was Lilli Vincenz, smiling. The inside article on Vincenz actually uses a pseudonym, Lily Hansen. "She is a member of the Daughters of Bilitis and oversees distribution of *The Ladder* to bookstores and newsstands in the Washington area, and is a member of the Mattachine Society of Washington, whose publication *The Gazette* she edits," *The Ladder* stated.

"The photo and interview of Ernestine Eckstein in June 1966 went one step further," Rubick said. "She was an African-American lesbian who talked about race as well as sexual orientation. … She drew parallels with the African-American civil-rights movement and suggested that more needed to be done to change society, rather than the homosexual." Her photo by Lahusen was a profile shot, and the caption on page 3 identifies her as Ernestine Eckstein—which Lahusen said was not her real name. Her real name may have been Ernestine D. Eppenger; a woman by that name, residing in San Pablo, California, died in 1992 around age 51.

In the lengthy interview, Eckstein said, in part: "Any movement needs a certain number of courageous people, there's no getting around it. They have to come out on behalf of the cause and accept whatever consequences come. Most lesbians that I know endorse homophile picketing, but will not picket themselves. I *will* get in a picket line, but in a different city. For example, I picketed at Independence Hall in Philadelphia on July Fourth last year, and at the White House in October, to protest discrimination against homosexuals."

Activism Push

Gittings continued to push the envelope. As Rubick writes: "In an August 1, 1964, editorial, Gittings openly criticized the Committee on Public Health of the New York Academy of Medicine for its negative views. It was, as she said, 'a medical group which myopically sees homosexuality only as a disease.' She went on to point out that '[t]he shoddy work behind this report is a discredit to a professional group in a scientific field.'

"More discussion about research followed. The East Coast Homophile Organizations, comprising the DOB and three other homophile groups in New York, Philadelphia and Washington, met in conference in 1964. *The Ladder* covered the conference in the January 1965 issue and again in the February–March issue, with a debate between activists Frank Kameny and Kurt Konietzko, the former advocating action and the latter education.

"The debate had been brewing for a while. One of the principles of the DOB had been educating the public, and many members were still in favor of a quiet, steady approach. Gittings and Lahusen were leaning toward action, and they supported Kameny's point of view. Again, in the February–March issue, Lahusen, writing as Kay Tobin, reported on the picketing of a lecture given on December 2, 1964, 'Homosexuality, a Disease.' Four picketers asked for rebuttal time and were given it [at the lecture]; the challenger pointed out that 'research on homosexuality is skimpy and has been conducted almost entirely with unhappy, ill-adjusted homosexuals who were patients undergoing therapy.'

"Although 'picketing was against DOB's philosophy,' both Gittings and Lahusen supported it. They 'put this debate in *The Ladder*' and called it 'Picketing: The Pros and Cons.'"

Kameny wrote in the October 1965 *Ladder*: "The homosexual's problems are political and social—not in essence psychological. They are problems of discrimination and prejudice, of law and custom."

When *Time* magazine published an essay, "The Homosexual in America," on January 21, 1966, referring to homosexuality as "a pernicious sickness," Lahusen responded in the April *Ladder* with "A Rebuke for TIME's Pernicious Prejudice," followed by "Letters TIME didn't print," criticizing the "crippling methodological flaws [in the *Time* article]."

The West Coast leadership of DOB became concerned about the direction of *The Ladder,* so Gittings and Lahusen were out by 1966. "She was fired, ostensibly because she was late with her pieces but also because the pair had a more activist stance than the DOB in California. They believed in picketing and joining with men; the California cohort was more interested in cautiously advancing the gay cause and promoting feminism over purely gay rights. The issue of August 1966, Volume 10, No. 11, was the last one listing Gittings as editor and Lahusen ('Tobin') as art director," Rubick said.

"[Gittings] wanted to drop 'For Adults Only' from the cover, but it wasn't allowed," wrote Lahusen in Bullough's book. "She wasn't allowed to change the magazine's name to *A Lesbian Review* so she added that as a subtitle. But the reason the board cited for firing her was her tardiness in shipping the monthly issues' mock-ups and covers to DOB headquarters in San Francisco. Mea culpa, says Barbara; she agrees her lateness was a hardship on the members there who physically produced the magazine."

Gittings seems to have moved on quickly from this setback. She was already engaging in bigger politics and protests, so producing *The Ladder* was not primary on her agenda. There were many other battles she was interested in fighting, including working alongside gay men. So Gittings and Lahusen climbed onto a larger platform, with Lahusen documenting their efforts every step of the way.

Gittings working on the Daughters of Bilitis New York newsletter, August 1962.
Photo by Kay Tobin Lahusen. Copyright Manuscripts and Archives Division, The New York Public Library

Gittings typing the DOB New York newsletter, 1962.
Photo by Kay Tobin Lahusen. Copyright Manuscripts and Archives Division, The New York Public Library

Left and below right: Gittings putting together issues of The Ladder, circa 1965.
Photo by Kay Tobin Lahusen. Copyright Manuscripts and Archives Division, The New York Public Library

Volunteers working on a mailing in Philadelphia, mid-1960s.
Photo by Kay Tobin Lahusen. Copyright Manuscripts and Archives Division, The New York Public Library

DAUGHTERS OF BILITIS

Third National CONVENTION

New York City
June 19-22, 1964

The Ladder promotion of the DOB 3rd national convention, in New York, June 1964.

THE THRESHOLD of the FUTURE

PROGRAM

Friday, June 19:   COCKTAIL PARTY AND RECEPTION

8:30 p.m.   New York Chapter Office, 441 West 28th Street, New York City. Speakers, guests, members and friends are invited.

Saturday, June 20:   PUBLIC FORUM

The Barbizon Room of the Barbizon-Plaza Hotel, 106 Central Park South, New York City.

9:00 a.m.   Registration. Forum sessions are open to the public.

9:30   ADDRESS OF WELCOME
Cleo Glenn, National President of Daughters of Bilitis, Inc.

10:00   HOMOSEXUALITY, THE PRESENT AND THE FUTURE
Wardell B. Pomeroy, Ph.D., co-author of Sexual Behavior in the Human Female and Sexual Behavior in the Human Male.

10:50   THE SOCIAL SITUATION OF THE HOMOSEXUAL
Ernest van den Haag, Ph.D., author of The Fabric of Society and Education as an Industry.

11:40   SOCIOLOGICAL RESEARCH TABOOS, PAST AND PRESENT
Sylvia Fava, Ph.D., co-editor of Sexual Behavior in American Society: An Appraisal of the First Two Kinsey Reports.

6:30   HOMOSEXUALITY AND THE CURRENT SCENE
Gerald Sabath, Ph.D., practicing psychoanalyst and lecturer associated with the Postgraduate Center for Mental Health.

7:20   COCKTAIL HOUR IN THE LOWER LOUNGE

8:30   BANQUET IN THE NORTH GALLERY
Speaker: Rev. C. Edward Egan, Jr., pastor of a Methodist church on Long Island; well-known counselor of "persons who by reason of their sexual deviation are in trouble with themselves, the law, or society."
Topic: WOMEN'S WORLD OF TOMORROW

Sunday, June 21:   GENERAL ASSEMBLY OF DAUGHTERS OF BILITIS, INC.

9:00 a.m.   New York Chapter Office, 441 West 28th Street, New York City. Business meeting for members of the organization only.

Monday, June 22:   CLOSE OF GENERAL ASSEMBLY. SIGHTSEEING TOUR.

10:00 a.m.   New York Chapter Office. Completion of unfinished General Assembly business.

Sightseeing tour of "The Big City." Non-members are welcome.

DAUGHTERS OF BILITIS, INC. wishes to take this opportunity to extend its gratitude to everyone who has helped in the presentation of this convention.

12:30 p.m.   MORE LESBIANS THAN NON-LESBIANS REPORT RAPE – WHY?
Ralph H. Gundlach, Ph.D., Associate Director of Research at the Postgraduate Center for Mental Health. (This preliminary report is the result of research being conducted with the cooperation of Daughters of Bilitis, Inc.)

1:20   LUNCHEON IN THE NORTH GALLERY
Speaker: Rev. Robert W. Wood, Pastor of the First Congregational Church of Spring Valley, New York; author of Christ and the Homosexual.
Topic: LYDIA AND DEBORAH

2:45   WHITHER THE HOMOPHILE MOVEMENT?
Donald Webster Cory, considered by many "the father of the homophile movement"; author of The Homosexual in America and the forthcoming The Lesbian in America.

3:30   THE ESSENCE OF FEMININITY
A Panel Discussion

Moderator: Jess Stearn, author of The Sixth Man and The Grapevine.

Panelists: Mrs. Lee Steiner, marriage counselor, author and eminent radio personality.

Adele Kenyon, author of Fourteen Days to a New Figure and How To Exercise Without Really Trying.

Florence DeSantis, Fashion Editor for Bell Syndicate.

4:50   SEXUAL FREEDOM AND HOPE FOR THE FUTURE
Robert Veit Sherwin, New York attorney; author of Sex and the Statutory Law.

5:40   IS CHANGE NECESSARY? or HOW TO ENJOY LIVING!
Mildred Weiss, Ph.D., former Captain of the Intelligence Corps of the U. S. Air Force; formerly Chief Psychologist of the Cleveland (Ohio) Center on Alcoholism; now Assistant Professor and Administrative Officer of the Psychology Dept., Western Reserve University.

1963 covers of *The Ladder*. Gittings became editor of the publication that year.

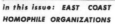

1964 covers of *The Ladder*. Lahusen's first cover photo was the for July issue, and was credited as "'Rhythm of the Sea' by Boris Blai. Photo by Kay."

The
LADDER

A LESBIAN REVIEW

FOR SALE TO ADULTS ONLY

April 1964

THE LADDER

a lesbian review   july 1964

(for sale to adults only) .50

THE LADDER

A LESBIAN REVIEW

FOR SALE TO ADULTS ONLY

AUGUST 1964

THE LADDER

a lesbian review   june 1964

3rd NATIONAL DOB CONVENTION

(for sale to adults only) .50

THE LADDER

A LESBIAN REVIEW   SEPTEMBER 1964

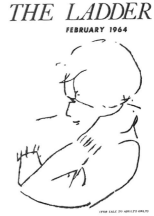

THE LADDER

FEBRUARY 1964

(FOR SALE TO ADULTS ONLY)

in this issue:
Lesbian Literature in '63

THE LADDER   MARCH 1964

A Lesbian Review

For Sale To Adults Only

In This Issue:
Dr. James Barry, The First Woman Doctor in Britain

More 1964 covers of *The Ladder*, including these with actual lesbians. The September 1964 photo, "September Sea," is credited Kay Tobin. October's photo is "October Evening, Beacon Hill," by Kay Tobin. The November cover is the first showing a woman in full face, "Ger van B, from Indonesia, photo by Rora". The December cover photo, by Kay Tobin, was called "Sizing Up the Tree," and was of Barbara Gittings.

Jan. 1965

1965 covers of *The Ladder*. Pics credited to Kay Tobin were the April "City Dwellers," the May issue, and the June issue (though the June issue says Day Tobin, an apparent typo).

More 1965 covers of *The Ladder*. Kay Tobin is credited with the ones for September and October (taken at the June 26 Civil Service Commission protest), but Lahusen said she did not take the top right image. It is by Eva Freund. Bottom left is a photo of artist "Jean" taken by Sandy. Bottom right December issue ballerinas Vera Zorina and Carmen de Lavallade in a photo by Werner Neumeister.

Lilli Vincenz, in a photo by Kay Tobin, on the cover of the January 1966 edition of *The Ladder*.

More 1966 covers of *The Ladder*.
The April cover was from the new
film The Group, featuring Lidia
Prochnicka as The Baroness and
Candice Bergen as Lakey. The May
issue (bottom right) featured "Carol"
on the cover, photo by Kay Tobin.

The June 1966 cover woman was Ernestine Eckstein, as photographed by Kay Tobin.
Copyright Manuscripts and Archives Division, The New York Public Library

The July cover photo (left) is
also credited to Kay Tobin.

PICKETING:

THE PROS AND CONS

The May 1966 *Ladder* carried an article on the pros and cons of picketing.

During the summer of 1965, for the first time in history, several homphile organizations sponsored picketing demonstrations in Washington, D. C. and elsewhere, primarily to protest the Federal government's anti-homosexual policies (especially in the Civil Service, in the military services, and in the State Department) and the steadfast refusal of government officials to meet with spokesmen for the homosexual community to discuss the government's discrimination against homosexuals.

The demonstrations were planned and conducted with great care. But the tactic itself evoked controversy within the homophile movement. Many people felt the tactic was not advisable. At this time, when those organizations that adopted picketing are preparing to demonstrate again this year, THE LADDER presents a sample of views pro and con. The following comments were made by heterosexual supporters of the homosexual cause.

+ + + + + + + +

Below: Phyllis Lyon and Del Martin, photographed by Kay Tobin Lahusen for her book *The Gay Crusaders*.
Manuscripts and Archives Division, The New York Public Library

(Statements made by Dr. Ernest van den Haag, psychoanalyst, educator, and social philosopher, at the East Coast Homophile Organizations conference in New York City in September 1965)

14

Chapter 3
Protests: New York, Philadelphia and Washington, D.C.

Gittings and Lahusen easily navigated the route from discussing homosexuality to marching in the streets. Influenced by Kameny's bold plan for equality, they acted up four years before the 1969 Stonewall rebellion, and two decades before the gay community took to the streets against AIDS.

Gittings was a charismatic personality, with unwavering energy for the cause. Lahusen's role was equally crucial—she used her camera to document almost everything significant happening around her. There are thousands of photos she took that serve as proof that militancy came earlier than many think. Those photos of Gittings, Kameny and the few dozen others who joined them at key protests in the 1960s are some of the most iconic images of the pre-Stonewall movement.

Gittings was featured in the documentary film *Before Stonewall*. "There were scarcely 200 of us in the whole United States. It was like a club; we all knew each other," Gittings said.

Gittings told author Eric Marcus: "Well, we were sort of itching under all of this, yet we stuck with DOB for several years, especially because it was then joining with several other gay groups in the East to form what was called ECHO—East Coast Homophile Organizations. The word *homophile* was very big in the late 1950s and early 1960s. If you wanted to be up front, the best you could do was to say *homosexual* or *homophile*. And very few used *homosexual*.

"Anyway, we met Frank Kameny at one of the ECHO conferences in the early 1960s. Frank was a fantastic man. He was a big influence on me because he had such a clear and compelling vision of what the movement should be doing and what was just," Gittings said. "He believed that we should be standing up on our hind legs and demanding our full equality and our full rights, and to hell with the sickness issue. *They* put that label on us! *They* were the ones that needed to justify it! Let *them* do their justification! We were not going to help them!"

Lahusen told Marcus: "Florence Conrad, from DOB in California, said, 'This isn't subject matter that can be marketed like toothpaste.' And Frank said, 'Unfortunately, this can be marketed just like toothpaste!' Poor DOB. They had never been grabbed by the short hairs and shaken up this way in their lives, these San Francisco ladies."

According to the Perry and Swicegood book *Profiles in Gay & Lesbian Courage*, Kameny declared, "We've been shoved around for three thousand years, and we're tired of it. We're starting to shove back. And we're going to keep shoving back until we are guaranteed our rights! I say it is time to open the closet door and let in the fresh air and sunshine … it is time to hold up your heads and look the world squarely in the eye as the homosexuals that you are … confident in the knowledge that as objects of prejudice and victims of discrimination you are right and they are wrong!"

By the early 1960s, homosexuals were used to being targets of the federal government and, especially, elected officials looking to score points with their constituents. Thousands of federal workers had lost their jobs. Kameny was just the highest-profile one—and the one who had gotten further than anyone else in fighting to keep his job.

Kameny was the battering ram for the gay movement when it came to the institutional discrimination taking place in Washington, D.C.

In 1963, he testified in the U.S. House of Representatives. Representative John Dowdy of Texas had introduced a bill, H.R. 5990, to oppose the District of Columbia's approval of charitable status for the Mattachine Society of Washington. According to the July 5 *Congressional Record*, Dowdy stated the group is "admittedly a group of homosexuals. The acts of these people are banned under the laws of God, the laws of nature, and are in violation of the laws of man."

"Homosexuals constitute a minority group no different, as such, from other minority groups," Kameny said in testimony August 8 before a House subcommittee on the District of Columbia. "We are working to achieve for the homosexual minority full equality with their fellow citizens. ... We are *not* a social organization. ... We are *not* interested in recruiting heterosexuals into the ranks of the homosexual—an impossibility anyway, despite popular belief to the contrary."

Kameny's Mattachine Society was the target of the Federal Bureau of Investigation, and he sent a letter June 28, 1962, to U.S. Attorney General Robert Kennedy requesting a halt to those investigations, which had included asking for membership lists for D.C.'s Mattachine. "One was even asked to act as an informer for the FBI," Kameny wrote to Kennedy. "We look upon this as grossly improper and offensive."

Even though most homosexuals wanted to stay behind the closet door and continue to meet and discuss issues in smaller groups outside public glare, Kameny and Gittings saw that there was no choice but to confront the bigots on their own turf. The anti-homosexuals were throwing down the gauntlet, and somebody had to respond—or discrimination might even have worsened and been further codified into U.S. law.

This was, after all, a time of great protests, of African-American civil-rights marches across the country, including the 1963 March on Washington for Jobs and Freedom. The homosexual civil-rights movement was not created in a vacuum; it was directly informed by the brave activism of Martin Luther King, Jr., Bayard Rustin (a gay man), and many more. In fact, many homosexuals had participated in these protests, learning first-hand the tactics of other civil-rights pioneers.

Merry Band of Protesters

Those few dozen people who dared to protest in public were a merry group, some staying friends for decades. John D'Emilio, writing about the life of Frank Kameny for the *Gay & Lesbian Review* in its March–April 2012 issue, noted that "Kameny was not, of course, alone in his work. The positions that he espoused were enthusiastically embraced by a core of other activists, and the actions that he proposed came to fruition because others took them up, side by side with him. People like Jack Nichols, Barbara Gittings, Craig Rodwell, Randy Wicker, and Lilli Vincenz were among his partners in crime in the 1960s."

Randolfe "Randy" Wicker was an early agitator who saw a need for a more aggressive approach to homosexual rights. In the August 1963 edition of *The Ladder*, he proposed picketing the White House "to highlight not only the homosexual movement but also discriminatory government policies in a variety of areas."

"I had been speaking at various events around New York in 1963–'64," Wicker recalled in 2015. "I joined the movement in 1958."

Wicker's first gay picket, believed to be the first in the country, happened September 19, 1964, at the U.S. Army's Whitehall Street Induction Center in lower Manhattan, to protest the Army's rejection of gays, and also the violation of confidentiality for gay men's draft records. About 10 people were there, including six straight allies. The sponsoring groups were the Homosexual League of New York and the New York League for Sexual Freedom. The Mattachine Society of New York urged Wicker and others not to protest.

"There was not much response, and the press didn't cover it," he said. "The next spring I announced a United Nations picket, and Kameny called for a White House protest the day before that."

The first White House picket for homosexual rights happened April 17, 1965. That year proved to be a pivotal one nationally for gays protesting in the streets.

The April 17 protest was against Fidel Castro's plan to put Cuban homosexuals in labor camps, and it also aimed to call attention to the bad treatment of homosexuals by the U.S. government. There were 10 picketers that day, and 29 picketers at Wicker's United Nations protest April 18. Another White House protest followed, on May 29, with about 13 people (signs included "We Don't Dodge the Draft, the Draft Dodges Us"). On June 26, more than 20 protested in front of the U.S. Civil Service Commission over its ban on the employment of gays.

The July–August 1965 edition of *The Ladder* covered the protests, as reported by Lahusen:

"After all efforts to negotiate with the Commission had failed, the homosexuals decided to stage a public demonstration and call attention to the problem. ... All were conservatively dressed and presented dignified appearance." The report noted that their neatly lettered signs carried such messages as:

"Government Should Combat Prejudice. Not Submit to It and Promote It."

"Discrimination Against Homosexuals Is as Immoral as Discrimination Against Negroes and Jews."

"Denial of Equality of Opportunity Is Immoral."

"We Want Federal Employment Based on Relevant Criteria."

The sponsoring groups were listed as Mattachine Society of Washington, ECHO (East Coast Homophile Organizations), Mattachine Society of Philadelphia, Mattachine Society Inc. of New York, and Chicago's newly formed Mattachine Midwest.

On July 31, there were 16 picketers at the Pentagon over military anti-gay bias. On August 28, there were 14 reported at the State Department to protest employment bias and security-clearance issues. On September 26, a total of 30 picketed at San Francisco's Grace Cathedral to protest discrimination against a pro-gay minister. And on October 23 of that year, there were 45 picketing the White House.

A press release for the October 23 picket stated four targets of the event: exclusion of homosexuals from federal employment; the military ban on homosexuals; denial of security clearances to homosexuals; and the "continuing refusal, by the White House and other agencies of the Federal Government, to accord even the common courtesy and decency of replying to letters written on behalf of the homosexual community (which, with its fifteen million members, is the nation's largest minority group after the Negro); and the refusal by the White House and most agencies and departments of the Federal Government to meet with spokesmen for the homosexual community ... ."

Gittings was at nearly all of those protests, and Lahusen was there to document. "Kay's grandfather died, and we came back [from Ohio] in time to take part in all the summer demonstrations that year," Gittings told Marcus. "We were at the first protest at the White House and the first one at the Pentagon."

Gittings and Lahusen were no longer as active with the DOB's New York chapter, because of their work on the national publication. Thus, when it came to deciding if the chapter would back protests, new chapter leaders Meredith Grey (the pseudonym of Marion Glass) and Shirley Willer declined. In the book *The Politics of Homosexuality*, Toby Marotta writes: "In May 1965 when Kameny proposed that ECHO sponsor monthly demonstrations in Washington during the summer, Willer and Grey objected. In June, the two submitted a resolution asking that the coalition 'not engage in any activity contrary to the policy or welfare of any participating organization.' When the resolution was voted down, the Daughters withdrew from ECHO."

The Ladder was full of articles and letters debating these street-based tactics. "The range of opinion is wide, with only one thing certain: virtually no one connected with the movement is indifferent on the subject," said one article on pickets in *The Ladder* of September 1965. It listed the "firm rules" followed by homosexual picketers, including: "Picketing is not an occasion for an assertion of personality, individuality, ego, rebellion, generalized non-conformity or anti-conformity. ... Therefore the individual picketer serves merely to carry a sign or to increase the size of the demonstration; not he, but his sign should attract notice. ...”

Wicker said he first recalls meeting Gittings and Lahusen through DOB and *The Ladder*. He subscribed to the newsletter, and his image was used on the back of one edition to show that the DOB had male support. He said he always got along with the women, and they were always positive about his work, even when other activists were critical of his efforts.

Also in 1965, on July 4, a series of annual protests began in Philadelphia that would further shape Gittings’ role as a leader in the movement. These protests were, after all, in her adopted hometown, one that in later years would honor her with street dedications, awards and special tributes.

The first of five Annual Reminder Day July 4 pickets at Independence Hall drew 44 people. “It was thrilling. You knew you were doing something momentous. People would stare at you. They had never seen self-declared homosexuals parading with signs,” Gittings told Marcus.

Lilli Vincenz did a film recording of the 1967 Philadelphia Annual Reminder Day, and a clip from that was used on an early 1980s talk show, *Our Time*, hosted by the noted gay film historian Vito Russo. Gittings was on the show with Harry Hay of the Mattachine Society. Asked by Russo if she was scared during these pickets, she said “Yes! There were very few people who really felt comfortable about being in one of these demonstrations. Because you didn’t know just what the consequences could be. Whether you might lose your job because your employer saw you on a television news clip, or somebody saw you on the street. It was rather scary.”

The Philadelphia events were called Annual Reminder Days to remind people that a large group of citizens was denied the rights promised in the Declaration of Independence, including “life, liberty, and the pursuit of happiness.” The fifth and final Annual Reminder Day was in 1969, just a few days after the Stonewall rebellion in New York City sparked the modern-day gay movement. The pre-Stonewall activists clearly had an influence on those Stonewall fighters, and in fact Wicker was a witness to the events in late June 1969 in Greenwich Village; he criticized the violent nature of the protests.

Gittings and Lahusen were not in New York City when the Stonewall riots occurred, but when they returned from vacation, they kept pace with the swift changes in the movement by joining protests and new organizations.

Gittings and other Philadelphia activists turned their focus in 1970 to the first anniversary commemoration of the Stonewall riots, with some 2,000 people attending the Christopher Street Liberation Day march in New York City.

Appearances Can Be Deceiving

In the pre-Stonewall era, a lot of attention was paid to appearance. With homosexuality perceived as perverted and criminal, activists, just as in the Black civil-rights movement, wanted the focus to be on the message, not the messengers. So women wore dresses, men wore suits, and Kameny made sure the signs were professional-looking.

Gittings told Marcus: “That was one of the few things that all the groups participating in the protests agreed on at the time. We decided that we were the bearers of a message. To keep attention on the message, not on ourselves, we had to look unexceptional and blend into the landscape. So the order went out, and everybody followed it. The stirrings to disobey the dress code didn’t really come up until 1969.”

“Also, at the Civil Service Commission, we were picketing for employment,” Lahusen told Marcus. “Frank Kameny’s thought was, ‘If you want to be employed, look employable.’ At the time, that meant turning out in a fairly conventional, respectable way.”

“And I think there was another element,” Gittings added. “The anti–Vietnam War protests had been mounting in size and fervor during this period. But by and large, these protesters were a really scruffy lot. The people who came out for those protests were flouting conventions—their hair, their dress, and everything was so wild as to turn off a lot of people to their message. We wanted to distance ourselves from this kind of protest and not have our message spurned because of who we were as the bearers. That's why there was this business of blending into the woodwork. Besides carrying signs, we handed out literature. We really had a great time."

"We needed the acceptance of society, we thought," Gittings told Katz. "So we geared ourselves to getting it. There was an incident at an early Daughters of Bilitis national convention (in Los Angeles, I think), where a woman who had been living pretty much as a transvestite most of her life was persuaded, for the purposes of attending that convention, to don female garb, to deck herself out in as 'feminine' a manner as she could, given that female clothes were totally alien to her. Everybody rejoiced over this as though some great victory had been accomplished—the 'feminizing' of this woman. Today we would be horrified at anyone who thought this kind of evangelism had a legitimate purpose. Yet at the time, I remember, I joined in the rejoicing.

"At the same time there was some kind of mental reservation in me. I felt there was something grotesque about this woman's trying to look 'normal' for the purpose of appearances at this convention. The resulting appearance simply wasn't that persuasive—and what was it really for, since we were essentially among ourselves? We always had the idea we were totally exposed to the world, but when you came right down to it, we were really mostly exposed to ourselves and those few non-gay speakers whom we invited.

"During the first years of New York DOB's existence there was another debate about a woman who lived as a transvestite, who was accepted even at her place of work as a woman who chose to live and dress as a young man. But in DOB there was discussion over her appearance, whether it was acceptable. It was a controversy that probably wouldn't even arise today, or would arise in a different form."

Wicker was one who disagreed with the appearance policies, but he followed them. "I always thought they were overdone," he said. "I could understand if you were in front of the White House, but when it got down to Philadelphia at Independence Hall, it was 100 degrees, and insisting that men wear suits and ties was difficult. I remember the two doctors, Dr. [Emery] Hetrick and Dr. [Damien] Martin [who in 1979 founded the Hetrick-Martin Institute for youth in New York], wearing shorts and alligator [polo] shirts, appropriate for that weather, and they were kicked off the picket line.

"In the *Gay Pioneers* documentary, I read out loud all those codes, and in the end I said that's why I left the gay movement. It was too micromanaged for me. I always wore a black suit and tie when representing gays on TV or elsewhere, it was important to making an official, formal, noncontroversial appearance. But it was different than being on a picket line. The rules mainly seemed aimed at the women, not men, since it was more an issue for women dressing [masculine]—there were almost no male cross dressers [at the protests]. I did understand it was a consensus viewpoint, so I followed it."

The Mattachine Society of Washington
Committee on Picketing and Other Lawful Demonstrations
Regulations for Picketing

A. Dress and appearance will be conservative and conventional

    1. Men will wear suits, white shirts, ties; women will wear dresses.

    2. When outer clothing is required, overcoats, topcoats, raincoats will be worn, not jackets or other more casual, less formal outer wear.

    3. Picketers will be well-groomed; men will have recent haircuts and fresh shaves; the wearing of beards will be discouraged.

B. Signs

    1. Legends on all signs must be approved in advance, through whatever coordinating machinery is set up for that purpose.

    2. Signs will be neatly and clearly lettered.

    3. Marchers will carry the signs assigned to them.

C. Marching

1. The order of the marchers and the signs will be established by those in charge of the demonstration. Signs will always be carried in the designated order.

2. All inquiries will be referred to a previously designated spokesman or spokesmen.

3. There will be no exchanges of remarks between picketers and passersby. Conversation and comments among the picketers will be kept to a minimum.

4. Picketers will neither smoke nor take refreshment on the line.

5. Picketers will leave the line only when absolutely necessary, as briefly as possible, and only a few at a time.

Helping Those in Need

After she left *The Ladder* in 1966, Gittings turned her focus to helping Kameny, who was acting as personal counsel to gays who had their security clearances suspended by the government. Gittings was assistant personal counsel.

"For gay men or lesbians in trouble, Frank and Barbara had explicit recommendations that boiled down to four vital points," Perry and Swicegood wrote. "(1) Say absolutely nothing, (2) sign nothing, (3) get counsel, and (4) fight back! Frank declared, 'It is the patriotic duty of every citizen to resist investigations and interrogations of homosexuals. Questions about homosexuals or homosexuality are never the proper concern of the government, and should not be answered.'

"Cases involving security clearances were often conducted in the Pentagon. Barbara, Frank, and whoever they were advising, would go to the meetings dressed very conservatively. 'I wore a dress, and heels and hose,' said Barbara, 'and Frank always had on a suit, white shirt, and tie. We looked great, but there was one jarring note we employed to unsettle the hearing examiners. We wore one or two slogan buttons with blatant messages that were completely out of step with the rest of our conventional attire. The little buttons made statements like 'Cheers for Queers,' 'Gay Is Good,' and one of the most deliberate eyepoppers of all time, 'Pray for Sodomy.'"

Gittings continued: "Publicity was the objective. So we held press conferences for the benefit of sharp-eyed reporters. And, when we first went into a hearing room, we made certain to shake hands with all adversary participants so those persons could not avoid reading our buttons. Throughout the rest of the day they had to either look at us or consciously ignore us, but they wouldn't be able to forget what our buttons said."

"Highly important was her participation with me as full formal co-counsels in Defense Department security clearance cases," Kameny recalled at Gittings' 2007 memorial ceremony. "Although not lawyers, we appeared in several such hearings at the Pentagon, commencing in 1967. At our first one, the department presented the late infamous Dr. Charles Socarides as an expert witness. Neither of us had heard of him before, although we heard lots of him thereafter. We listened in fascinated horror as he testified under direct examination. We then cross-examined him for three hours. We discredited him sufficiently so that shortly thereafter, the Pentagon announced that as a result of our cross-examination, Dr. Socarides had been removed from their list of expert witnesses." (In an ironic twist, Socarides' son Richard is a gay man and prominent in national Democratic politics.)

Also at Gittings' memorial, Bobbie Dallas, a woman Gittings and Kameny helped, spoke up. She told the story of what happened to her some 40 years earlier. "I am very proud to say, I was [Gittings' and Kameny's] first case when we went up against the government [to protect Dallas' job against allegations of homosexuality]. … They accompanied me to an interrogation the FBI had set up. … They counseled me, and they showed the compassion that I truly needed at that time," she said through tears.

Kameny and Gittings helped in the landmark case of *Scott v. Macy*, where Bruce Scott was denied a Defense Department job because of "immoral conduct." Kameny had urged the National Capital Area affiliate of the American Civil Liberties Union to take on Scott's case, and it eventually did—

after much pressure from Kameny. Ultimately, the U.S. Court of Appeals for the District of Columbia Circuit said the charge was too vague, handing Scott the first major court victory for homosexual employment rights. [The case was argued December 17, 1964 and decided June 16, 1965.]

David Johnson documents this era in his book *The Lavender Scare: The Cold War Persecution of Gays and Lesbians in the Federal Government*. "The total number of men and women affected by the anti-homosexual purge is incalculable ... [but] as many as five thousand suspected gay or lesbian employees may have lost their jobs with the federal government during the early days of the Cold War. At the very least, these partial statistics suggest that the total number of federal employees fired for homosexuality is well into the thousands."

One of Kameny and Gittings' higher-profile cases, on which they also worked with the ACLU, was that of Benning Wentworth, an electrical technician who worked for a private company that did secret work with the federal government. *The Philadelphia Inquirer* reported November 25, 1967, that Wentworth had been notified that his security clearance was revoked in 1966, after his name was found in the address book of a homosexual Air Force service member who was just an acquaintance, not a sexual partner. *Harper's Magazine* noted that the question was not whether Wentworth was homosexual; "rather, it was the essence of his defense that he was a publicly admitted, openly practicing, mentally competent adult homosexual, and was not, therefore, liable to the possibilities of blackmail, bribery, coercion, and pressure to have caused other homosexuals to be regarded as 'security risks.'"

Gittings is quoted as saying the only relevant question should be, "Is this person capable of safeguarding classified material?"

The New York Times reported on Wentworth's victory in May 1972, stating that "a district judge ordered the Defense Department to restore the security clearance it had revoked from Benning Wentworth."

The Associated Press reported July 2, 1969, on a victory in a similar Kameny-and-Gittings case, for Clifford Norton in *Norton v. Macy*: "The U.S. Court of Appeals ruled 2–1 Tuesday that federal civil service workers may not be fired solely on grounds that they are homosexuals." The unfortunate headline read: "Can't Fire Deviates, U.S. Told."

Norton was a budget analyst in the National Aeronautics and Space Administration who was discharged for "immoral conduct" and for possessing personality traits that rendered him "unsuitable for further Government employment." The court ruled: "Since the record before us does not suggest any reasonable connection between the evidence against him and the efficiency of the service, we conclude that he was unlawfully discharged." Norton had been arrested by D.C. Morals Squad police officers six years earlier, on October 22, 1963, after picking up a man allegedly for sex.

While previous cases made it more difficult for the Civil Service Commission "to exclude gay people from federal employment, these rulings did not question the agency's fundamental policy that homosexuality is always incompatible with government service," noted author Genny Beemyn in *A Queer Capital: A History of Gay Life in Washington, D.C.* "But in *Norton v. Macy* in 1969, the same Court of Appeals challenged the rationale for the government's automatic ban on gay employees. ... This decision established what became known as the 'rational nexus' test: agencies had to demonstrate that a person's behavior in their private life 'demonstrably affects the employee's performance on the job or the efficiency of his [*sic*] department.'"

Wicker pointed out that these efforts by Gittings, Kameny and others to help people were common expectations that came with little reciprocation from those who benefited from their services: "Hundreds of people needed help, but they only came to us when *they* needed something, like legal help. They asked for something, but they were not joining the movement to do something."

At the same time they were defending gays in federal employment and military cases, Kameny and Gittings were still protesting in the streets and in other venues. Kameny, at Gittings' memorial event, said the East Coast Homophile Organizations coalition was succeeded by the North American Conference of Homophile Organizations in 1966. Both Kameny and Gittings attended the 1968 NACHO conference in Chicago, when Kameny revealed his "Gay Is Good" campaign. He said

Gittings "actively supported" his efforts at NACHO.

Gittings also strongly backed Kameny in his 1971 run as an openly gay man for U.S. Congress, to represent the District of Columbia (a non-voting seat in the House of Representatives). He didn't win, but he made history as the first openly gay person to run for Congress. His campaign organization morphed into the Gay and Lesbian Activists Alliance of Washington, D.C.

Gittings and Lahusen also actively participated in a mixed-gender Philadelphia group, the Homophile Action League, which branched off from the local DOB chapter in 1968. The group, which focused on political work as opposed to the social gatherings of DOB, stayed active through the early 1970s. [See Marc Stein's books for more on Gittings in Philadelphia.]

Gittings worked for change both inside and outside the political system. One of her bigger insider posts was a 1975 appointment by Pennsylvania Governor Milton Shapp to the state's Council for Sexual Minorities. This was the first official government body in the U.S. focused on gay issues, and it worked on regulatory changes at a wide range of state agencies.

Changing With the Times

Gittings was curious about the Gay Liberation Front that formed after Stonewall, but she was disheartened by what she saw as its lack of purpose and lack of leadership. GLF was eventually overtaken in New York by that city's Gay Activists Alliance. "The dignified pickets of the 1960s were replaced by the boisterous, free-wheeling Gay Pride marches that began in 1970. Barbara joined in, moving with the times, and was asked to be a main speaker at the 1973 march in New York," Lahusen wrote in the Bullough book.

Marcus wrote this about Lahusen and Gittings: "By the fall of 1969, Barbara and Kay had become symbols of the past, 'Establishment accommodationists,' who, according to gay liberationists, represented everything that was wrong with the movement before the Stonewall riots. But unlike many of their friends from the homophile movement, Barbara and Kay had no intention of being dismissed. Instead, they became deeply involved in the newest phase of the struggle for gay rights, including the battle to convince the American Psychiatric Association to remove homosexuality from its list of mental disorders. Barbara and Kay were vacationing on Fire Island, a gay resort off Long Island, when they first heard about the Stonewall riot."

"I don't like violence but I was pretty elated to hear that GLBT people were standing up and fighting back in the midst of a police [raid] on a seedy, Mafia-run gay bar," Lahusen said in a 2012 *Philadelphia Gay News* interview with Jen Colletta. "Gay people were largely outwitting the police. News of their bravery galvanized gay people in New York and across the country really. The riots were a flashpoint, Barbara used to say, in the gay-rights movement and inspired gay people to get further organized and step up their efforts to improve the lives of their minority. ... Early picketers inspired gay people to go a step further and fight back at Stonewall."

"All hell broke loose after Stonewall," Lahusen said in a 2001 interview with *Visions Today* magazine. "But the movement didn't start with Stonewall."

"When we came back into the city that September, I immediately started attending the meetings of a new organization called the Gay Liberation Front," Lahusen told Marcus. "They were huge meetings. It was the best theater in town. This was the heyday of radical chic. These people were out there in million-dollar rags, each more far out than thou in terms of their leftist ideology. They were spouting stuff that I had never heard before. And here I was, the plain-Jane dinosaur out of the old gay movement.

"They didn't know me from anybody. Barbara and I would sit there in amazement. It was a whole new lingo of oppression. ... There were endless guilt trips against the gay white males. These meetings were really wild. ... It was a total emotional blowout at every meeting. It was like going through a catharsis every time. It was unlike anything we had ever seen, and it just came out of the blue!

"I was convinced that this was a Communist or a New Left plot. I even made an effort to investigate these people for taking over our movement. I think most of them were gay, but they had been tucked away in other leftist causes and suddenly saw the gay bandwagon as the one to hop on. There were still a few of us around from the old gay movement, but suddenly we were drawn into all this radical hoopla, with all these different factions and endless blowouts.

"Even though I wasn't interested in advancing some leftist ideology, I went to GLF meetings because I always cared passionately about what happened to gay people. I certainly didn't think that this ideology would save the gay minority. They were pointing to Cuba and to Russia and constantly trying to make the good case for how great it would be under socialism and how our cause was really an economic cause. That we really needed to overthrow capitalism and have a socialist regime, and blah, blah, blah."

Gittings added: "Suddenly, here were all these people with absolutely no track record in the movement who were telling us, in effect, not only what we should do, but what we should think. The arrogance of it was what really upset me. I remember a meeting I attended, along with Frank Kameny and a gay activist woman from Philadelphia, as well as a couple of others, all of whom had long track records in the movement. Would you believe, the gay liberation people called us on the carpet during the meeting and asked us to explain who we were and what we were doing at a GLF meeting? They wanted to know, 'What are your credentials?' It was incredible! For once, I think even Frank was dumbfounded. As if we owed them an explanation. The meetings were advertised as being open to everyone. I think I finally said, 'I'm gay. That's why I'm here.' It was outrageous."

Toby Marotta wrote about this meeting in his book, noting that Foster Gunnison, Kameny and Gittings were targeted by Jim Fouratt as "lackeys for the Establishment!" "whose very presence compromised GLF's commitment to a radical new consciousness. Although GLF's general assembly eventually voted to let the homophile delegation remain, they spent more than an hour and a half discussing whether 'pigs' should be permitted to participate in a collectivity that was trying to embody a humane new society. Though the experience was disconcerting, it helped the homophile militants to clarify how their political perspectives differed from those of the radical gay liberationists."

Lahusen recalled that she and Gittings tried to turn a negative—being called "dinosaurs" by their own community—into positive public relations. The couple would often bring two stuffed dinosaurs to community meetings and events, and their photo was taken with the props.

Dudley Clendinen and Adam Nagourney also wrote about this episode in *Out for Good: The Struggle to Build a Gay Rights Movement in America*: "Three of the original GLF members were particularly distraught at the turn of events, convinced that the GLF was talking itself into impotence. They were Marty Robinson, who had led the post-Stonewall demonstration at Washington Square Park; Jim Owles, a waifish Wall Street clerk, and Arthur Evans, a Columbia graduate student studying philosophy. ... The GLF was crumbling, Robinson, Owles and Evans argued, because its foundation—its broad interest in a catalogue of causes—was cracked."

"But, of course, the new wave frequently tries to put the last wave out of business," Lahusen told Marcus. "Certainly, we had our differences with Del Martin and Phyllis Lyon at DOB [Daughters of Bilitis]. We had said to them, 'You're over the hill. Your thinking is out of date.' So GLF did the same to us."

Gittings added, "We didn't do that in a public setting."

"But we took [DOB's] magazine in a totally different direction, and they weren't happy with that. We thumbed our noses at them—almost," Lahusen answered.

While New York's Mattachine Society still existed, Lahusen told Marcus it was slow to respond to Stonewall, and like all organizations, there was a built-in life expectancy. "GLF was here today, gone tomorrow. Even they said, 'We're just here as a catalyst to push things in another direction. We'll push this into a movement of people, and we'll all be up front.' It could be said that, in a sense, they did just that," Lahusen said.

"They got people to picket at the Women's House of Detention on Sixth Avenue. They got them to picket for the Black Panthers. Finally, a lot of people started saying, 'Who's coming out for the gay cause? What are we doing for the gay issues? I'm going out for the Blacks. I'm going out for the women. But what am I doing for myself?' Out of that kind of feeling was born Gay Activists Alliance," Gittings added.

GAA was launched four days before Christmas 1969, with Owles as its first president. The group's constitution was "a rejection of both the assimilation strategy of the Mattachine Society and the view of the Gay Liberation Front that the homosexual struggle was a small part of a larger movement," wrote Clendinen and Nagourney in *Out for Good.* In part, the group's constitution read, "Before the public conscience we demand an immediate end to all oppression of homosexuals and the immediate unconditional recognition of these basic rights," including a "right to our feelings." The new group would be "completely and solely dedicated" to gay rights.

Lahusen was one of the original dozen-or-so members of GAA, which was seen as a single-issue group. "We didn't want somebody telling us we had to go out and picket for all these other causes," she told Marcus. "We also wanted a structured group. GLF was always chaotic. The GLF people, of course, said they had no leaders. That was part of their thing. We didn't want chaos. We wanted a structured group. So we decided on *Robert's Rules of Order.* We decided to have officers, elections, and all those standard things. GAA was almost totally political. Politics was everything. You had to have your meetings with the police, to put the squeeze on. Organize gays as a voting bloc. That was GAA's big thing."

Lahusen also organized the Gay Women's Alternative in the early 1970s in New York City.

For his part, Wicker was moving away from an exclusive focus on gay rights, going even further than GLF. "I saw the gay movement as my main movement, but I started being active in the Sexual Freedom League, worked on abortion rights, marijuana legalization, anti–Vietnam War protests, and more," he said. "I felt the parameters of the gay movement were too narrow." Wicker also started a pin-back button shop in Greenwich Village which he quickly turned into a profitable concern. The first successful button produced by Wicker, who became known as "The Button King," was one that proclaimed "Equality for Homosexuals."

Movement Mavericks

"Kay and I are considered mavericks within our movement," Gittings said to Perry and Swicegood for *Profiles in Gay & Lesbian Courage,* "because we don't always agree with some of the other women's views on sexism and the use of language. But Kay was a co-founder of the Gay Activists Alliance because we were fed up with leftist shenanigans and a waste of our time by the Gay Liberation Front. ... The GAA was also firm in its belief that although it's very nice to get support from existing groups, it was an error to depend on others. When the crunch comes, outside associations will always use their money and energy for pressing needs of their own. Issues of gay employment, antigay church attitudes, homosexual parents, and so on, have to be dealt with by gay people. Groups like NOW and the NAACP will sometimes give us friendly assistance, but I would never expect organizations with nongay priorities to be a major resource in the gay rights battle.

"I want to deal with gay issues—first and foremost! For that reason, the National Organization for Women obviously was not for me. I have more in common with homosexual men than with heterosexual women. The last place I want to be in is a room with women talking about their babies. Child care is important, but let somebody else worry about it. There are millions of heterosexual women who can be tapped to fight for those concerns. But there aren't that many homosexual women and men willing and able to be upfront in our battle for gay rights."

"We did all sorts of public protests," Lahusen told Marcus. "We lay in wait for Mayor Lindsay to come out from the Metropolitan Museum and then stormed up the steps and got right in front of him and asked him embarrassing things. When the U.S. ambassador to the United Nations came out of some meeting and got in his big black limousine, I remember going crazy, rocking and beating on the limousine. He didn't know what was going on. He had never been besieged by a bunch of homosexuals before. But he had said something that got us going.

"Leafleting was a lot of fun. I was the first to leaflet the men's department at Bloomingdale's. I stood just outside the entrance to the men's department and handed out leaflets that explained where the various political candidates stood on gay rights. Those uptown faggots, their minds were blown. They didn't know whether to take the pamphlets or not."

Lahusen also wrote and took photos for New York's *GAY* newspaper in the early 1970s. *GAY* was edited by Jack Nichols and his partner Lige Clarke.

"We did plenty of things, and I covered it all for the *GAY* newspaper," she told Marcus. "I was interviewing and writing news stories and taking pictures. I would confront politicians and say, 'I'm with *GAY* newspaper. Where do you stand on …?' I would dutifully write down their answers. I would even tape their answers, so I would be dead accurate. It was a very exciting time."

Gender Divides

Gittings also spoke about the male-female splits in the movement.

"Since men come first in most people's minds, lesbian speakers are expected to understand gay men and tell about their lives and concerns—and we do," she said in Lahusen's *Crusaders* book. "On the other hand, a gay male speaker alone may neglect lesbianism and his audience will rarely think to question him about it. Whenever possible, I suggest that the host group invite a gay man to be co-speaker with me, so that the audience can talk with gays of both sexes and get both subjective viewpoints. I think that's fair. Unfortunately, only some gay men are attuned to the idea of equal representation. And it falls to us lesbians to force the issue so that more gay men will reciprocate and regularly ask that lesbians accompany them on speaking engagements. Ours should not be a male movement! It should be for gays of both sexes."

Lahusen wrote that Gittings' strong primary identification with the gay cause rather than the women's movement stemmed from her difficult years of isolation. Gittings said: "In high school, for instance, where the boys and girls were being groomed for their social roles as heterosexuals, I felt I had little in common with either the girls or the boys. So [who] was there I could reach out to? Later I realized there had been other gay people around, both faculty and students. But at the time I didn't know about them; we were all wearing the mask! If I'd had a single homosexual friend, male or female, student or teacher—just *one of my own kind,* someone I could be myself with—it would have made a world of difference and would have saved me a lot of heartache later on.

"For me at least, the struggle to be gay and feel good about it overrode the struggle of trying to be my own person as a woman. I feel that gay people of both sexes do have certain common problems as gays which transcend the different socializations of females and males. For example, most gay women are still in the closet, as are most gay men. Both are pretending to be what they're not—straight. Both often have trouble meeting other gays. Both have to worry about the consequences of being discovered as gay—losing their jobs, being alienated from their families, being shunned in their churches. These are gay problems that put homosexuals of both sexes into the same boat."

During the 1970s, many lesbians started to separate from gay men, because of the sexism in the gay movement, and also because of the growth of the women's movement. It took the AIDS crisis, starting in the 1980s, to bring the two groups back together somewhat. Gittings, during her entire activist career, always wanted the two factions to work together. "Since leaving DOB she has always worked in mixed-membership groups such as the Homophile Action League, Gay Activists Alliance, and the library task force," Lahusen wrote. "While keenly aware of male-centeredness within the gay movement as well as outside it, she maintains it's more effective to work with gay men and confront and criticize them for their male chauvinism when necessary than to be separatist and let the men continue to go their heedless way."

"No one was surprised that I, a lesbian, knew the literature on male homosexuality well enough to draw up the short general bibliography for the library Task Force on Gay Liberation," Gittings said. "But try asking most men in the movement about books or articles on lesbianism, and almost 100 percent of the time they're at a loss to mention any, let alone discuss them sensibly. One man in the task force who was collecting gay periodicals for a microfilm project came to me for help, complaining he couldn't find any other lesbian who knew enough about gay women's publications to assemble them for his project. I pointed out that *The Ladder,* for example, is 15 years old and nationally circulated. It was baloney for him to claim he couldn't get hold of it! And I asked him, why should he expect a woman to do the work of gathering women's materials and hand them to him on a silver platter?

"The general male attitude—with both gay and straight men—is that what men are and do is of interest to everybody, whereas what women are and do is of interest only to other women. That's no longer tolerable! Gay men especially owe gay women reciprocity, since many of us have traditionally worked with them on gay issues despite their male-centered outlook on these issues. We can hardly afford to be divided in the face of the deep prejudice against homosexuality. And if gay people of both sexes don't act together to fight this prejudice, nobody else is going to do it for us.

"But gay men need to do a lot of head-changing to merit lesbians' continuing with them in a joint effort. Instead of our working with them as in the past, hereafter gay men must learn to move our way, to work with us. Otherwise we'll be in for a long period of separatism."

There were such sharp divisions along gender lines that during one visit to Chicago in the 1970s to speak at the Lesbian Feminist Center, Gittings was banned because she worked with men in the movement. She gathered those who wanted to hear her and spoke down the street at the Beckman House gay center, according to historian Marie J. Kuda in her December 9, 1999, column for *Outlines* newspaper (now *Windy City Times*). Beckman House was created primarily by gay men but named for a lesbian activist, Barbara Beckman, who had died in an automobile accident.

Chicago-based *Lavender Woman* newspaper covered a rap session Gittings held at the Women's Center in its May 1974 edition. "I make no apology for working with gay men to educate the straight public," Gittings said. "Damn it, someone has to do it. You can work if you choose within the community of your choice, but don't put down other people who choose a different kind of work."

There were also difficulties within the movement along racial and class lines, as well as between gay men and lesbians and the transgender community, which was also just beginning to find its voice. Many lesbians who attended the 1973 New York pride parade and rally were complaining about transgender presence on the stage, and it caused community strife for many years. Transgender activist Sylvia Rivera had also tried unsuccessfully to increase transgender prominence in the parade—at the front. Some lesbians were also upset that the bars were big sponsors of the event, and many of those businesses were controlled by the Mafia.

But Gittings spoke to the estimated 20,000 people in New York's Washington Square just before major strife happened. She was introduced by gay activist Vito Russo, who would go on to write the groundbreaking *Celluloid Closet* book. In the 2011 book *Celluloid Activist: The Life and Times of Vito Russo*, author Michael Schiavi reports on that hot summer day:

"In skintight slacks and a wildly printed shirt unbuttoned to his breastbone, [Vito] introduced Barbara Gittings, who got things off to a rousing start by proclaiming, 'We are everywhere!' She informed her ecstatic audience that not only were sodomy laws falling, 'like autumn leaves in state after state,' but the psychiatric establishment was about to legitimize gay mental health as well. Majestic under the arch, Gittings assured the crowd, 'Those of us who are out are oiling the closet door hinges as fast as we can.' She whipped the park into an evangelical frenzy by directing them to chant after her, 'Gay is good! Gay is proud! Gay is natural! Gay is normal! Gay is gorgeous! Gay is positive! Gay is healthy! Gay is happy! Gay is *love!*' His voice trembling, Vito pronounced Barbara 'beautiful' and read a letter from Bella Abzug, urging the community to keep fighting … ."

Gittings told Perry and Swicegood, for their 1991 book, that she thought "one of the better aspects of our movement today is the mingling of men and women. My affinity has always been for all gay people on the basis of our common interest, not on the basis of gender.

"I grew up homosexual in a void, when there was virtually no literature. What did exist was most often dismally incorrect. There was little with which to identify. I had to find my own way, without any role models that I could talk to. I suffered a lot of anguish, alone, until a gay man befriended me."

Continued Fight

Though she was part of numerous short-term projects, Gittings also played an important role in organizations that have lasted for many decades.

In 1973, she was a founding member of the National Gay Task Force, now known as the National LGBTQ Task Force, alongside board members and key supporters Dr. Howard Brown, Martin Duberman, Ron Gold, Frank Kameny, Nathalie Rockhill, Bruce Voeller, Joseph Norton, David Rothenberg, Pete Fisher, Marc Rubin, "Bebe" Scarpi, Sidney Abbott, Barbara Love, Ginny Vida, and Meryl Friedman, according to Toby Marotta's book. It was quite a mix from all factions of the movement, new and old.

As Toby Marotta wrote, "NGTF would ask that homosexuals be acknowledged and rewarded for the ways in which they were as competent and ethical as straights. ... In addition to staging initiatives that would politicize and mobilize homosexuals, NGTF would take advantage of the status of homosexuals as a recognized bloc to command responses from the Establishment that, by further changing popular attitudes about homosexuality and providing protections for homosexual rights, would encourage more and more gay people to come out and to become political. ... They believed that by having their organization press for recognition to the ways in which homosexuals resembled heterosexuals, as well as those in which they were different, they could win the support of other gay professionals," whose skill and status would help convey the message "that homosexuals were as well-adjusted, competent, and ethical as heterosexuals even though they had special ways of fulfilling themselves sexually and emotionally."

Gittings was also a charter member of the Gay Rights National Lobby, a major national gay political group. Steve Endean had been its leader from 1978, and he founded the Human Rights Campaign Fund as a political action committee to raise funds for candidates in 1980. There was a lot of debate about the need for two separate groups, so eventually GRNL and HRCF merged and became the Human Rights Campaign in 1985. The Human Rights Campaign Foundation was launched in 1985 as a tax-exempt partner agency.

Like so many groups, GRNL had controversial roots.

On the first anniversary of his ownership of *The Advocate* national gay magazine, publisher David Goodstein tackled the internal strife in the gay movement in his January 14, 1976, "Opening Space" column. He criticized leadership of many gay groups, saying they hijacked them "from more responsible persons. ... They appear unemployable, unkempt and neurotic to the point of megalomania." He attacked those who wanted to fight "oppression, persecution, personal hurt, fascism, sexism, or whatever." Six of his own writers criticized him in a letter of response, according to authors Dudley Clendinen and Adam Nagourney in their book *Out for Good.*

Soon after that column, Goodstein announced a national conference to create a new national gay organization. *The Advocate* Invitational Conference was in a hotel meeting room near Chicago's O'Hare International Airport in March 1976—and no "obstructionists" were allowed. The invitation list was secret, and some who agreed to attend had to defend themselves against harsh criticism of the event. Clendinen and Nagourney note that Task Force Co-Executive Directors Bruce Voeller and Jean O'Leary were at the meeting, even though they knew Goodstein was trying to create a new group aimed at killing the Task Force.

The group that was formed that weekend was the Gay Rights National Lobby. Goodstein was attacked by attendees for his narrow views of the movement and lost many votes for his agenda.

Two decades into their gay activism, Gittings and Lahusen remained critical parts of post-Stonewall activism and organizing. But even into the 1980s and 1990s, they continued to be on the front lines of the movement, even if the front lines were far more crowded by then.

Gittings used her theatrical side to protest the U.S. Supreme Court's decision upholding sodomy laws in *Bowers v. Hardwick.* The Philadelphia event is recalled in Bullough's book, in the chapter by Lahusen: "In 1986, gays staged a 'Burger Roast' at Independence Hall to protest the decision by the

Supreme Court under [Chief Justice] Warren Burger to uphold Georgia's sodomy law. Barbara, draped in a white sheet, played the allegorical figure of Justice in a tableau, but instead of the traditional scales, she held a Bible, and instead of a blindfold, she had binoculars 'to peer into the nation's bedrooms.' For a gay cabaret in 1998, Barbara donned other costumes to read a piece by Gertrude Stein and to sing a duet with the cabaret's lead drag performer."

Lahusen, for her part, participated in AIDS Coalition To Unleash Power (ACT UP) demonstrations.

Both women were also involved in various efforts to make religious denominations more inclusive of the gay community, including the Episcopal Church. They especially supported the work of the Reverend Troy Perry, founder of the Metropolitan Community Churches movement.

Gittings and Lahusen were proud ACLU members for decades, and Lahusen still is. Gittings' ACLU card came in handy during a police raid on a gay bar in the mid-1960s. Ada Bello, a Cuban immigrant, was celebrating her pending citizenship test at the bar when the officers entered and asked for everyone's identification. Gittings pulled out her ACLU card, and no one was arrested that night.

The Earliest Gay Pickets: When, Where, Why

Gittings prepared this list in 2005. It has been edited for style.

September 19, 1964
The first gay picket! Ten women and men (four gay and six straight supporters) picket at the U.S. Army induction center on Whitehall Street in lower Manhattan to protest Army rejection of gays and issuance of less-than-honorable discharges ("We Don't Dodge the Draft—The Draft Dodges Us").

December 2, 1964
Four gay men and women picket a psychoanalyst lecturing on "Homosexuality: A Disease" at Cooper Union in New York City. They demanded and got 10 minutes' rebuttal time for their spokesman [Randy Wicker].

April 17 and 18, 1965
Pickets spurred by news that Fidel Castro was going to put Cuban homosexuals into labor camps. Ten picketers at the White House on April 17. Twenty-nine picketers at the United Nations on April 18 ("Cuba's Government Persecutes Homosexuals: U.S. Government Beat Them to It"). Brief article in *The Washington Afro-American*. April 20, 1965. Reporters present from *The New York Times* and WTOP-TV.

May 29, 1965
Thirteen people picket at the White House ("Government Should Combat Prejudice. Not Submit to It and Promote It"). Coverage either on the scene or by prior interview by AP, UPI, Reuters, Agence France Presse, *New York World-Telegram and Sun*, TV networks and White House press corps. Stories reportedly appeared in *The New York Times,* New York's *Daily News, The Evening Star* in Washington, *Orlando Sentinel*, and *Chicago Sun-Times*.

June 26, 1965
Eighteen men and seven women picket at the Civil Service Commission over ban on employment

of gays ("The American Way: Employment Based Upon Competence, Ability, Training—Not Upon Private Life"). Brief mention next day in *The Washington Post*.

July 4, 1965
Forty-four take part in the first of five annual July Fourth pickets (Annual Reminder Day) at Independence Hall in Philadelphia to remind the public that a large group of citizens is denied the rights and equality promised by the Declaration of Independence, including "life, liberty, and the pursuit of happiness." Demonstration shown on late-night TV in Philadelphia and given a brief front-page mention in next day's *Philadelphia Inquirer*.

July 31, 1965
Sixteen picket at the Pentagon over anti-gay policies of armed services ("Homosexuals Died for Their Country Too"). Covered on scene by CBS-TV; shown on evening TV in Washington.

August 28, 1965
Fourteen picket at the State Department on employment and security-clearance issues ("Government Policy Creates Security Risks"). Story in *The Washington Post*, August 29. Reporters on hand also from CBS-TV, Agence France Presse, *The Kansas City Star*.

September 26, 1965
Thirty people picket at San Francisco's Grace Cathedral to protest discrimination against a minister who was a straight ally ("A True Christian"). Stories next day in *San Francisco Chronicle* and *The San Francisco Examiner*.

October 23, 1965
Forty-five picket at the White House ("Denial of Equality of Opportunity Is Immoral").

July 4—1966, 1967, 1968 and 1969
Second, third, fourth and fifth Annual Reminder Day pickets at Independence Hall. Almost 150 picketers in 1969, a week after the Stonewall rebellion in New York City. Coverage in *The New York Times,* July 5, 1967 (only four column inches under "Pickets and Homosexuals"); in Rose DeWolf's column in *The Philadelphia Inquirer,* July 6, 1967; "Another Minority Bids" in *The Philadelphia Tribune,* July 12, 1969; "150 Homosexuals Parade Before Independence Hall to Protest Maltreatment" photo in *The New York Times Magazine,* November 12, 1967, with article by Webster Schott, "Civil Rights and the Homosexual: A 4-Million Minority Asks for Equal Rights."

(Notes: Published accounts vary on the exact number of picketers at these events. Information on mainstream news coverage is incomplete. Also, there were other protests during this time that were of national importance, including on April 25, 1965, when young people confronted anti-gay treatment at a popular hangout for gays in Philadelphia, Dewey's Lunch Counter. There are some reports that Gittings participated in the Dewey's protests. Historian Marc Stein reports that one person he interviewed said Gittings was there. See http://outhistory.org/exhibits/show/deweys-sit-in, http:// historynewsnetwork.org/article/11652, and also http://ebar.com/openforum/opforum.php?sec=guest_ op&id=510.)

Civil Service Commission in Washington, D.C., June 26, 1965. Lilli Vincenz is front left, in front of Reverend Robert Wood.
Photo by Eva Freund. Copyright Manuscripts and Archives Division, The New York Public Library

Picket at the Pentagon, July 31, 1965. In front are Dick Clark and Lilli Vincenz.
Photos by Kay Tobin Lahusen. Copyright Manuscripts and Archives Division, The New York Public Library

Picketers at the Pentagon, July 31, 1965.
Photo by Kay Tobin Lahusen. Copyright Manuscripts and Archives Division, The New York Public Library

White House, October 23, 1965. Gittings in front of the line, top, and Ernestine Eckstein, bottom, in skirt.
Photos by Kay Tobin Lahusen. Copyright Manuscripts and Archives Division, The New York Public Library

**White House, October 23, 1965.
Ernestine Eckstein in photo
at left, Randy Wicker in photo
below.**
Photos by Kay Tobin Lahusen. Copyright
Manuscripts and Archives Division, The
New York Public Library

Gittings in one of the Philadelphia protests mid-1960s.
Photo by Kay Tobin Lahusen. Copyright Manuscripts and Archives Division, The New York Public Library

Philadelphia mid-1960s protests. Top photo: Gittings and Kameny.
Photos by Kay Tobin Lahusen. Copyright Manuscripts and Archives Division, The New York Public Library

Kay Lahusen in one of the Philadelphia protests of the mid-1960s.
Copyright Manuscripts and Archives Division, The New York Public Library

Barbara Gittings in one of the Philadelphia protests of the mid-1960s.
Photo by Nancy Tucker. Copyright Manuscripts and Archives Division, The New York Public Library

Photos from Philadelphia protests from 1965–1967. Frank Kameny, holding leaflets, on the right. Leo Skir, below, with the American flag.
Photos by Kay Tobin Lahusen. Copyright Manuscripts and Archives Division, The New York Public Library

Frank Kameny marching in one of the Philadelphia protests, mid–1960s.
Photo by Kay Tobin Lahusen. Copyright Manuscripts and Archives Division, The New York Public Library

Kameny, delivering a letter to the White House, 1965.
Photo by Kay Tobin Lahusen. Copyright Manuscripts and Archives Division, The New York Public Library

The two photos below are from the East Coast Homophile Organizations (ECHO) conference, 1965. Below left, Jack Nichols addresses the audience. At right are participants.
Left photo by Kay Tobin Lahusen; right, photographer unknown. Copyright Manuscripts and Archives Division, The New York Public Library

Barbara Gittings at Frank Kameny's Washington, D.C., office, working with him on gay discrimination cases against the federal government, mid-1960s.
Photos by Kay Tobin Lahusen. Copyright Manuscripts and Archives Division, The New York Public Library

Kameny and Gittings working together, mid-1960s.
Photos by Kay Tobin Lahusen. Copyright Manuscripts and Archives Division, The New York Public Library

Kameny runs for U.S. Congress, 1971. Below: Gittings campaigning for Kameny.
Photos by Kay Tobin Lahusen. Copyright Manuscripts and Archives Division, The New York Public Library

Lige Clarke, Jack Nichols, Frank Kameny and Barbara Gittings at Kameny's election night party, waiting for returns.
Photo by Kay Tobin Lahusen. Copyright Manuscripts and Archives Division, The New York Public Library

Below left: Kameny in New York City's Christopher Street Liberation Day Parade, 1970.
Photo by Kay Tobin Lahusen. Copyright Manuscripts and Archives Division, The New York Public Library

Below right: 1969 Village Voice clipping titled "Gay Is Good," a news item about the 5th annual Philadelphia Reminder Day. This clipping was hanging on Lahusen's wall at her residence in 2014.

Some of the buttons in Kay Lahusen's collection.

Additional buttons. The "Gay Love, It's the Real Thing" Coke-parody button was created and produced by Michael Bergeron of Chicago. New York activist Randy Wicker owned a button store in New York City, and produced many popular gay movement buttons.

Above left photo from the M. Kuda Archives, Oak Park. Other photos by Kay Tobin Lahusen. Copyright Manuscripts and Archives Division, The New York Public Library

Christopher Street Liberation Day parade, 1970. Above: Vito Russo holding the banner up on the right side, marching with New York's Gay Activists Alliance. Bottom: Nancy Tucker (left) and partner.
Photos by Kay Tobin Lahusen. Copyright Manuscripts and Archives Division, The New York Public Library

Christopher Street Liberation Day marchers in the early 1970s
Photo by Kay Tobin Lahusen. Copyright Manuscripts and Archives Division, The New York Public Library

Below: Kay Lahusen with camera at an early-1970s New York City gay march, with Gay Activists Alliance contingent.
Photo by Fred Orlansky. Copyright Manuscripts and Archives Division, The New York Public Library

Gay Activists Alliance actions in New York City, early 1970s.
Above, left: Arthur Evans at the Board of Education. Photo by Rich Wandel. Above, right: Marty Robinson with police officers. Below: A picket for rights in 1970s. These last two photos are by either Wandel or Lahusen, according to Lahusen. They are marked as Lahusen's in the library's collection. Copyright Manuscripts and Archives Division, The New York Public Library

Gay Activists Alliance early-1970s pickets.
Photos by Kay Tobin Lahusen. Copyright Manuscripts and Archives Division, The New York Public Library

Top: Peter Ogren, Prescott Townsend, Tom Doerr, Mark Golderman and Randy Wicker, 1970, Sheep Meadow, Central Park, New York, during the Christopher Street Liberation Day.
Bottom: Transgender activist Sylvia Rivera in New York City.
Photos by Kay Tobin Lahusen. Copyright Manuscripts and Archives Division, The New York Public Library

Gay Activists Alliance "Rockefeller Five" giving peace signs to supporters and the media, and then pictured on the cover of *GAY* newspaper, early 1970s. Bottom: GAA athletes, with Barbara Gittings front, right, early 1970s.

Photos by Kay Tobin Lahusen. Copyright Manuscripts and Archives Division, The New York Public Library

Barbara Gittings speaks at Philadelphia Pride, 1972.
Photos by Kay Tobin Lahusen. Copyright Manuscripts and Archives Division, The New York Public Library

Barbara Gittings at Philadelphia Pride, 1972.
Photos by Kay Tobin Lahusen. Copyright Manuscripts and Archives Division, The New York Public Library

Philadelphia Pride, 1972. Below: Gittings being interviewed by a reporter during the march.
Photos by Kay Tobin Lahusen. Copyright Manuscripts and Archives Division, The New York Public Library

Philadelphia Pride, 1972.
Photos by Kay Tobin Lahusen. Copyright Manuscripts and Archives Division, The New York Public Library

Gittings at New York Pride 1972.
Photographer unknown. Copyright Manuscripts and Archives Division, The New York Public Library

This page, Rutgers University Gay Lib event. Top: Frank Kameny, Randy Wicker and Jim Owles, 1971. Middle and bottom: Showing some love at Rutgers.
Photos by Kay Tobin Lahusen. Copyright Manuscripts and Archives Division, The New York Public Library

**Rutgers University, 1971
conference on Gay Lib.
Top photo: Gittings
at the table leading
discussions.**
Photos by Kay Tobin Lahusen.
Copyright Manuscripts and
Archives Division, The New
York Public Library

Columbia University gay event in 1971. Top: Lige Clarke, Jack Nichols, Jim Owles and Marty Robinson. Below: The Reverend Troy Perry, Clarke and Nichols.
Photos by Kay Tobin Lahusen. Copyright Manuscripts and Archives Division, The New York Public Library

Barbara Gittings and fellow Gay Lib conference attendees at Columbia University, 1971. Below: The Reverend Troy Perry (left) leads discussions.
Photos by Kay Tobin Lahusen. Copyright Manuscripts and Archives Division, The New York Public Library

An early-1970s national church conference on homosexuality. Gittings and Lahusen were active in the movement to change homophobia in religious communities. Bottom left is the Reverend Robert W. Wood, bottom right is Foster Gunnison Jr. Wood was author of the first book published in the U.S. on Christianity and homosexuality, *Christ and the Homosexual*, in 1960. He was the only member of the clergy among those who picketed in front of the Civil Service Commission in Washington, D.C. on June 25, 1965. In the mid-1960s, Gunnison encouraged the homophile movement to find and work with allies in mainstream institutions such as the church. Gunnison was an archivist of the gay and lesbian movement.
Photos by Kay Tobin Lahusen. Copyright Manuscripts and Archives Division, The New York Public Library

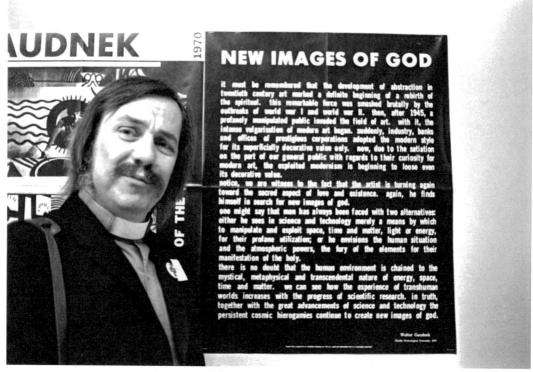

Father Robert Clement, at an Integrity Episcopal conference, 1970. Clement was not an Episcopalian but had been ordained a priest in the Old Catholic Church of America and then in other independent Catholic churches. At the time of the photo, he was leading Manhattan's Church of the Beloved Disciple, which he co-founded to serve primarily LGBT New Yorkers. There he helped to create the term "holy union" for couples of the same sex and in July 1970 is said to have been the first to celebrate such a union publicly.

Photos by Kay Tobin Lahusen. Copyright Manuscripts and Archives Division, The New York Public Library

Kay Lahusen, the Reverend Troy Perry, writer/activist and pioneering gay journalist John Paul Hudson and Morty Manford. In 1968, Manford helped found Gay People at Columbia University, one of the nation's first gay campus groups, and in 1969 he helped found Gay Activists Alliance. His mother Jeanne founded what later became Parents and Friends of Lesbians and Gays. Photo by Barbara Gittings. Copyright Manuscripts and Archives Division, The New York Public Library

Below: Gittings doing a skit protesting the 1986 U.S. Supreme Court *Bowers v. Hardwick* decision upholding sodomy laws.
Photos by Kay Tobin Lahusen. Copyright Manuscripts and Archives Division, The New York Public Library

A protest at the state Legislature in Albany, New York. Pictured is Arnie Kantrowitz.

Below: Craig Rodwell, owner of Oscar Wilde Memorial Bookshop, the first bookstore for gays and lesbians in the U.S. It opened in 1967 in New York City.
Both photos circa 1971. Photos by Kay Tobin Lahusen. Copyright Manuscripts and Archives Division, The New York Public Library

Jack Nichols and Lige Clarke, founders of *GAY* **newspaper.**
Copyright Manuscripts and Archives Division, The New York Public Library

Below: Kay Tobin Lahusen.
Photographer unknown.

Bottom left: Ros Regelson, who taught an informal course on homosexuality at NYU. The women are pictured during their early-1970s *GAY* **newspaper days. Bottom right: Lahusen and Marcia Blackman with Congressional candidate Paul Rao, 1970. Kay sometimes used just Tobin as her last name, or Tobin Lahusen, or just Lahusen**
Photo of Regelson by Kay Tobin Lahusen. Courtesy of The New York Public Library Manuscripts and Archives Division

May 18, 1970, Volume 1, Number 15

GAY's News Editor Kay Tobin *(left)* and Advertising Assistant Marcia Blackman with Congressional Hopeful Paul Rao   *(photo by Ken Gaul)*

Gittings at the National Student Association meeting, 1977.

Below: Jack Baker, Michael McConnell and Barbara Gittings, 1972.
Photos by Kay Tobin Lahusen. Copyright Manuscripts and Archives Division, The New York Public Library

Lige Clarke, Barbara Gittings, Kay Lahusen and Jack Nichols.
Photographer unknown, circa 1971. Copyright Manuscripts and Archives Division, The New York Public Library

Chicago's *Lavender Woman* covered Gittings' trip to the city for its May 1974 edition.

DISCUSSIONS WITH BARBARA GITTINGS

Lesbian political organizing tactics have got to present some of the most knotty problems of all times. I started really thinking this after a stormy rap session at the Women's Center with Barbara Gittings of the American Library Association's Gay Task Force. The quotes interspersed in this article are from that session.

For those of you not familiar with the name Barbara Gittings or the Gay Task Force, a little background. Barbara has been out of the closet since the 1950's when she was a member of D.O.B. She edited THE LADDER from 1963-1966. In 1970 she got involved with the Gay Task Force. As she has said, the non-fiction books about lesbians were full of crap and though some of the fiction was better it was often out of print or didn't make it to the booksellers in the first place. She is not a professional librarian but saw the Task Force as a chance to work for change.

"The people who need to be reached are the straight public who hate our guts."

and

"I make no apology for working with gay men to educate the straight public. Dammit, someone has to do it. You can work if you choose within the community of your choice, but don't put down other people who choose a different kind of work."
—Barbara Gittings

The Task Force is a run-away committee of the ALA's. It is made up entirely of volunteers and receives very limited funding. They've sponsored annual gay book awards beginning in 1971 with PATIENCE AND SARAH. Probably their greatest effort has been directed toward putting out a gay bibliography. It is a listing of non-fiction gay books, periodicals, pamphlets, articles, audio-visuals, and directories to gay groups. Not all works about gays get listed. LOVE BETWEEN WOMEN by Charlotte Wolff was deliberately omitted as well as other materials that have obviously distorted viewpoints. Of course some books are omitted because they don't know about them. The Bibliography is free to librarians and to anybody else who will provide postage. (Write to Barbara Gittings, P.O. Box 2383, Philadelphia, P.A. 19103)

The 1974 Gay Book Award and ALA convention is coming up this summer. Gay

Task Force is sponsoring a "Take a Homosexual to Lunch" campaign and skits dramatizing gay issues. They also will demand that ALA support the Supreme Court appeal of Michael McConnell who was fired from a librarian job at the University of Minnesota when he married Jack Baker.

"I'm upset because you are working with men and spending energy on the straight public. We need each other. Nobody is going to take care of lesbians but lesbians."
—A Chicago Lesbian

"That's not true. Where it's a gay issue men can be very helpful."
—Barbara Gittings

The moving force behind the Gay Task Force is none other than Barbara Gittings. She was in town the week of April 15th to address a conference of educators about gay issues on campus. She wanted to talk with Chicago lesbians and came over to the Women's Center for a rap session. It got stormy.

For a while the talk was about the Task Force and the things Gittings was into. Then the conversation started getting empassioned with questions about

working with gay men and being concerned about straight opinion. Of the twenty five or so lesbian women there, about six took strong positions of either challenging Gittings or agreeing that what she was doing was worthwhile. There were more than a few fence-sitters.

The phrase putting "energy into men" was argued as both valid and invalid. To one woman it was like a principle of physics—you have so much energy, therefore the energy you spend on men is wasted for women. Another woman argued that it wasn't a question of putting energy into men but into women to build the power to tell the men to move over. Barbara and several other vocals staunchly argued that women can disagree but have a right to be where they are...that

"You can't ignore the enemy (men and straight society) and hope they'll go away."
—A Chicago Lesbian

"I'm not ignoring them. I'm outright rejecting them!"
—Another Chicago Lesbian

there is no one best way but a lot of good ways of doing things. The question of support or validation came up. Probably neither side felt the other could support them, although it was admitted that the feeling of support is tricky in that it is given on a lot of different levels.

"Just building the community and rejecting the rest of society sounds incestuous and I'm really bored...people are saying they can respect you, but you also should respect Barbara for doing what she's doing. All your anger says you can't."
—A Chicago Lesbian

In the end, this rap session was draining for all involved and caused a lot of emotional hangovers the next day. The issues and the way they were argued out of heavy conviction adds significance to the words "can not support". They are fertile grounds for serious splits and factions. While maintaining the right to disagree, we should be able to make it known in this society that calls us "queers" that we are together. There simply aren't that many of us.

Judy Whitaker

Rape News ....

Cont. from page 3

The first training session for lay advocates is already underway at the Loop Y. Interested women should contact CWAR (372-6600) for details on the next session, which is scheduled for Sept.

The second bit of good news is that special emergency room facilities for rape victims may be set up at three Chicago hospitals. Alderwoman Marilou Hedlund (48th Ward) made the proposal in an April 15th City Council meeting.

What it means is that police would take any rape victim to one of three hospitals - one each on the North, South and West sides - instead of the nearest emergency room, where the victim may get improper treatment or be refused treatment. After the woman has been taken to the center, police responsibility for her "care" would end and considering police treatment and attitude toward rape victims the proposal makes sense. The centers, as envisioned by Hedlund, would have a gynecologist and a woman psychiatric social worker on call at all times, besides trained personnel to take care of the victim from admission to discharge.

Workers in the center would be trained in handling evidence that could be used later in court.

Alderwoman Hedlund expects the City Council's health committee to hold hearings on the proposal in late May at which she is planning to have representatives of women's groups, the rape crisis centers, AMA, and the policy testify. The proposal seems to be a step in the right direction in terms of the woman who is raped, but how the centers are approved, planned, set up, staffed and operated will determine this. We must make certain that our influence and impact is made at the hearings and thereafter to guarantee that the centers, if established, will be in the best interests of the woman who has been raped.

And so much for progress in the war against rape. A state legislative committee that conducted hearings recently in Chicago and downstate (discussed in the last issue of LW) has made no noise in Springfield yet about changing the rape laws. Write your representative.

Page 4 LAVENDER WOMAN May 1974

LUCY PARSONS

WOMEN STRIKE 26 AUG

Gittings with military activist Leonard Matlovich, mid-1970s.

Middle: Activist Vito Russo.

Below: Jim Owles and Morty Manford, in front of Owles' campaign office when he ran for New York City Council.
Photos by Kay Tobin Lahusen (Russo photographer unknown). Copyright Manuscripts and Archives Division, The New York Public Library

The founding board of the National Gay Task Force, circa 1973. Gittings is front row, second from left. Front, left, is Dr. Howard Brown.

Below: Bruce Voeller in the NGTF office.
Photos by Kay Tobin Lahusen. Copyright Manuscripts and Archives Division, The New York Public Library

It's Time

Monthly Newsletter of the National Gay Task Force

Early Task Force literature, 1975.
From Kay Tobin Lahusen's archives

CAMPAIGN BEGINS FOR HR 5452

By NATHALIE ROCKHILL
and BRUCE VOELLER

Twenty-four sponsors introduced a gay rights bill into Congress on March 25, and the National Gay Task Force simultaneously launched the first nationally coordinated gay lobbying effort in history.

The bill, HR 5452, would amend the 1964 and 1968 Civil Rights Acts to prohibit discrimination, based on a person's "affectional or sexual preference," in the areas of employment, housing, public accommodations and facilities, education, and federally funded programs.

First introduced as HR 166 in January by Rep. Bella Abzug (D-NY) and four cosponsors, the bill was circulated by Abzug among her colleagues in the House of Representatives for additional support.

Working closely with the Abzug office, NGTF contacted potential sponsors directly and relayed information to and from gay groups in several states. Key roles were played by lesbians and gay men in Northern California, Minnesota, Massachusetts, Denver, Washington DC, Philadelphia, and New York City. The result is a geographically diverse list of sponsors (see box).

—Photo by M. J. VILARDI

REINTRODUCTION OF HR 5452 was announced at a press conference organized by NGTF in Washington on March 25. Speakers included (left to right) NGTF Legislative Director Nathalie Rockhill, Rep. Bella Abzug (D-NY), Rep. Edward Koch (D-NY), and Executive Director Bruce Voeller. Also participating were Rep. Pete McCloskey (R-Cal), National Organization for Women President Karen DeCrow, Marilyn Haft of the American Civil Liberties Union, Dr. Fred Strassburger of the American Psychological Association, and Herb Gant of the American Psychiatric Association.

The representation of minority and mainstream politicians from both political parties illustrates the growing belief among legislators that civil rights are not divisible and that no segment of the population can be denied their constitutional rights.

The climate for such legislation is changing rapidly. Gay civil rights laws have already been passed in twenty American cities, including Seattle, Minneapolis, Detroit, San Francisco, and Washington DC, and are close to passage in several states.

New attitudes toward the gay minority are demonstrated in the growing list of organizations which have adopted policy resolutions pressing for legal reform. These include th- A------- D-- A------ tion, American
American Fede-
al Education A:
Organization of
Liberties Union
Christian Assoc
National chu
adopted gay rig
Lutherans, Unit
Church of Chris
tion of Priests C
about half the F
the United Stat
In addition,
by NGTF revea

corporations as AT&T, IBM, Bank of America, American Airlines, Eastern Airlines, Citicorp, CBS and NBC have stated policies of nondiscrimination against gays in hiring or promotion.

The federal bill now goes to the Civil and Constitutional Rights Subcommittee of the House Judiciary Committee. Sponsors for a companion bill in the Senate are currently being sought.

WHAT YOU CAN DO
To help secure passage of the federal bill:

Write to your Representative and urge her/his support for HR 5452. Write to Rep. Don Edwards (D-Cal), chairman of the House Judiciary Subcommittee on Civil and Constitutional Rights and ask

Honor Roll

The 24 Representatives cosponsoring HR 5452 are:

Bella Abzug (D-NY), Herman Badillo (D-NY), Jonathan Bingham (D-NY), George Brown (D-Cal), John Burton (D-Cal), Shirley Chisholm (D-NY), Ronald Dellums (D-Cal), Walter Fauntroy (D-Wash DC), Donald Fraser (D-Minn), Michael Harrington (D-Mass), Elizabeth Holtzman (D-NY), Edward Koch (D-NY), Paul McCloskey, Jr (R-Cal), Norman Mineta (D-Cal), Parren Mitchell (D-Md), Robert Nix (D-Pa), Charles Rangel (D-NY), Fred Richmond (D-NY), Benjamin Rosenthal (D-NY), Patricia Schroeder (D-Colo), Steve Solarz (D-NY), Pete Stark (D-Cal), Gerry Studds (D-Mass), H. A. Waxman (D-Cal).

IT'S TIME.

It's time for all gay people to work together and support the growing gay movement. It's time for people who care about the rights of the gay minority to take a stand and come out in some way for the dignity of 20-million Americans.

It's time — to join the National Gay Task Force.

In our first year, NGTF has become a strong, active force in reshaping public attitudes about lesbians and gay men. We have made progress — thanks to the support of over 2000 women and men who have joined us and helped make NGTF the largest gay civil rights organization in this country's history.

Some highlights of our work have been:

- Spearheading the national push for federal civil rights legislation for gay people, which has led to the introduction of House bill 166 on March 25th, sponsored by over twenty members of Congress.
- Persuading the American Psychiatric Assoc. to remove the "sickness" label.
- Identifying and publishing job protection policies for gays at IBM, AT&T, American and Eastern Airlines, Bank of America and many others.
- Coordinating the national protest of "Marcus Welby: The Outrage."
- Spearheading the drive for positive film and TV portrayals of gay people.
- Securing job protection for gays at the NBC and CBS television networks.
- Launching, with the American Civil Liberties Union, court cases challenging the state "sodomy" laws. Our goal — a decision by the US Supreme Court.
- Supporting local gay organizations' efforts for gay civil rights legislation, e.g., in California, Colorado, Idaho, Pennsylvania, Illinois, Ohio, Massachusetts, Texas, Minnesota and Georgia.
- Challenging the media blackout of gay ads in some national publications by running a full page ad for NGTF in the New York Times.
- Helping to found an international organization to work on gay rights through the United Nations and other international bodies.
- Challenging the Immigration and Naturalization Service's discriminatory policies towards foreign gays in obtaining visas and citizenship.
- Working with the National Council of Churches on their recent, very strong gay rights resolution.
- Initiating a major court challenge on custody rights of lesbian mothers and gay fathers.
- Obtaining the gay rights resolution of the American Association for the Advancement of Science.

. . . . and much more.

BUT SO MUCH MORE NEEDS TO BE DONE!

**NATIONAL
GAY
TASK
FORCE**

It's Time

Newsletter of the National Gay Task Force

Vol. 2, No. 4   Single Copy: 25 cents   January, 1976

Task Force newsletter, 1976
From Kay Tobin Lahusen's archives

NGTF HOLDS PUBLIC FORUM; QUARTERLY SERIES BEGINS

GAY/LESBIAN/FEMINIST MOVEMENTS EXPLORED

By Scott Anderson

At its quarterly event on December 6, NGTF sponsored a public forum on "The Relationship of the Feminist, Lesbian, and Gay Movements." Charlotte Curtis and Roger Wilkins, both members of the N.Y. Times Editorial Board, participated as questioners for six panelists representing the three groups. It marked the first time that members of the "establishment media" have lent their names and support to a gay-sponsored event. Over three hundred people attended the forum and a reception following the event at the N.Y.U. School of Medicine's Schwartz Auditorium.

Jean O'Leary, NGTF National Coordinator and Legislative Director, acted as moderator. Panelists included Betty Powell, language professor and activist in the Gay Academic Union; Martin Duberman, playwright, historian, and NGTF Board member; Bert Hansen, history professor and GAU activist; Kathy Samuels, Project Director, Women's Action Alliance; Charlotte Bunch, lesbian-feminist theoretician and editor of *Quest*; and Ronni Smith, Director of Special Projects, N.Y. State Division of Human Rights. Ms. Bunch is also active on the NGTF Board of Directors. Charlotte Curtis, Op–Ed Page editor of the *Times*, commented, "The discussion was the broadest range of views on the subject I have ever heard."

Ms. Smith mentioned in her remarks, as in fact did all of the panelists, that "all three groups share discrimination because of sexism, and all three groups have the same targets—groups we need to reach; the establishment, those in power; and the misinformed and frightened general public, those that need educating." She added that her goal of feminism was to "give women options, not functions."

Both Duberman and Hansen commented on the applicability of a feminist perspective and analysis to the concerns of gay men in particular, and in general, to

NGTF Board Member Betty Powell speaking at Dec. 6 Forum. Other participants (l. to r.) are Jean O'Leary, N.Y. Times editors Roger Wilkins and Charlotte Curtis; Charlotte Bunch, Ronni Smith, Bert Hansen, Martin Duberman and Kathy Samuels. Photo by Bettye Lane.

needed social change. But Duberman added that he felt many gay men were "men first, gay second" and that consequently a significant number of gay men were interested in assimilating the values and privileges of our "patriarchal" society, i.e., maintaining the status quo.

Ms. Bunch stated that the passage of civil rights legislation for gays would not be enough; what is needed is a fundamental change in society, and in particular in the concept of power and its relationship to economics, class, race, sex roles, etc. The new structure would not substitute women for men in decision-making roles, but would instead replace heterosexual power structures with a new system where all groups have equal access to those decision-making roles. She saw lesbians as a possible bridge between the feminist and gay movements.

Remarks by the panelists were followed by questions submitted by the audience and by Ms. Curtis and Mr. Wilkins. Ms. Curtis commented that she felt gays deserved "more support in the media." Her participation in the event, and that of Wilkins, the Times civil rights specialist, demonstrated support for a cause in which they believe. As Wilkins put it, "I am participating in this event because I support the gay movement and the feminist movement, and I want to know more about them and help them."

Gay Academic Conference

NGTF STAFF AND BOARD TAKE ACTIVE ROLES

By Barrett Brick

The third annual conference of the Gay Academic Union, held at Columbia University the weekend of November 28-30, drew over 1,000 men and women from across the country, among them many NGTF members. The three-day gathering featured over forty workshops and panels on a wide range of subjects including anthropology, legislation, religion, literature, the military, sexuality, and the media. NGTF Staff and Board members at the conference included Dr. Bruce

Media Notes

NGTF MEETS WITH NBC; HATCH PLANS FOR SOAP OPERA AND DOCUMENTARY

By Ginny Vida

An east coast gay media delegation organized by NGTF met with NBC-TV network president Bob Howard and executives from the Standards and Practices, Programming, and News Departments on December 5. The meeting was the third in a series of meetings with NBC brass to review progress toward positive representation of gay people on the network.

Following the first meeting with Mr. Howard in November 1974, NBC agreed not to rerun the "Flowers of Evil" episode from the Policewoman series, and issued a statement to their employees pledging nondiscrimination in employment with respect to sexual preference. They also agreed to hold regular meetings with the gay community to review progress.

Principal complaints to the network this round were the rebroadcast of "Born Innocent" (still offensive despite editing), a gay stereotype on "Saturday Night Live," and the virtual invisibility of gay people on the network during the last year (with the exception of positive gay characters in "Doctors' Hospital" and the "Bob Crane Show").

Lin Bolen, VP of Daytime Programming, assured the delegation that there is no taboo against gay themes in serial dramas, and she agreed to encourage a gay storyline in "Another World." Bolen would like to do one gay story as a trial run, and have gay media representatives share in reading the mail when viewers respond.

Russ Tornabene of NBC News expressed an openness to doing a documentary on the gay movement. He offered to set up and attend a meeting with Al Perlmutter, head of documentary productions for NBC News, and gay media reps to discuss the project.

Bob Kasmire, VP of Corporate Relations said that NBC policy on representation of lesbians and gay men on the network is basically in agreement with NGTF's guideline: i.e., that "until such time as positive images are regularly appearing on the network, no negative images will be permitted." (Unfortunately, they have not followed that policy thus far.)

Mr. Howard told the group that NBC producers and Standards and Practices personnel were informed last April-May at a west coast meeting that the network is open to shows with gay themes and gay characters. Nonetheless, few scripts with gay storylines have been submitted, especially stories about lesbians. The network will provide us with a list of producers of all NBC programs t. which we are encouraged to submit storylines.

If you would like to help by submitting your storylines (very brief, a paragraph will do) for particular programs on NBC, send them to Ginny Vida, NGTF Story-Line Project, 80 Fifth Ave., Rm. 506, NY, NY 10012. The idea is to use whatever familiarity you may have with primetime or daytime network series by thinking up specific ways in which gay characters or issues could fit into the format of particular shows. Don't limit yourself to ideas that make gay characters or issues the focus of an episode, but think as well how minor characters could be simply identified as gay, and then go about their business. If storyline or news account ideas spring to mind from your experience, that you can't readily mesh with a particular series, send those along too, and we can try to think of a series in which it would work.

NGTF could use your help with another project, too. The president of Viacom Enterprises, the company that owns the syndication rights to "Born Innocent," has refused to meet with NGTF to discuss our objections to this film (it includes the most violent and brutal rape scene ever on television—performed by lesbians). Please send your letter urging Viacom's cooperation to: Larry Hilford, President, Viacom Enterprises, 345 Park Avenue, New York, NY 10022.

Vida Joins Staff As Media Director

Ginny Vida, educator and activist in gay groups for several years, recently joined the NGTF staff as Media Director. She is a former English teacher and textbook editor. Spokeswoman for Lesbian Feminist Liberation, and Vice-President of the Gay Activists Alliance in New York. Ms. Vida has also served on the NGTF Board of Directors since its inception in October 1973.

Ginny commented that "the position of Media Director involves constant communication with people in the broadcast and print media including the gay press. It also involves publicizing gay news of national significance as well as special NGTF projects. Through our Gay Media Alert Network we keep in touch with gay media groups throughout the country and help coordinate actions directed toward the straight media."

Ginny feels that media work is of critical importance to the movement. "The media is an important means of changing attitudes. Lobbying helps to inform and involve the politicians; the media helps to reach their constituents and the general public. Erasing the negative image and myths about lesbians and gay men is only the tip of the iceberg. We have to foster a positive image to replace those old notions and prejudices. That is where the hard work really begins—and that is my top priority."

Gay Academic Union

(Continued from page 1)

Coordinator of the Task Force, Nath Rockhill, and former Media Coordinator Loretta Lotman also had active roles.

Among the first panels was one entitled "Gay Religion," moderated by NGTF Financial Director, the Rev. Robert Herrick.

Bob stated that "the large attendance at the GAU religious panel demonstrated the increasing role of gay religious groups within the gay movement. Religion is coming alive within the gay movement in a way that non-gay churches seem to have lost." NGTF Executive Director Bruce Voeller spoke at a seminar on "Gays as Parents." Other seminars and workshops included "Gay Psychological Counseling," "Teaching Gay Courses," "Class and Feminism," and "Legislation Affecting Gays." In the latter panel, Jean O'Leary, NGTF Legislative Director, spoke about the relationship between Gay Civil Rights and the Equal Rights Amendment, and the importance of that bill's success to lesbians and gay men.

NATIONAL GAY TASK FORCE
FRANCES DOUGHTY, *Board Co-Chairperson*
DAVID ROTHENBERG, *Board Co-Chairperson*
BRUCE VOELLER, *Executive Director*
ROBERT HERRICK, *Program Director for Finance, Planning and Religion*
JEAN O'LEARY, *Legislative Director and National Coordinator*
GINNY VIDA, *Media Director*

IT'S TIME   Vol. 2, No. 4   January 1976
Edited by Ginny Vida
Scott Anderson, Assistant Editor
Graphics by Nick Curto
Typeset by Inter Typographics, Inc.

Published by the National Gay Task Force, Inc., Room 506, 80 Fifth Avenue, New York, New York 10011. Single copy 25 cents. Subscription to IT'S TIME by membership in NGTF. Please notify us of any change of address. Entire contents copyright © 1976 by the National Gay Task Force, Inc.

Chapter 4
Taking on the American Psychiatric Association

Gittings' efforts at *The Ladder*, as well as protesting in front of the White House and Independence Hall, led her in the direction of tackling powerful, institutional homophobia head-on. It seems almost obvious in retrospect that making changes in how psychiatrists treated homosexual patients was a key to the movement's success, but many in the community did not agree with this tactic. Taking on the American Psychiatric Association seemed an insurmountable task.

But not for Gittings, Lahusen, Kameny and a few others who went after the head of the monster.

In advance of their appearance on a 1972 APA Dallas conference panel that would become historic, Gittings and Kameny issued "Gay, Proud, and Healthy," a statement regarding the psychiatric profession:

> *"In recent years, an adversary situation has developed between the psychiatric profession and the homosexual community. While much of psychiatry seems unaware of this, it is felt with growing resentment and bitterness by the homosexual community, who increasingly see psychiatry as THE major enemy in a battle against deeply-rooted societal prejudice, and see psychiatrists as singularly insensitive and obtuse to the destruction which they are wreaking upon homosexuals by their negative attitudes and pronouncements. We consider such an adversary situation undesirable and reconciliation to be to the advantage of both parties. This is why we, as homosexuals, are here at the Dallas conference of the American Psychiatric Association. In our view, homosexuals are the people most knowledgeable about, and certainly most concerned with these questions. We have traditionally been the people last consulted while others, self-appointed and never authorized to represent us, have talked about us instead of with us, and set themselves up, without our permission, as our spokesmen. We are bringing that to an end.*
>
> *"Central to the conflict between psychiatry and the homosexual community is the 'sickness theory' of homosexuality and the whole related complex of negative attitudes toward homosexuality, which try to make of homosexuality something inferior to and less desirable than heterosexuality. It matters not whether the word used be sickness, disorder, affliction, disturbance, dysfunction, neurosis, immaturity, fixation, character or personality disorder, pathology, or any other—or whether homosexuality be considered as merely symptomatic of these—the effects are the same: (1) To support and buttress the prejudices of society and to assist the bigots in the perpetration and perpetuation of their bigotry; and, at least equally important (2) To destroy the homosexual's self-confidence and self-esteem, impair his or her*

self-image, degrade his or her basic human dignity."

Four decades after she started fighting the APA, Gittings accepted the APA's first John E. Fryer, M.D., Award, on October 7, 2006, in New York City. The award is presented to a person who has made significant contributions to LGBT mental health, and it is named for the once-anonymous doctor who helped change the world for homosexuals. Kameny also received the Fryer award at the event.

What follows is Gittings' speech from that event. It also appears as the "Preface: Show-and-Tell" in the 2007 book *American Psychiatry and Homosexuality: An Oral History*, edited by Jack Drescher, M.D., and Joseph Merlino, M.D., M.P.A.

In Gittings' Own Words: Taking on the APA

When our American movement for full civil rights and equality for homosexuals got launched 56 years ago, we had a huge range of basic problems to tackle. We were denounced as immoral and sinful. We were punished as criminals and lawbreakers. We were labeled as "sick" and needing a "cure." We were mostly invisible as gay, which made it hard for gay men and lesbians to develop good social lives and to create a movement to battle injustice and prejudice.

It's difficult to explain to anyone who didn't live through that time how much homosexuality was under the thumb of psychiatry. The sickness label was an albatross around the neck of our early gay-rights groups—it infected all our work on other issues. Anything we said on our behalf could be dismissed as "That's just your sickness talking." The sickness label was used to justify discrimination, especially in employment, and especially by our own government.

Some brutal methods for curing us in vogue at one time included incarceration in mental hospitals, lobotomies, and aversion therapy. The latter is where they show you pictures of the "wrong" kind of sexual partner and give you an electric shock, and then show you pictures of a person you *should* like and play nice music to persuade you to change your choice of sexual partner.

There were of course other efforts at curing homosexuality that were less physically brutal, including psychotherapy, but they all thrived on the notion that homosexuality was bad for the individual and for society and should be fixed. You can see more on this in a documentary video called *One Nation Under God*. Though the film is mainly about the faith ministries that try to convert gays to heterosexuality, it's chock full of anecdotes on psychiatric cures and footage of psychiatrists expounding on how sick homosexuals are.

You all know about one book that especially popularized the sickness view. *Homosexuality: A Psychoanalytic Study*, published in 1962, claimed to be a scientific study comparing a group of gay men in psychoanalysis with a group of heterosexual men also in analysis. The authors, including Dr. Irving Bieber, pumped in at the beginning their belief that homosexuality was psychopathological, and they worked their meager statistics up and down and sideways, and lo! At the end they plucked out those beliefs as scientific conclusions.

What a shameful work. More shameful is that it was uncritically accepted at the time. I'm not aware of a single review or comment in the contemporary psychiatric literature that pointed out that the Bieber authors failed to follow science. This bothered me. I talked to a psychologist, Dr. Fritz Fluckiger. He wrote a detailed critique of the Bieber study called "Research Through a Glass, Darkly." It was published in 1966 in *The Ladder,* the magazine of the national lesbian organization the Daughters of Bilitis, which I was editing at the time. Unfortunately, Dr. Fluckiger wasn't an MD analyst and his review wasn't published in a professional journal.

But reaction was building to the sickness label's bad effect on gay individuals' self-image and on our movement's fight for equality. One of the psychoanalysts who participated in the Bieber study gave a public lecture in December 1964 plainly titled "Homosexuality: A Disease." Four gay protesters showed up; they demanded and got ten minutes of rebuttal time for their spokesman [Randy Wicker].

Another key event was the antisickness statement adopted in 1965 by the Mattachine Society of Washington, D.C., and many other gay organizations. Eventually gay groups were demanding official reconsideration of homosexuality as sickness. A petition to the American Psychiatric Association (APA) appeared in a lesbian newspaper in 1971. We were also taking a proactive stand, saying, "We Are the Experts on Homosexuality."

Changes in thinking were brewing among psychiatrists, spurred in part by the pioneer work in the 1950s of psychologist Dr. Evelyn Hooker, which challenged traditional views about homosexuality. Psychiatrist Dr. Judd Marmor was especially influential because of his own evolution from the old orthodoxy. A good account of the developing shift is in Ronald Bayer's book *Homosexuality and American Psychiatry: The Politics of Diagnosis,* published in 1981.

Things came to a head in 1970 when gays invaded several psychiatric meetings, targeting in particular sessions on aversion therapy. Protesters seized microphones and denounced psychiatry for hurting instead of helping us. The angry disrupters said, "Stop talking about us and start talking with us."

Wisely, the APA met this demand. At its 1971 meeting in Washington, D.C., there was a panel of gay people including Frank Kameny titled "Lifestyles of Non-Patient Homosexuals." We jokingly called it "Lifestyles of Impatient Homosexuals." But it was the first time the APA acknowledged that there are homosexuals who aren't in therapy and have no need for it.

Also Frank and I disrupted a lecture on aversion therapy and forced an exhibitor of aversion therapy materials to remove the slides he was selling for use on homosexuals.

The next year, 1972, Frank and I were invited to be on a panel in Dallas called "Psychiatry: Friend or Foe to Homosexuals—A Dialogue." My partner Kay said, "This isn't right. Here you have two psychiatrists pitted against two gays and what you really need is someone who is both." The panel moderator, Dr. Kent Robinson, agreed to add a gay psychiatrist if we could find one. In 1972, who would come forward? Oh, how we searched! Kay and I wrote letters and made phone calls around the country. (Remember, no e-mail in those days.)

At last, John Fryer said yes, provided he could wear a wig and mask and use a voice-distorting microphone. Dr. H. Anonymous was born.

We smuggled him in his disguise through back corridors into the packed lecture hall. He really rocked the audience, speaking as a closeted gay person to his own colleagues, telling why he couldn't be open in his own profession. To back up John Fryer, I read excerpts from letters I'd solicited from the other gay psychiatrists who felt they had to decline to be on the panel.

Also at the 1972 APA meeting, Frank and I were given a booth in the exhibit hall. With much help from friends, I set up an eye-grabbing display, "Gay, Proud, and Healthy: The Homosexual Community Speaks." Frank wrote the flyer. This exhibit featured the word LOVE in big letters. I think it was the *only* place in the whole convention where the word LOVE appeared.

There were more eye-openers for the psychiatrists. At APA's dinner-dance, at the conclusion of the conference, Frank took as his date Philip Johnson, a gay activist from Dallas. And when the band struck up a waltz, Frank and Phil sailed out onto the dance floor. The other heterosexual couples all pretended they didn't see what they saw!

Meanwhile, behind the scenes in APA, the wheels were already moving to consider taking homosexuality off the list of mental disorders as part of a general revision of the *Diagnostic and Statistical Manual.* This long and difficult debate is well recounted in Bayer's book. When the Board of Trustees endorsed the recommendation to delist homosexuality in December 1973, a major Philadelphia newspaper headlined its story "Homosexuals Gain 'Instant Cure.'" The trustees also passed a civil rights resolution opposing laws and official discrimination against gay people.

Of course a stroke of the pen doesn't change attitudes. Objections to the "official cure" were contested by psychiatrists who petitioned for a referendum of APA membership that took place in 1974. This political battle is told in detail in Bayer's book *Homosexuality and American Psychiatry.*

Mindful of the need for continuing education, APA gave the National Gay and Lesbian Task Force exhibit space at several later conventions. In 1976, in Miami, we did "Homophobia: Time for Cure," with displays of materials illustrating anti-gay attitudes and policies and practices. Part of our prescription to cure homophobia included photos of gay couples. Surprisingly, they drew strong reaction. One dubious doctor asked, "Do these relationships really work?" Many psychiatrists were used to thinking of us as miserable patients with troubled lives, and they needed to see some reality.

At this time, 1976, gay psychiatrists were coming out of the closet and had launched a GLB Caucus, whose newsletter was on hand. Its members helped staff the booth to talk to colleagues.

My last APA exhibit, "Gay Love: Good Medicine," was in Atlanta in 1978. Again we featured gays not as patients but living happy and healthy. And this time I was able to get five gay psychiatrists willing to be in the exhibit with their photos and credentials—quite a breakthrough! The GLB Caucus in APA was now taking steps to become an official subgroup of APA.

Still the closet was emptying slowly. One psychiatrist wrote the piece "The Invisible Gay Psychiatrist" for distribution at that 1978 conference; he urged those who couldn't come out to take other specific steps to push things along.

By 1979, the GLB Caucus went fully public by taking part in the gay community's first National March on Washington. You know well the rest of your history.

I am thankful to the American Psychiatric Association and to the Association of Gay and Lesbian Psychiatrists for recognizing my and Frank Kameny's work toward healing the wounds of prejudice and discrimination. I'm sure John Fryer would be thrilled and deeply gratified, as I am, for having an APA award presented in his name and for the first one going to Frank and myself. By drawing attention to the mask and the damage it does, Dr. H. Anonymous helped tear away disguise and secrecy. He gave courage to his fellow gay and lesbian psychiatrists to be fully themselves and to affirm, in Frank's great motto, that Gay Is Good.

The gay community's mental health improved dramatically when we spoke up for ourselves and took charge of our own destiny. I'm so glad I was a player in this part of gay history and that I got to know the incomparable John Fryer.

Leading the Charge

Gittings and others were forever indebted to Fryer for his efforts at helping change the APA.

David Scasta interviewed Fryer for the *Journal of Gay & Lesbian Psychotherapy* in 2003. Fryer recalled attending the APA convention with other closeted gay men who were part of an underground group, the "Gay-P-A," in 1970, and "all of us watched" Gittings and Kameny "picketing the APA. We in the Gay-P-A commented, 'Isn't that nice,' but we weren't about to do anything that might expose us."

After Fryer agreed to do the panel in disguise, he had the task of figuring out how to do that at 6 feet 4 inches and about 300 pounds. "Fortunately, my lover at that time was a drama major and, with his assistance, we created an outfit," he told Scasta.

At that 1972 meeting, Fryer said, in part: "I am disguised tonight in order that I might speak freely without conjuring up too much regard on your part about the particular *who* I happen to be. ... As psychiatrists who are homosexual, we must know our place and what we must do to be successful. ... Much like the black man with the light skin who chooses to live as a white man, we cannot be seen with our real friends—our real homosexual family—lest our secret be known and our dooms sealed. ... Just as the black man must be superperson so must we, in order to face those among our colleagues who know we are gay."

Fryer died in 2003, at age 64. The *British Medical Journal*'s obituary noted that he had been "forced out of his third year of residency at the University of Pennsylvania when it was discovered that he was gay" and that he "had insisted on delivering his Dallas speech in disguise not only through fear for his job. It was also 'a bit of calculated theatre,' said Barbara Gittings. Flamboyant and outspoken, Fryer often used a bit of theatre to good effect. ... During his famous 1972 speech, Fryer spoke directly to the 'more than a hundred [gay] psychiatrists' he claimed were registered at the convention, urging them to find ways to help change the attitudes of both heterosexual and homosexual patients towards homosexuality. He warned them that it would be risky, but added, 'We are taking an even bigger risk, however, not accepting fully our own humanity, with all the lessons it has to teach all the other humans around us and ourselves. This is the greatest loss: our honest humanity.'"

Katherine Fryer Helmbock, Fryer's sister, told the *Journal*: "To people who knew John, this was only one of the many things he did, but changing *DSM* [*Diagnostic and Statistical Manual*] was a momentous thing. This label, mental illness, was one of the bases for treating gay people badly. This took away a huge cudgel used against gay people for so many years."

Kameny had been opposed to having anyone appear in a mask at the APA. As Lahusen told Rubick: "Frank said, 'This goes against everything we've been fighting for.' So we [Lahusen and Gittings] had a terrific argument with Frank. People thought we were just rubber stamps for Frank, but that wasn't true—because we were all so strong-minded."

Rubick added: "Lahusen, as usual, took photographs of the panel, one of which promptly appeared in *GAY* newspaper. … In 1972, the same year as the panel, Lahusen published a book called *The Gay Crusaders*. The publisher preferred to have a man's name on the cover of the book (the book had been sold to the publisher as having a gay man and a gay woman as authors), so Randy Wicker lent his name, but Lahusen, with Gittings' help, wrote the book."

Wicker admits to this, saying in 2015: "It's absolutely her book, I wrote maybe one paragraph in that whole book." During promotions, Lahusen wanted Wicker to be the public face of the book, because she preferred to be behind the scenes.

Like Gittings, Lahusen was positive in her outlook. In a December 23, 1970, letter to Craig Rodwell, who was a friend and owner of Manhattan's Oscar Wilde Memorial Bookshop, Lahusen wrote, "We want our book to be the most positive statement possible about the men and women who have been gay crusaders."

Gittings, in *Crusaders*, summarized their goals: "The whole point of gay liberation is that gay people are no longer willing to live by heterosexual expectations and values, as codified by the psychiatrists or anyone else. We're defining our own lives for ourselves, we're setting our own expectations for ourselves, we're developing our own value systems. For almost a century psychiatry has poisoned the whole climate of thinking about homosexuality! But at last good antidotes are being produced."

The American Psychiatric Association convention in 1972 was in Dallas. It was the first to feature a gay psychiatrist—but he wore a mask. On the panel were Barbara Gittings, Frank Kameny, Dr. H. Anonymous and Dr. Judd Marmor (at mic in top photo).
Photos by Kay Tobin Lahusen. Copyright Manuscripts and Archives Division, The New York Public Library

Text is a statement Gittings and Kameny handed out in advance of the panel discussion.

GAY, PROUD AND HEALTHY

In recent years, an adversary situation has developed between the psychiatric profession and the homosexual community. While much of psychiatry seems unaware of this, it is felt with growing resentment and bitterness by the homosexual community, who increasingly see psychiatry as THE major enemy in a battle against deeply-rooted societal prejudice, and see psychiatrists as singularly insensitive and obtuse to the destruction which they are wreaking upon homosexuals by their negative attitudes and pronouncements. We consider such an adversary situation undesirable and reconciliation to be to the advantage of both adversaries. That is why we, as homosexuals, are here at the Dallas conference of the American Psychiatric Association. In our view, homosexuals are the people most knowledgeable about, and certainly most concerned with these questions. We have traditionally been the people least consulted while others, self-appointed and never authorized to represent us, have talked *about* us instead of *with* us, and set themselves up, without our permission, as our spokesmen. We are bringing that to an end.

Central to the conflict between psychiatry and the homosexual community is the "sickness theory" of homosexuality and the whole related complex of negative attitudes toward homosexuality, which try to make of homosexuality something inferior to and less desirable than heterosexuality. It matters not whether the word used be sickness, disorder, affliction, disturbance, dysfunction, neurosis, immaturity, fixation, character or personality disorder, pathology, or any other—or whether homosexuality be considered as merely symptomatic of these—the effects are the same: (1) To support and buttress the prejudices of society and to assist the bigots in the perpetration and perpetuation of their bigotry; and, at least equally important (2) To destroy the homosexual's self-confidence and self-esteem, impair his or her self-image, degrade his or her basic human dignity.

Above: Dr. H. Anonymous listens as Gittings speaks. Bottom left: Dr. H. Anonymous with moderator Dr. Kent Robinson. Bottom right: Dr. Anonymous and Dr. Judd Marmor.
Photos by Kay Tobin Lahusen. Copyright Manuscripts and Archives Division, The New York Public Library

Above: Gittings and Kameny in Dallas at the APA. Bottom left: The duo talk with psychiatrists. Bottom right: Gittings confronts Dr. Richard Green and colleague at the APA.
Photos by Kay Tobin Lahusen. Copyright Manuscripts and Archives Division, The New York Public Library

The gay activists had a "Gay, Proud, and Healthy" display at the APA in Dallas. Gittings and Kameny are featured in the top photo. Below: A conference attendee looks at the display.
Photos by Kay Tobin Lahusen. Copyright Manuscripts and Archives Division, The New York Public Library

Gittings at the 1972 APA display.
Photos by Kay Tobin Lahusen. Copyright Manuscripts and Archives Division, The New York Public Library

**Gittings
and Phil
Johnson, a
Texas gay
activist,
staff the
APA booth.**
Photo by Kay
Tobin Lahusen.
Copyright
Manuscripts
and Archives
Division, The
New York
Public Library

Bottom left: coverage in *GAY* newspaper of the APA participation.

Bottom right: Gittings, Johnson and Kameny at the APA.
Photo by Kay Tobin Lahusen. Copyright Manuscripts and Archives Division, The New York Public Library

The Chicago Gay Crusader was among the many gay and mainstream papers that headlined the APA's change in diagnosis of homosexuality.

Below: Gays protesting at one of the annual APA meetings.
Photo by Kay Tobin Lahusen. Copyright Manuscripts and Archives Division, The New York Public Library

Gittings and Kameny returned to the APA for several years. Here is their 1978 booth.
Photo by Kay Tobin Lahusen. Copyright Manuscripts and Archives Division, The New York Public Library

Chapter 5
In the Stacks:
American Library Association

Even as she was helping to take on the formidable American Psychiatric Association, Gittings had her sights on another major institution: the American Library Association. Gittings was a bibliophile, hunting to find her own life reflected in the library stacks from the first inkling she was gay. She knew the power of books, both in their ability to undermine or to uplift. So, even though she was not a librarian by training, she joined forces with a new group for librarians, the Task Force on Gay Liberation, to make significant change at the ALA.

"Bells rang for me!" Gittings told Perry and Swicegood in *Profiles in Gay & Lesbian Courage*. "It seemed absolutely wonderful, and I had a sudden urge to be a part of that group. I knew the power of books. I could never forget how the heroines of novels had taught me something of gay life, how they helped me in a quest to find my people, and instilled in me the idea that we, as homosexuals, deserve the same opportunities as everybody else for the pursuit of happiness. Therefore, since the notice didn't say the new organization was for librarians only, I went to their next meeting. It turned out to be a very small gay group gathering in somebody's New York apartment, and they welcomed newcomers who could help, librarians or not."

She wrote an article about her ALA efforts for the 1990 book *Gay and Lesbian Library Service*, edited by Cal Gough and Ellen Greenblatt, but she missed the deadline for the book and instead put out the material as a pamphlet. What follows is Gittings' piece, "Gays in Library Land: The Gay and Lesbian Task Force of the American Library Association: The First Sixteen Years."

Barbara Gittings: Gays in Library Land

"I don't see why those people are getting all the publicity when we have so many famous authors in town." — Librarian at 1971 American Library Association conference in Dallas, commenting on TV coverage of the Task Force on Gay Liberation's kissing booth in the exhibit hall

A kissing booth at a librarians' convention? A *gay* kissing booth? What on earth were Those People up to?

Getting ourselves noticed, that's what. Making a gay presence to highlight gay issues in a setting where homosexuality wasn't typically viewed as a concern for the profession.

When the gay group in the American Library Association formed in 1970, it was the first of its kind, the first time that gay people in any professional association had openly banded together to advance the gay cause through that profession. Why didn't this happen first among gay professionals in law or religion or the behavioral sciences, the fields that had been treating homosexuality as a special concern?

It was just good luck for ALA to be the pioneer.

A year before, at ALA's annual conference, social activists had launched a new official unit of ALA, the Social Responsibilities Round Table (SRRT), under whose wing self-created task forces began to tackle neglected issues in librarianship.

Janet Cooper and Israel Fishman met at SRRT gatherings at ALA's 1970 conference in Detroit. They talked about not running scared anymore, and about using their professional standing and skills to openly influence library holdings on homosexuality. The Task Force on Gay Liberation was born. It was promptly endorsed by SRRT and was allocated a share of SRRT's small money pie (derived from dues separate from ALA dues). The TFGL drew a handful of other gay librarians who were fired up by the Stonewall Rebellion in 1969 and were eager to change gay literature and gay people's lives.

I, too, was keen to push for change. Back in 1949, when I was a freshman in college, the confusion finally cleared and I put the label on and said to myself, "Homosexual—that's what I am, I'm one of those." So what were "those"? What did it mean to be a homosexual? What was in store for me? There wasn't anyone I could ask. So naturally I went to the library for information.

Today when I speak to gay groups and mention "the lies in the libraries," listeners over 35 know instantly what I mean. Most gays have at some point gone to books in an effort to understand about being gay or to get some help in living as gay. In my time, what we found was strange to us (they're writing about me but I'm not like that!) and cruelly clinical (there's nothing about *love*) and always bad (being this way seems grim and hopeless).

I flunked out of college at the end of my freshman year because I had stopped going to classes in order to run around to libraries and spend my time reading—reading about myself in categories such as "Sexual Perversions"—and wondering and worrying. When I returned home in disgrace, I couldn't explain to my parents what was wrong, and I still knew no one I could approach to talk to—so back to the stacks I went.

This time I was luckier. I found the fiction of homosexuality. In these stories homosexuality often was an agony and the endings usually were unhappy. Still, the characters weren't case histories but people who had feelings and who loved and who even had times of happiness. From Stephen Gordon, the earnest strong dyke of Radclyffe Hall's *The Well of Loneliness*, to Compton Mackenzie's *Extraordinary Women,* the exotic figures of fun, they all made me feel much better about being a lesbian.

Soon I had my first mutual love affair, and soon after it ended I left home and landed in the nearest big city. After seeing to my most urgent needs—a job, a place to live, and a choral group to sing with—I devoted most of my spare time to my continuing education. I spent hours in the Rare Book Room reading Havelock Ellis and John Addington Symonds, and many more hours browsing in second-hand bookshops hoping to turn up gay novels.

Eventually I read [Donald Webster] Cory's *The Homosexual in America* and was thrilled to find extensive checklists of literature in the back of his book. I arranged to meet Cory, and through him I found the then-tiny gay movement, which I officially joined in 1958. Now I had less time for reading and collecting. At first I did social and political organizing. Later I was picketing and marching for gay rights, battling homophobic bureaucrats, appearing on radio and later on TV, and editing *The Ladder,* the first national lesbian magazine.

But working in the movement kept reminding me that the written word has such a long-range effect, that the literature on homosexuality was so crucial in shaping the images that we and others have of ourselves, and that these distorted images we were forced to live with must not be allowed to continue. I knew that the lies in the libraries had to be changed, but I didn't have a clear sense that we gay people could do it.

Then for a few months in 1970 I was asked to report gay news on New York's WBAI-FM. One day, in the station's mail slot for the gay broadcast, I found a news release from the Task Force on Gay Liberation of the American Library Association. A group of gay librarians had formed and was inviting others to join.

Gay books? Libraries? That rang bells for me!

I went to early meetings of TFGL in New York in the fall of 1970 and was welcomed. The group was ambitiously planning a sizable annotated bibliography. Meanwhile, a short list of the most positive materials available was wanted for distribution at the Midwinter conference of ALA, and I helped put together that first non-fiction bibliography, dated January 1971, with 37 entries—books, pamphlets, and articles. That first list was easy. We were still 10 years away from the great explosion of gay materials that would mean Reader's Delight Equals List-Maker's Plight.

Israel Fishman was TFGL's first coordinator and his talent for making a flamboyant presence helped put the group boldly on the ALA map that first year. For the annual conference in June 1971 in Dallas (I was there, I was now thoroughly hooked!) the group planned solid, professional program events: the first Gay Book Award; talks by Joan Marshall and Steve Wolf under the joint title "Sex and the Single Cataloger: New Thoughts on Some Unthinkable Subjects"; and a talk by Michael McConnell, who had lost a new library job in 1970 after he and his lover Jack Baker applied openly for a marriage license [in Minnesota], and who was fighting his job discrimination case in the federal courts.

But solid, professional program events need audiences. We needed publicity. At the biggest meetings during the conference, we aggressively leafleted with 3,000 copies of a revised edition of our list, which now was titled "A Gay Bibliography" and had 48 entries including a few periodicals and featured a bold "Gay Is Good" logo at the head. We posted notices of our activities all around the conference premises—and kept replacing them as they disappeared. We ran a hospitality suite in the main convention hotel where we offered free copies of gay periodicals and a place to relax and talk.

We took over the microphones at a huge meeting of the Intellectual Freedom Committee that was playing fictitious "value games" and [we] claimed the audience's attention with a real example of intellectual freedom abuse: the case of Michael McConnell, whose earlier appeal to the IFC had been brushed aside even though IFC's own policies were clearly applicable to his situation. We weren't afraid to pre-empt a tame meeting and give it some guts.

And we learned, with the help of McConnell's lover Jack Baker, how to do news releases. Late each night we were in ALA's on-location offices using the typewriters and Xerox machines to produce short write-ups of our past or coming activities, always including not only the main facts but a lively quote or two ("Catalog librarians declare that 15 million gay Americans refuse to be called Sexual Aberrations"). Then we went around Dallas hand-delivering the releases to newspapers, wire services, and radio and broadcast stations.

What a heady time! We were activists. We were innovative, bold, imaginative, full of fun and energy, full of love for promoting our cause.

Predictably, it was our gay kissing booth that really threw us into the limelight. All the SRRT task forces had been invited to use a booth in the conference exhibit hall for a couple of hours each. We could have devoted our turn to a nice display of books and periodicals and our "Gay Bibliography." But Israel Fishman decided to bypass books and show gay love, live.

We called it Hug-a-Homosexual. On the bare gray curtains forming the back wall of the booth, we hung signs reading "Women Only" at one end and "Men Only" at the other, and there we waited, smiling, ready to dispense free (yes, free) same-sex kisses and hugs.

The aisles were jammed. But no one entered the booth. They all wanted to ogle the action, not be part of it. Maybe the *Life* photographer and the glaring lights from the two Dallas TV crews made them feel shy.

Hundreds of exhibit visitors crowded around and craned their necks as the eight of us in the booth hugged and kissed each other, called encouragement to the watchers, kissed and hugged each other some more—and between times handed out our bibliography to those in the throng.

Librarians at that 1971 conference learned fast that lesbians and gay men are here and everywhere, that we won't go away, and that we will insist on our rights and recognition. Result: In the last days of the conference, we got both the Council (the elected policy-making body of ALA) and the general membership to pass our pro-gay resolution. ["The American Library Association recognizes that there exist minorities which are not ethnic in nature but which suffer oppression. The association recommends that libraries and members strenuously combat discrimination in services to, and employment of, individuals from all minority groups, whether distinguishing characteristics of the minority be ethnic, sexual, religious, or any other kind." (Passed by ALA Council and ALA membership, June 1971.)]

Maybe some librarians voted for it because it seemed innocuously vague, and maybe others voted for it in hopes we wouldn't embarrass ALA with another Hug-a-Homosexual stunt. Still, the resolution did become official policy of ALA.

Our group's aim to change library holdings on homosexuality coincided with a shift in the book business itself. In 1969, even the best non-fiction writing on gays was mostly by non-gay authors, and it hedged about us, sniped at us, clucked over us, or dissected us.

But the Stonewall uprising of 1969 galvanized many gay people to new action. Some produced book manuscripts that caught editors' fancy as the major trade publishers sighted a whole new market. At the time our gay group sprouted in ALA, publishers were processing the first major crop of gay-positive books by gay authors. There were a dozen of them, and they boosted by 50 percent the books section of the June 1972 edition of our "Gay Bibliography." Now the first title on the list was no longer *Sexual Morality* but Abbott and Love's *Sappho Was a Right-On Woman.*

Our first Gay Book Award in 1971 also reflected the publishing transition. Isabel Miller, a published writer under her own name Alma Routsong, could not, in 1968–'69, sell her novel about a lesbian couple homesteading in the early 1800s. So she published it herself in 1970. At the time she came to Dallas in 1971 to receive our Gay Book Award for *A Place for Us,* she was negotiating with McGraw-Hill for a hardcover edition of her novel to be retitled *Patience and Sarah*—and McGraw-Hill was one of the publishers who had turned it down before. We had found a way to honor our own gay authors just as the first wave of general recognition was breaking.

I loved working with the Task Force on Gay Liberation. So when Israel Fishman wanted to step out as coordinator and suggested me for the job, I was delighted to accept. I took out membership in ALA (ALA accepted lay members) to facilitate the necessary working-through-channels within the association.

Since we now had a formula for success at ALA conferences, we used it in Chicago in 1972. Again, posting notices and handing out the "Gay Bibliography" at large meetings kept people aware of us, and this time our main events were also listed in the official conference programs.

Michael McConnell brought an overflow audience up to date on his case: a federal appeals court, reversing a lower court's ruling in his favor, had said that while there was no question he was fully qualified for the library job he was denied, the university was entitled to renege because he demanded "the right to pursue an activist role in *implementing* his unconventional ideas" (court's emphasis).

Joan Marshall spoke again wittily on the queer ways gay books are classified, and she told about one positive change, the Library of Congress's new number, HQ 76.5, for works on "Gay Liberation Movement."

The authors of *Lesbian/Woman,* Del Martin and Phyllis Lyon, and *The Gay Mystique,* Peter Fisher, were on hand to receive jointly the second Gay Book Award. And there were poetry readings from Sappho, Walt Whitman, Constantin Cavafy and Gertrude Stein, reminding our audience of 250 that these writers whose works they value on library shelves had a homosexual dimension to their lives and art.

Our hospitality suite that year was large and, thanks to enthusiastic gay friends in Chicago, was kept open 12 hours a day for people to talk, browse in gay books, walk through a display of photos of gay love and gay liberation activities and examine a set of art works by famous artists (Rodin, Homer, Hockney, etc.) showing same-sex couples. When the wife of the ALA president came to look us over, we felt we'd really arrived.

But our job was as much to unsettle ALA over gay issues as to settle into the ALA fabric. With good gay reading for adults fairly launched, what about gay reading for kids? In February 1972, *School Library Journal* published an article about our group led by Mary McKenny, who noted that school libraries owe, but rarely give, good service to young gay people or to any students who want sensible information about homosexuality.

At the ALA conference in June of that year, we unveiled our first gay primer, *Fun With Our Gay Friends,* in which Dick and Jane and their playmates casually meet same-sex adult couples as a natural part of the world around them. Frances Hanckel, another non-librarian in TFGL, insisted the primer deserved more attention than mere display. So, spoofing ALA's [Newbery and Caldecott medals for children's books], we created and bestowed the New Raspberry–Cold Cut Award. Alas, there was no rush of publishers to put this winner into mass circulation. But we knew we'd come back to the theme of gay reading for youngsters.

We skipped the 1973 conference and the Gay Book Award for that year. None of our core members could get to Las Vegas, and there was no outstanding book we wanted to honor. Still we tried to maintain our presence at ALA by means of a flier which we asked friends in SRRT to post and hand around the conference.

We were unmistakably present in New York City in 1974. Our smiling leafleteers, all two of them, blitzed the conference in its first three days with 4,000 copies each of our "Gay Bibliography" and a flier announcing our activities. Almost 300 people turned up to hear "Let's Not Homosexualize the Library Stacks," Michael McConnell's reasoned appeal to move from "Homosexual" to "Gay" in subject headings in order to spur needed changes in attitude.

Appropriately, our first Gay Book Award author, Isabel Miller, presented the 1974 award to *Sex Variant Women in Literature* by Jeannette Foster, a retired librarian. Dr. Foster too had had publishing trouble. When in the mid-1950s she finished her critical survey of lesbianism and sexual variance in literature from Sappho through 20th century writings in English, German, and French, no publisher would touch it, not even a university press. She had to go to a vanity house in 1956 to see it in print, and then wait almost 20 years more to see it properly republished. We were pleased to recognize her pioneer work.

By now we had a reputation for putting on programs that appealed to librarians' professional interests and were also entertaining. Over 400 people attended our 1975 program on negative gay themes in teenage novels, "The Children's Hour: Must Gay Be Grim for Jane and Jim?"

It struck sparks. The lively debate it triggered convinced us to do a follow-up panel discussion as part of the next year's program. And the energy momentum drove the program's architects, Frances Hanckel and John Cunningham, to prepare a set of "Guidelines for the Treatment of Gay Themes in Children's and Young Adult Literature" (September 1975), to write an article for the library press called "Can Young Gays Find Happiness in YA Books?" [*Wilson Library Bulletin*], and to collaborate on a trade book titled *A Way of Love, a Way of Life: A Young Person's Introduction to What It Means To Be Gay* (Lothrop, Lee and Shepard, 1979).

Other popular programs:

— "Serving the Fearful Reader" (1976), a series of skits about what can happen when patrons who are timid or confused about homosexuality approach the reference desk, plus a superbly acted pantomime on the stolen-book problem called "Now You See It, Now You Don't"

— "Gay Film Festival" (1978), 18 non-fiction gay/lesbian films including the just-released blockbuster *Word Is Out*

— "An Evening With Gertrude Stein" (1979), a re-creation by actress Pat Bond that was so moving that one librarian told us afterwards, "You know, I've never read Gertrude Stein, but I'm going to read her now"

— "Gay Materials for Use in Schools" (1980)

— "It's Safer To Be Gay on Another Planet" (1981), about gay themes in science fiction/fantasy, with author Robert Silverberg as panel moderator

— "The Celluloid Closet: Lesbians and Gay Men in Hollywood Film" (1982), Vito Russo's now-famous lecture with film clips from 1895 to today, including several startling outtake scenes

— "Why Keep All Those Posters, Buttons, and Papers? The Problems and Rewards of Gay/Lesbian Archives" (1983)

— "Closet Keys: Gay/Lesbian Periodicals for Libraries" (1984)

— "You Want To Look Up WHAT?? Indexing the Lesbian and Gay Press"; also "Blind Lesbians and Gays: The Lavender Pen on Cassette and in Braille" (1985)

Our programs were always open to the gay community in the host city. We publicized our ALA events through local gay groups and publications, and we let people know they didn't need to be registered for the conference, they didn't even need to be librarians. They were welcome to walk in— and they did.

Also we weren't shy about asking host-city people for help with everything from bringing refreshments, to donating flowers to dress up podiums, to leafleting with us around the conference. Occasionally, local activists would set up a bonus event for the benefit of TFGL members. Examples: in Los Angeles, the national president of Parents and Friends of Lesbians and Gays, Adele Starr, and her husband Larry Starr came to our business meeting to talk about their work with libraries and to exchange ideas; in New York City, we went to showings of films about May Sarton and Christopher Isherwood, arranged by the Gay Teachers Association.

Our open-door policy was partly due to our having, in the early years, several non-librarians besides myself in key roles in the Task Force—most notably Jack Baker; Frances Hanckel, who was active in the group for over seven years; and Kay (Tobin) Lahusen, who for 15 years contributed vision, practical help, and a photo history of our activities. Publicity and propaganda were as much needed as librarian skills, and there was plenty of work for everyone who wanted to boost gay materials and their handling in libraries.

Participation by non-librarians not only brought extra energy and talent to our group, it also was good for ALA's image. Hundreds of gay men and lesbians across the United States who wouldn't dream of being involved in professional meetings of doctors, historians, and the like—except perhaps to demonstrate against them—found themselves happily rubbing elbows with librarians at ALA conferences.

The lay-professional mix in the Gay Task Force (as it was renamed in 1975 so the word Gay would hit the eye first) was aided by ALA's and SRRT's few rules about structure and membership, and by the very loose organization of GTF itself. For its first 16 years, including the 15 years I served as coordinator, GTF had no elected officers, no membership requirements, no dues. As coordinator I handled most of the ongoing scut work: ALA paperwork and deadlines; SRRT meetings and reports; correspondence; set-up and printing of fliers and the "Gay Bibliography" and other publications; the jobs were done by those willing to do them, for the fun and satisfaction.

In outreach beyond the library field we scored best with "A Gay Bibliography." We had begun this list as a selective guide to the small crop of gay-supportive books just beginning to appear in 1970–'71, plus a few key gay periodicals and pamphlets. Naturally we wanted the list to reach not only librarians who buy for their libraries, but also gay people who might be searching for the sparse gay material available in libraries and bookstores.

By dint of our efforts to promote our one-of-a-kind guide, we began getting mentions of our bibliography and our group in books then being published, such as *Sappho Was a Right-On Woman* (1972) and *Lesbian/Woman* (1972). Even in 1990, the GTF hears from people who have just come across these books and who write, "I hope there's still somebody at this address after all these years."

For some who write to us, it's their first contact with a gay/lesbian group. The "information" they often need is more than finding gay reading—it means finding other gay people. What a boon it's been to have *Gayellow Pages* to steer them to!

Our "Gay Bibliography," issued yearly at first, soon got harder to revise so often. The 6th edition, in March 1980, with 563 entries including audio-visuals, took more than a year to put together and cost several thousand dollars to produce. We had to take a breather. Fortunately we had ordered a big printing run, and over the next few years more than 38,000 copies of that edition were distributed in and out of libraries.

As gay materials grew in quantity and quality, we began getting requests for shorter lists, lists crafted for a particular audience or focusing on one topic. For example, an aide to a Midwestern state legislator asked for no more than a dozen basic gay items to start educating lawmakers who knew little about homosexuality. "If you give them a long list, it's too much to grasp and they won't look at anything," she said. We complied.

Other inquiries came from lesbians and gay men who wanted guidance to novels, since our bibliography's book titles were non-fiction and biography. Founders of the early Parents-of-Gays groups sought to pinpoint materials about gay people's relationships with their families. And once a librarian at a men's prison wrote that some inmates wanted to be able to use gay materials without advertising the fact; would we make up a list of gay male books without the words "gay" or "homosexual" in the titles or showing on the covers? We did.

There was one challenge we couldn't meet: the occasional request to "Please send all available information on homosexuality. My term paper is due next week."

Out of the requests we got most often came a series of short lists, including "Gay Resources for Religious Study," "Gay Materials for Use in Schools," and "Gay Aids for Counselors," all launched in 1978 and revised several times, and "Gay Teachers Resources" (1979, 1980). "A Short Lesbian Reading List" (also first issued in 1978) prompted more than one reader to ask, "Is it for tall lesbians too?"

One special list we started in 1976, "Gay Books in Format for the Blind and Physically Handicapped," was eventually adopted, with our gratitude, by another organization far better equipped to keep it up to date and circulate it, the Lambda Resource Center for the Blind in Chicago [which in 2015 no longer operates as a free-standing organization].

We also drew up a short list aimed specifically at librarians. In 1976, John Cunningham pointed out that H. W. Wilson's *Public Library Catalog* recommended only two books on homosexuality: Merle Miller's *On Being Different* and Peter and Barbara Wyden's anti-gay *Growing Up Straight*. Cunningham's efforts to deal directly with the catalog editors got mired in the Wilson company's complicated national-jury system for its selections. So we prepared a "Gay Materials Core Collection List" (1976, updated annually through 1980) as a buying guide for small and medium-sized public libraries. For five years we did our best to counteract the inadequacies of Wilson's recommendations, which continued to lag far behind publishing trends in the choice of gay titles.

As more good gay literature came out, lay people too were itching to get the stuff into libraries. Stuart W. Miller headed our committee of eight who produced a pamphlet of tips for non-librarians, "Censored, Ignored, Overlooked, Too Expensive? How to Get Gay Materials into Libraries" (1979). This booklet explained library selection policies in a general way, and told what groups and individuals could do to promote gay books and periodicals in their public and college libraries. It included sections on what to do if your request is turned down, on why gay books are sometimes kept where you have to ask for them, and on donating materials to the library.

Ordinary libraries weren't our only concern. Gay and lesbian libraries and archives had begun forming in the 1960s, to provide concentrated collections and preserve materials that wouldn't be acquired by most mainstream libraries. Each such library/archive had to create its own classifications and subject headings, because existing schemes for organizing information, such as Dewey and Library of Congress, weren't intended for the depth and scope of specialized collections. But why keep inventing the wheel? In 1985 Joseph Gregg and Robert Ridinger began developing a master thesaurus of subject terms that will make it easier for gay libraries to coordinate with each other and for their users to find materials.

Much of GTF's work was guidance and encouragement with respect to gay materials produced by others. The one kind of information on homosexuality we hoped to influence directly was encyclopedia articles. Encyclopedias are a first source of information for many readers, and they carry authority, especially with school students who assume the material in them is the best available. What students read about us in encyclopedias in the 1970s ranged from dismal to depressing. As for accuracy, it had as much relevance to our lives as though a skin doctor were to write about black people. Our committee on encyclopedia changes reviewed the major encyclopedias and also planned to ask gay psychiatrists and psychologists, whose "expert" credentials might more readily impress encyclopedia editors, to work with us to effect changes. [Dale C. Burke, "Homophobia in Encyclopedias," *Interracial Books for Children Bulletin* Vol. 14, Nos. 3 and 4 (1983).]

So many avenues for us to explore! For a few years in the early 1980s we turned our Midwinter meetings into mini-programs—"mini" only in the size of the rooms allotted us, since at the smaller Midwinter conference of ALA each January, ALA units were supposed to have only working sessions for their members, no programs for large audiences. Thirty to 40 people would cram GTF's small room to hear our unofficial programs:

— In 1981, two librarians who came to explain the case of a Virginia Beach gay newspaper that was removed from a freebie table in the public library's lobby
— In 1982, "The Family Protection Act vs. First Amendment Rights"
— In 1984, "Gay-Lesbian Publishing and the Library of Congress: Coming Out and Going In"
— In 1985, "Gay Materials in Smalltown, USA?"

At the 1986 Midwinter conference we did arrange a full-scale, big-room program on "AIDS Awareness: The Library's Role." Despite co-sponsorship by the Public Library Association, a major division of ALA, there was a very disappointing turnout for this excellent presentation of the AIDS Information Project at the Chicago Public Library in cooperation with the Chicago Department of Health. For shame, that we were ahead of our time in raising the AIDS issue in ALA in early 1986.

We had other disappointments too.

For instance, there was our experiment with sign language interpretation. Lyn Paleo, a speaker at our 1981 panel "It's Safer To Be Gay on Another Planet," happened to be a signer, and she offered to interpret the whole program. We announced this in advance. A number of deaf librarians attended the program and told us afterwards how pleased they were to have something they could go to at the conference outside of the few signed sessions devoted to deaf concerns.

We thought we'd latched onto a good thing. So the next year we paid for interpreters for our main and secondary programs, both lectures with audio-visuals: "The Celluloid Closet: Lesbians and Gay Men in Hollywood Film" by Vito Russo, and "From 'Boston Marriage' to the Tell-All 1970s: One Hundred Years of the Lesbian in Biography" by Marie Kuda. Again, we advertised the signing. This time, not a single person wanting sign interpretation showed up. It was a worthy but expensive gesture and we didn't repeat it.

Then there was the fizzle of our gay mediagraphy for teenagers. After Frances Hanckel and John Cunningham set ALA buzzing about young-adult gay materials in 1975–'76, the Media Selection and Usage Committee of the Young Adult Services Division invited two GTF members as consultants to help MSUC prepare a mediagraphic essay on the gay experience. Here was a great chance for us to influence a recommended basic-collection list to be issued by an influential group in ALA. After a couple of productive meetings to review films and books, the project fell apart, then was put back on track by a new MSUC chair, then collapsed again. Why was never clear.

We also fared badly with a project strictly our own, our discrimination survey in 1978. We wanted to know, beyond our small group, what are the concerns of gay and lesbian library workers about discrimination and/or censorship on the job? We crafted a questionnaire to find out. To reach as many people as possible, we saturated the 1978 conference with the questionnaire: copies in stacks right near conference registration documents that everyone would pick up, copies handed out to everyone at doorways to meetings big and small, even copies laid on audience chairs in advance of some meetings. No one needed to feel singled out in getting a copy.

The result after several thousand questionnaires were distributed? Only 135 were returned. Most of the respondents reported they didn't feel any pressures strong or subtle affecting themselves or gay materials for their libraries. This "No Problem" picture struck us as skewed, but at the time we had no other way to discover different stories.

Certainly there *was* prejudice in library land. We had a prime case to prove it: Michael McConnell. For four years starting in 1971, McConnell and others in GTF protested his job loss at Council and Membership meetings. Each time his case was bumped along for "study" or "investigation"—to the Intellectual Freedom Committee, to the desk of ALA's Executive Director, to the Staff Committee on Mediation, Arbitration and Inquiry.

Each report recommended No Action, citing in part such technicalities as the fact that the university which dumped McConnell in 1970 wasn't violating any ALA policy in force at that time. Since ALA did adopt our 1971 gay support resolution and in 1974 an equal-employment policy including the phrase "regardless of ... individual lifestyle," it's plain that ALA failed the spirit if not the letter of fairness by refusing even in 1975 to go to bat for McConnell.

ALA was a bit less squeamish about gay rights by the time Anita Bryant launched a national crusade against gay rights in 1976. Anita Bryant, until then best known as a Christian singer and a publicist for Florida orange juice, expected her "Save Our Children" campaign to roll back gay civil rights laws and to undo other gains toward equality achieved by our movement.

The Gay Task Force got ALA Council to pass in 1977 a resolution reaffirming "its support for equal employment opportunity for gay librarians and library workers" and reminding libraries of "their obligation under the Library Bill of Rights to disseminate information representing all points of view on this controversial topic."

[Author's note: Anita Bryant's crusade lent itself to being spoofed. GTF member Kay Lahusen wrote an ultra-short puppet play, *Flaming Fundamentalist Meets Football Faggot*, in which gay football player Dave Kopay applies for a coaching job at Anita Bryant's Christian school—and worlds collide. The playlet was performed by puppet artist Jim Moyski at the 1977 ALA conference in Detroit.]

By 1985 ALA was ready to take a stronger stand on a case of actual rather than anticipated censorship. England's only gay/lesbian bookstore, Gay's the Word, had been raided in 1984 by British customs officers who arbitrarily seized as "obscene and indecent" quantities of books and periodicals imported from Giovanni's Room, one of the largest American gay bookstores and a major distributor of gay/lesbian materials to Great Britain and other countries. The manager and directors of Gay's the Word were up for trial for criminal conspiracy.

In the resolution we proposed, we were asking ALA to criticize a foreign government. So we sought and got endorsements from no less than seven sub-groups of ALA, including two international-relations groups. After the resolution passed, ALA wrote to the British ambassador in Washington expressing "concern ... about the restrictions on access to information in the United Kingdom" because of the raid on the London gay bookstore. [In 1986 the British government finally got itself off the hook of international embarrassment by dropping all the charges.]

The one section of ALA we could always count on to support our actions was our parent group, the Social Responsibilities Round Table. In addition, the SRRT was as generous with money as it could be. Still, the few hundred dollars we got each year never covered our expenses for all our busy doings. So we cheerfully dipped into our own pockets, hustled donations, and became adept at doing things frugally but with flair.

For instance, our awards for the Gay Book Award were usually items that cost very little or were donated, tokens of symbolic value or of personal interest for the author: hand-lettered scrolls, a lavender commencement cap, mounted copies of gay art works, a butterfly kite, a movie poster, a lavender cape.

At first, decisions about the title or titles for the Gay Book Award were made by consensus. When that became impractical, Frances Hanckel set up a committee to get nominations and make choices. By 1981 we had settled on formal guidelines and procedures for the award.

It was time to get our Gay Book Award inside the ALA tent. I applied to ALA's Awards Committee in 1982; the matter went on hold for a while, but finally I propelled it through. My last public act as coordinator of the Gay Task Force was to announce at our 1986 program that our Gay Book Award was now an official award of ALA.

I had fun in library land those 16 years. I'm proud of our accomplishments. And I think it was more than chance that ALA was the first professional association to be liberated by gay activists. Librarians are after all committed to inquiry, the open mind, and dissemination of information. We worked in a truly civilized setting.

We got the gay tide rolling in ALA. Librarians: Run with it, get more and better gay materials in libraries. Library users: Do the same. Take a librarian to lunch, if you will, and enjoy yourself while making your pitch. After all, what is activism without fun? I can almost guarantee results!

Gittings the Editor

The foregoing essay by Gittings also ran in the book *Daring To Find Our Names: The Search for Lesbigay Library History*, edited by James V. Carmichael, but Gittings was concerned about some errors in the piece as printed there and sent Carmichael an email June 19, 2003. Lahusen asked for the letter to be in this book, to clarify the historical record.

Hello Jim:

Well, Kay and I waffled for weeks about going to Toronto because of my compromised health (the cancer is growing again and I have to have another round of heavy chemotherapy). But I really wanted to get my ALA Honorary Membership award in person and my doctor said okay. Will we meet you at the conference?

Recently I was rummaging in *Daring To Find Our Names* and got a surprise. In several places in my chapter "Gays in Library Land," phrases I wrote in the negative were rendered in the affirmative, and that changed the meanings. For example:

— p. 83, I had written "we weren't afraid to pre-empt a tame meeting and give it some guts." In the book it's "We were afraid ..."

— p. 87, I had written "Also we weren't shy about asking host-city people for help..." In the book it came out as "Also we were shy..."

— p. 88, I had written "There was one challenge we couldn't meet..." and it came out as "There was one challenge we could meet..."

These are the three typos I spotted. Don't know if there are more. The odd bit is that these are all the same sort, eliminate the negative.

Jim, is it likely that your book will be reprinted? I hope so because it's a real treasure trove. And maybe the typo errors in my chapter could be fixed then?

In gay spirits, Barbara

A Natural Home

American Libraries magazine Editor Leonard Kniffel interviewed Gittings in June 1999 at the annual ALA conference in New Orleans, published in its December edition that year.

The librarians group, she said, "seemed to be my natural home in the gay rights movement. I just found that librarians have a good spirit and a good sense of fun, and all you need to do is tap it a little bit and they can really let loose—better than most other professional groups. ...

"What has changed, in the nearly 30 years since the task force started, is simply that librarians have not only become accustomed to gay literature—which is now, happily, a flood of gay literature—but they have embraced it and taken it up. You don't have to have quite the nudging and pressure that we had to use in the early years to get librarians to pay attention to all the emerging gay literature. I think that's somewhat taking care of itself now, but the task force still has a lot of issues it has to deal with."

Gittings said she was still concerned about access to books at libraries, including censorship battles around the country focused on children's books *Heather Has Two Mommies* and *Daddy's Roommate*.

"The fights have their good side because at least you now have something out in the open that you can have a dialogue about, which is much better than the total invisibility in the 1950s, and 1960s, when there was no material and nobody talked about it, and you could hardly even find anything under 'sexual deviation' or 'sexual aberration,'" she said.

ALA provided Gittings with her "best experience" in networking for the movement, because the meetings were in different cities each year. "Today, I know thousands of people, and a lot of it is thanks to ALA and the conferences in different cities," Gittings told Kniffel. Asked how she would like to be remembered, it was as "someone who helped make complete turn-arounds in the attitude toward homosexuality in the library field and the field of psychiatry."

Reflecting Ourselves

Isabel Miller, in accepting the first Task Force on Gay Liberation Book Award for *A Place for Us* in Dallas in 1971, said she felt the existence of the award "tells gay people something we've been needing to hear—that homosexuality is an interesting and valid source of subjects for artists, that it is worth the full concentration of artists, and that the true things we observe in it have a general meaning," as reported in the August 2 issue of *GAY* newspaper. "I hope gay artists will more and more stop withholding themselves from their work. I hope we will more and more look to our own lives and our friends' lives and to our great secret history for subjects and inspiration, and I hope organizations like this will more and more confirm us when we do."

Chicago's *The Paper*, a short-lived gay newspaper, covered the ALA Task Force gay book awards in Chicago in its July 1972 issue. Marie J. Kuda and George Alexander wrote the report, which detailed the honors and performances at the event, including a presentation by Chicago lesbian poet Vernita Gray. Gittings said of the books being honored: "They are a step in getting the lies about homosexuality out of the libraries." The books were *Lesbian/Woman* and *The Gay Mystique*.

In accepting his Gay Task Force award in 1975 for the Arno Press reprint series *Homosexuality: Lesbians and Gay Men in Society, History, and Literature*, Jonathan Ned Katz sent an acceptance speech read by Jack Latham. Katz stated, in part: "The development of gay studies is not a matter of academic interest only. Our rediscovery of our forgotten history, and our new knowledge of ourselves, will provide us with the spiritual nourishment we need for living, loving, and surviving in a genocidal society—for militant struggle against what Christopher Isherwood called the 'heterosexual dictatorship.' In the process of recovering our suppressed history, gay librarians have the special knowledge, resources, and interest to play a major role, as the pioneering bibliographic research librarian Jeannette H. Foster indicates. Lesbian and gay male librarians can play a vanguard role in that progress of self-determination represented by gay studies research. I view the whole movement for lesbian and gay male self-determination as a major link between ourselves, heterosexual women, Blacks, Mexican-Americans, and all ethnic, national, and economic groups and classes, who, feeling their own particular oppression, are now organizing to create a radically new society, more responsive to their human needs."

On June 24, 1995, for the 25th anniversary of the renamed Gay and Lesbian Task Force, at a Chicago event managed by former Co-Chair Roland Hansen, Gittings received a Special Recognition Award for her 15 years of ALA work. Gittings tapped Kuda to accept the award on her behalf. Kuda later spoke about that moment during a 2009 speech to the now-named Gay, Lesbian, Bisexual, and Transgender Round Table of the American Library Association.

In the remarks read by Kuda, Gittings said she was "delighted" to receive the award. "For us who put our energy and time and money into creating a better life for gay men and lesbians now, a big pat on the back is always welcome, even if you believe that the change you bring about is its own reward.

"Maybe some of you voted for me because you remember me personally, and others because you've heard about me, because my 15 years of activism with the Task Force has had a high profile. But George Eliot wrote in her novel *Middlemarch* that 'the growing good of the world is partly dependent on unhistoric acts.' So I hope you will find a way to recognize and honor the contributions of the scores of people who've done special jobs for our growing good—but whose names usually don't turn up in the written stories about us. People like Marie Kuda, who has been a mover and shaker in this organization for 20 years. Marie, I salute you. And I salute all those others who for a day, for a week, or for years, have given our Task Force their time and talent just for the fun of it and as its own reward.

"As for your 50th anniversary, when I'm interviewed at the Lavender Light-Years Retirement Home and I'm asked what has most gratified me as a gay activist since 1958, I'll probably say it was putting other people up to things for the cause, stirring up gay gumption whenever I could. Keep up the good work!

"And I'll say now what I know I'll say then: to paraphrase the title of one of the first crop of gay books coming out at the time the Task Force itself got launched: *I've Had More Fun With You Than Anybody*."

Wayne Dynes, who helped work on the gay bibliographies put out by ALA's Gay Task Force, wrote on the LGBT-Today website that his work on the project "made a personal difference to me, because my continuing reflection on the matter led finally to my book *Homosexuality: A Research Guide* of 1987, fully annotated and still the largest work of its kind. Some activists (like most people, I fear) are 'underwhelmed' by bibliographies. Such indifference is a mistake, because these research tools are vital underpinnings of any valid understanding of sexual orientation—and ultimately of the social and legal changes which were such a necessary component of the last 50 years."

Fairy Godmother

Gittings' work went beyond the APA and ALA in the 1970s.

"In the fall of 1973 I persuaded Barbara to serve as a keynote speaker at [a] convention of the just-organized Gay Academic Union at John Jay College in New York City. The title of her presentation was 'Take a Lesbian to Lunch,'" Dynes wrote. "It was a humorous talk that addressed a serious problem, the shroud of invisibility that we had to contend with. Even now, some of our 'respectable' opponents insist that if only we would be quiet and remain in the closet, all would be well. Barbara would have none of this. She insisted that we activists must always be busy oiling the hinges of the closet doors so that everyone could come out.

"Perhaps Barbara's most outstanding quality was her universality: She could talk to anyone and was not shy about doing so. In part this ability stemmed from her family's background in the diplomatic corps. But it was also personal, relying upon her natural warmth and strength of character.

"Because of the Vietnam War and other issues, the 1970s, which saw the birth of the modern GLBT movement, were a very turbulent era. From my vantage point in the New York Chapter of the Gay Academic Union I saw, close up, the conflicts between the radicals and the reformers, the hippies and the squares, and the separatists and the integrationists. Only time could heal these splits, as it did, but Barbara Gittings played a very important role in hastening our progress towards the relative unity we now enjoy."

"Barbara loves fairy-godmothering: it gratifies her to stir up gay gumption," Lahusen wrote in *Before Stonewall*. "She also inspired nurses to form the Gay Nurses Alliance in 1973 and advised start-up gay groups in the American Public Health Association and the American Association of Law Librarians."

By the 1970s, Gittings was also a popular Grand Marshal for pride parades across the country, especially along the East Coast, and was a speaker at universities and gay events up until shortly before she died. Her illustrated lecture was titled "Gay and Smiling: Tales From Fifty Years of Activism." She also addressed high school students, often through Gay, Lesbian and Straight Education Network events in the 1990s.

Is society responding to the initiatives of gay pride? Lahusen asked Gittings in her 1972 *Crusaders* book. "I see response every day," said Gittings, "when I open my P.O. box and get letters from libraries and schools all over the country wanting to know about materials on gay liberation. Remember how I talked about encountering the lies in the libraries at Northwestern and in Chicago? Well, when both these libraries wrote me asking for our bibliography, I was especially touched. For me it was a very personal triumph. Maybe today someone 17 looking in those libraries will find right away what I couldn't find 20 years ago—reinforcement and a positive view of gay love and the gay world."

Mark Meinke, founder of the Rainbow History Pages website, remembered Gittings' appearance at the first GLBT ALMS (Archives, Libraries, Museums, and Special Collections) conference in May 2006 at the University of Minnesota. "She mesmerized the audience with her plenary speech," he said. "I remember speaking with other conferees who had never heard her before: the commanding tone, the warm smile and stories, and the eyes that asked, 'What more are you going to do for our cause?' They were agog."

American Library Association Social Responsibilities Round Table Task Force on Gay Liberation, 1971. Gittings is front row, left. Below: Jack Nichols and Lige Clarke. Photos by Kay Tobin Lahusen. Copyright Manuscripts and Archives Division, The New York Public Library

At the 1971 American Library Association conference in Dallas, Gittings helped create a kissing booth to call attention to efforts toward a more inclusive ALA. Above: Gittings and author Isabel Miller (a published writer under her own name, Alma Routsong) kiss for the crowd. Photos by Kay Tobin Lahusen. Copyright Manuscripts and Archives Division, The New York Public Library

Gittings presents Isabel Miller with the first Gay Book Award in 1971 at the ALA. Photos by Kay Tobin Lahusen. Copyright Manuscripts and Archives Division, The New York Public Library

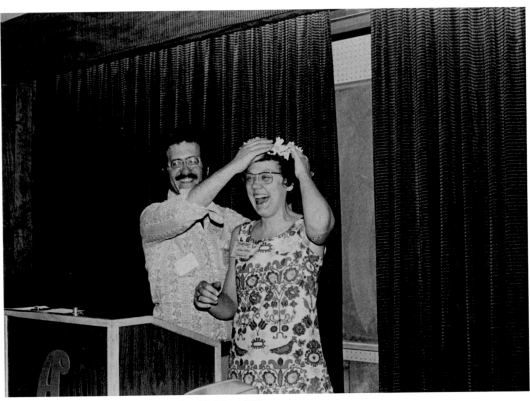

Israel Fishman and Gittings at the ALA in 1971.

Below: Members of the ALA Task Force on Gay Liberation in 1971. Librarian Michael McConnell and Jack Baker in foreground next to Gittings.
Photos by Kay Tobin Lahusen. Copyright Manuscripts and Archives Division, The New York Public Library

Michael McConnell and Jack Baker were early marriage-rights pioneers. They fought for a marriage license in Minnesota, and lost their case when the U.S. Supreme Court declined to overturn a lower court's decision. Above: McConnell, who lost his library job in 1970 as a result of their case, spoke at the ALA 1971 convention in Dallas. Below: McConnell and Baker in an intimate pose.

Photos by Kay Tobin Lahusen. Copyright Manuscripts and Archives Division, The New York Public Library

Del Martin (above left) and Phyllis Lyon received the 1972 Gay Book Award from The ALA Task Force on Gay Liberation, for their book *Lesbian/Woman*. Right: *The Paper*, a short-lived Chicago gay newspaper, covered the conference in July 1972 because it was in the Windy City. Peter Fisher, author of *The Gay Mystique*, shared in the award that year.
Photo by Kay Tobin Lahusen. Copyright Manuscripts and Archives Division, The New York Public Library

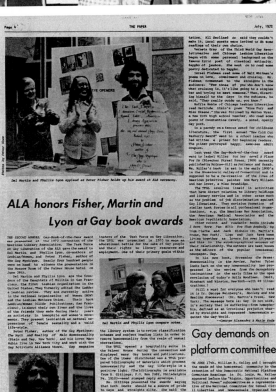

Gittings at the 1972 ALA convention in Chicago.
Photo by Kay Tobin Lahusen. Copyright Manuscripts and Archives Division, The New York Public Library

Gittings with Michael McConnell at the 1972 ALA convention in Chicago. Below: Gittings with a blowup cover of Lahusen's *The Gay Crusaders* book, promoted at the ALA that year. Photo by Kay Tobin Lahusen. Copyright Manuscripts and Archives Division, The New York Public Library

Authors and activists at the ALA convention in Chicago, 1972. Back row, from left: Kay Lahusen, Michael McConnell, author Karla Jay, Phyllis Lyon, Del Martin and Herbert Kovasznay, a Chicago activist who enthusiastically volunteered to help the Task Force. Gittings is in the front row, second from right. Also in the front row, on floor at left, is Steve Todd, another Chicago activist who helped, next to Israel Fishman.

Photo by Jack Baker. Copyright Manuscripts and Archives Division, The New York Public Library

ALA / SRRT
TASK FORCE ON GAY LIBERATION

Task Force on Gay Liberation, American Library Association (Social Responsibilities Round Table), Box 2383, Philadelphia, Pa. 19103
Barbara Gittings, Coordinator　　　　　　　　　　　　　　　　　　　Tel: (215) 382-3222

ALA Social Responsibilities Round Table Task Force on Gay Liberation 1977 letter.

April 12, 1977

Donald B. Reynolds, Jr.
2880 S. Locust - 400 S
Denver, CO　　80222

Dear Don,

Thanks for your phone call this morning and our good talk.
Do please let me know where our joint meeting lands in the Detroit schedule.
As for the other part of our discussion: It's time, really, for you to do puppet theater for our program! And it's timely to air the matter of homophobia on the job for librarians, notwithstanding the failure of the McConnell case in ALA.
You could work up to the subject of librarians' problems with a non-librarian opening scene making use of the Anita Bryant campaign plus the Dave Kopay book which I hear has just reached the top ten best sellers list!
Anita Bryant Meets Dave Kopay in the Lavender Orange Bowl!
What fun it would be making the puppets! Bryant of course would have an orange head. Kopay would have that nice blond hair, a lavender jersey with padded shoulders, and a white lambda on the jersey in lieu of a number.
Here's a sample script Kay wrote after overhearing your and my phone talk.

KOPAY: Miss Bryant, I understand you've got a coaching job open in your Christian school, coaching 7th and 8th graders in football, and I'd like to apply. I need a coaching job real bad.
BRYANT (aside): Oh dear God, the Lavender Menace has come to my very door! I pray for the strength and wisdom to Save Our Children!
BRYANT: Young man, I've heard about you, since your ratings on the talk shows are better than mine. You are a DECLARED homosexual, and I do not want you acting as a role model for our children. Don't you know what the Good Book says about homosexuality?
KOPAY: Yes, I surely do. I read all that in my years in seminary. I tell all about that in my book, THE DAVID KOPAY STORY, which has sold 50,000 copies, has gone to 6 printings, and is due out from Bantam any day now. By the way, do you have it in your school library?

- 2 -

BRYANT (aside): Oh God, may I find the strength and wisdom to Save Our Children. And the dollars too, That's very important.
BRYANT: Young man, you should ask God's loving forgiveness for your sins every morning of your life--while you drink your Florida orange juice, of course. I'm not prejudiced against homosexuals, in fact some of my best friends are homosexuals, it's just that I don't want my children to see any. They might get the wrong idea that gay is good when we know it's bad and sinful.
KOPAY: That's a moralistic judgment. Anyway, what does that have to do with the fact that I'm a well-qualified coach? I could bring fame and fortune to your school. Just let me at those kids and I'll really show them how to play!
BRYANT: I'll bet you will!
KOPAY: Don't get snide with me. Sin can be in the eye of the beholder, you know. Pure thoughts are as important as pure orange juice.
BRYANT (aside): Oh God, give me the wisdom, the strength, the dollars, the TV shows, the sponsors, the Nielsen ratings to fight this menace and Save Our Children.
KOPAY (seeing her lost in prayer): Anyway, I may not be available for a coaching job after all. You see, Miss Bryant, I've been talking to the California orange growers about promoting California oranges.
BRYANT (aside): Oh God, the ultimate Lavender Menace is in the fruit business! (Hoists sign "Save Our Citrus, O Lord")

# # #

Well, Don??????

As ever,

Barbara Gittings

Gay Task Force NEWS

Task Force on Gay Liberation, American Library Association Annual Conference 1978, Chicago

Gay Film Festival

Starts Sun. June 25 & runs for four days. Features eighteen documentary gay films! Complete schedule on reverse. Our members and friends who want to help usher, handle literature, etc., please show up early.

Mon. June 26, 7:00-8:45 pm.

RECEPTION for our task force and our friends, co-hosted by Gay Academic Union, Chicago Chapter & by area members of the National Gay Task Force. At YWCA, 37 S. Wabash (across street from Palmer House).

This reception follows the SRRT Open House from 4-7 pm. at the Jane Addams Bookstore, Rm. 1508, 5 S. Wabash (one block north of Palmer House). Jane Addams Bookstore has new and out-of-print feminist, children's, men's liberation, and lesbian materials.

Everyone is welcome at both our Reception and SRRT Open House. At both, meet Ginny Vida, editor of OUR RIGHT TO LOVE: A LESBIAN RESOURCE BOOK (Prentice-Hall 1978).

* * * * * * * * * * * * * * * * * * * *

Tues. June 27, 2 pm.

GAY BOOK AWARD Presentation, prior to Gay Film Festival III. Conrad Hilton Hotel, Boulevard Room.

* * * * * * * * * * * * * * * * * * * *

Wed. June 28, 10 am.-Noon

BUSINESS MEETING of Gay Task Force. Gold Room, Blackstone Hotel. All are welcome!

* * * * * * * * * * * * * * * * * * * *

WHAT ELSE?

Help us get the facts on gay job discrimination in libraries. Copies of survey questionnaire on hand at all our events.

For info on gay places, events, services in Chicago: 337-2424 or 929-HELP.

About Our Group

Our group was launched in 1970; we're just a year younger than our parent division in ALA, the Social Responsibilities Round Table. We work to get more & better gay materials into libraries & out to readers, and to deal with discrimination in libraries. (For our story up to summer 1975, see chapter "Combatting the Lies in the Libraries" in THE GAY ACADEMIC, edited by Louie Crew, ETC Publications 1977). Our membership is informal & consists of those individuals who are actually working on one or more projects. We get about $200 a year from SRRT (about the most SRRT can give any of its task forces). For the rest of our expenses we count on donations & taking out of our own pockets. So we're happy to get contributions for our work! Make checks payable to "Barbara Gittings-- TFGL." Every bit helps & is appreciated! Where will your donation go?

- Our how-to booklet, for gay groups and individuals, on ways to get gay materials into their public & school libraries. Due fall 1978. Estimated printing cost, $125.

- Our survey of gay job discrimination in libraries. Copies of the questionnaire are available at all our events at this ALA conference, and by mail on request. Printing questionnaire, $90.

- Gay Film Festival. Far costlier than our usual program-on-a-shoestring. While the films are supplied on courtesy basis, we have to rent screens & projectors at set prices, pay union operators, return films, etc. Each show costs about $110.

- A completely new, 6th edition of our Gay Bibliography, due early 1979. Cost not yet known but letter postage alone to collect and check info may run to $100.

- An examination of what encyclopedias say--and don't say--about homosexuality, and recommendations for changes.

Task Force on Gay Liberation, American Library Association (Social Responsibilities Round Table), Box 2383, Philadelphia, Pa. 19103
Barbara Gittings, Coordinator   Tel: (215) 382-3222

ALA Social Responsibilities Round Table Task Force on Gay Liberation 1978 newsletter.

AMERICAN LIBRARY ASSOCIATION--MIDWINTER 1986 CONFERENCE--CHICAGO

GAY TASK FORCE - BUSINESS MEETINGS

Saturday, January 18, 1986
8 - 10 p.m.
Hilton--Williford Room A

Sunday, January 19, 1986
2 - 4 p.m.
Palmer House--Parlor H

AIDS Awareness:
The Library's Role

Sponsored by: Gay Task Force (SRRT) and Public Library Association

Sunday, January 19, 1986, 5 - 6 p.m.

Chicago Public Library Cultural Center Theatre 78 E. Washington St.

A discussion of the AIDS Information Project at the Chicago Public Library in cooperation with the Chicago Department of Health. Participants will include members of the AIDS Information Project Committee at CPL and health professionals from the Chicago Department of Health's AIDS Awareness Program, the Sable/Sherer AIDS Clinic of Cook County Hospital, and the Howard Brown Memorial Clinic's AIDS Action Project.

Copies of informational brochures, flyers and bibliographies on AIDS will be shared.

OPEN TO ALL INTERESTED PERSONS

Gay Task Force, American Library Association (Social Responsibilities Round Table) Box 2383, Philadelphia, PA 19103. Coordinator: Barbara Gittings (215) 471-3322.

ALA Social Responsibilities Round Table Gay Task Force 1986 program, perhaps the first library program on AIDS, held in Chicago.
Courtesy of the M. Kuda Archives, Oak Park, Illinois

Above: In 2003, the American Library Association honored Gittings with a lifetime honorary membership.

Left: Lahusen photo-edited this card featuring one of Gittings' favorite quotes.
Photos by Kay Tobin Lahusen. Copyright Manuscripts and Archives Division, The New York Public Library

Chicago-area activist Marie J. Kuda with Gittings and Philadelphia activist John Cunningham in an uncredited photo. Kuda and Cunningham were instrumental in the work of the ALA Task Force on Gay Liberation.

Chapter 6
A Public Face: Making the News

Telegenic, articulate personalities who can resonate in the mainstream media are rare in movements for social change. For the burgeoning homosexual-rights movement of the 1960s, Barbara Gittings was the perfect mix of charm and intelligence.

Putting oneself in the spotlight comes with a cost. Early movement leaders sacrificed more lucrative careers and risked personal safety for the cause. But more difficult were the movement's internecine battles. If you put yourself out on television and in newspapers as a spokesperson, be prepared to deal with the conflicts within your own community. The battles are legend from that era, and because the movement was so much smaller, the wounds ran much deeper. There was almost no place to hide.

While much of the strife was around strategy, there were also at times petty jealousies and personality clashes. In the end, Gittings found it still worth the trouble.

In her early activist years, she noted how difficult it was to get gay people to even want to fight back.

"While I think the word 'oppression' has been trivialized by overuse and abuse, it's plainly the only word that fits here, the only word that describes the constraint and fear that keep many gay people from fighting back," she told Lahusen for her 1972 *Gay Crusaders* book.

Her first radio and TV appearances started in 1964, around the time the mainstream media finally started to tiptoe into the rarely covered world of homosexuality.

"At first when other gay people and I did broadcasts, we were confined to late-night shows," Gittings said. "The assumption was that our subject was suitable fare for adults only, and children would be in bed by then. Now that's all changed. We get evening prime time or daytime. We're no longer shoved into the gloom of night!"

Gittings and Lilli Vincenz were the first lesbians to go on a nationally syndicated TV show, *The Phil Donahue Show,* then produced in Dayton, Ohio, in May 1970. Gittings told Lahusen for the Bullough book that she remembered the live audience as "hostile housewives."

Gittings was one of the regular newscasters handling the pioneer weekly radio series *Homosexual News and Reviews* on New York's listener-supported station WBAI. When TV stations in Philadelphia, Baltimore, Dayton, Chicago, New York City, Pittsburgh, and Dallas were ready for gay guests, she was happy to oblige, according to *Crusaders*. Then, in the fall of 1971, the nationally syndicated *David Susskind Show* devoted an entire program to lesbianism. Most of Susskind's millions of viewers no doubt had never seen this many open lesbians in one place.

David Susskind Meets His Match

A flier was circulated by Gay Activists Alliance of Philadelphia for the show. Titled "7 Gay Women Speak with David Susskind," the flier noted discussion groups being hosted to mark the screening of the show, which aired December 10 and 11 on WHYY-TV and stations across the country.

A typed list for the September 27, 1971, taping of the show lists the following as guests, along with Gittings: Lilli Vincenz, the Reverend Magora Kennedy (the only Black woman on the panel), Lyn Kupferman, Diana Travis, Anna Salvato, Barbara Love and Adrienne Parks under the name Rachel Parker. Since that makes eight names, one must have been a no-show. Based on a viewing of the program, Travis was the one not at the taping.

Gittings and the six other gay women tangled with Susskind, "who kept the show moving by advancing popular myths about homosexuality in general and lesbianism in particular. The guests neatly disposed of such fictions as: gay people are more promiscuous than straight people; gay couples usually engage in butch-femme role-playing; lesbians dislike men; lesbians want to seduce straight women," Lahusen wrote in *Crusaders*.

Watching the program on a tape more than 40 years later, it's interesting to see how some of the same arguments and stereotypes still exist about homosexuality, and lesbianism in particular.

"You keep wanting to put us in your boxes," Gittings said to Susskind. "The whole point of our movement is that we're making our own boxes, if there are to be any boxes whatsoever. We are no longer going to live by your expectations and your value systems, and your demands for us. ... If only this thing had been on the air 20 years ago when I was trying to come out as a homosexual, it would have made all the difference to me. We are defining our own lives for ourselves, we are setting our own expectations for ourselves, we're developing our own value systems. This is what it's about. You can't force us into your boxes anymore, we are not going."

Kennedy, a mother of five, urged parents to be more open with their children, including gay parents. Susskind asks if this dealt severe emotional damage to her children. She answered: "The severe blow would have come from the hiding. I am thankful that today we no longer have to hide."

Parker mentioned two women she knew, who were in their 50s, together for 30 years, and who adopted a boy and a girl. "Children who have both homosexual men or lesbian parents need not become that, a homosexual," Parker said.

Gittings added: "I think the children who are going to grow up to be homosexual anyway, should get this kind of encouragement [like on a TV show] ... it should be in the air, in the society, that homosexuality is perfectly all right and that it's to be just as much valued and desired as a heterosexual orientation. To that extent, yes, it should be encouraged, so that it would be available for those who were going to grow up that way anyway, so that you can avoid the problems of telling people who are perfectly all right that they're not all right." Susskind did agree with that Gittings statement.

"I think society has the problem," Parker said. "If they could only understand us as human beings, not as a lesbian, not as a homosexual, not as someone who has a problem. We have no problems."

"Your attitudes toward us are the problem," Gittings interjected. "There's nothing wrong with homosexuality, the only thing wrong with it is that you people are upset about it. Why?" She directed this question to Susskind. He said he agreed with the great body of evidence saying homosexuality is an illness, or a mental aberration. He later even compared it to drug use as an affliction.

Susskind was flustered when asked if he would teach his children about lesbians. "It's one of those human illnesses that I don't choose to educate my children too deeply about," he said.

Gittings jumped in: "It wasn't very long ago that left-handedness, which we now accept as perfectly natural and perfectly normal ... there is a parallel in how society views them. ... I remember when I went to primary grade school there was a boy in one of my classes, who had his left hand tied behind his back. ... [Then] people stopped fussing about it ... . The day you people stop worrying about us, and stop fussing about it, will be a day of liberation.

"This body of psychiatric literature you are so devoted to, I don't like going back this far, but 450 years ago or so, it was absolutely the only way to look at the whole world, that the sun revolved around the Earth ... all supported this belief. ... It was outrageous [what Galileo Galilei said challenging this]. ... The body of knowledge had to be challenged. I say that the body of knowledge which claims sickness for homosexuality has to be challenged."

Later in the discussion, Gittings commented on diversity. "In this country, we have policy statements of various kinds, which give lip service to the idea of diversity and variety, but when it comes down to emotional and affectional life, bang, the door is closed shut," she said. "And we are programmed and processed to go into this one way, lockstep forever and forever, male and female, shall they go into the ark. Now, this is cutting off all of the other possibilities for people to love. One of the reasons I'm in gay liberation is to broaden the choices, to open up the possibilities for people, to make it possible for more diversity and variety. Isn't it what we believe in in this country? I believe in it and I'm practicing it. Why do you have such a vested interest in trying to channel people, narrow down, to program them for this one thing, this one way of life?"

Some gay men in the audience were concerned about divisions in the community between men and women, and the panelists, including Vincenz and Gittings, refuted this with credentials of working with men.

"I have been in the gay movement since 1958," Gittings said. "Except for membership in an all-women's organization during a part of that time, I have been involved for the most part in organizations which are mixed, that is, men and women both as members, and my current major commitment in a subgroup of the American Library Association, the Task Force on Gay Liberation, is a mixed group, men and women, librarians and nonlibrarians, who are trying to revolutionize libraries, and serving the needs of gay people."

Gittings pointed out that not just colleges were getting gay groups, but "it's coming in the high schools."

"Oh, that's thrilling," Susskind said sarcastically. Then he said if he were a college president and a homosexual group were suggested, "I'd throw the outfit right off campus." Gittings assured him he would face a court challenge.

The audience for the taping was very supportive of the panelists. At the end, Susskind, who had been corrected not to call the women "ladies," stated: "The lad- … the women want me to say that they are here tonight to change the society, or try to, and not to have society change them. I think they've done well in that direction."

Response to the *Susskind Show*

"The show hit major cities everywhere, including Barbara's home town of Philadelphia," Lahusen wrote in *Crusaders*. "[P]hone calls and letters poured in to her for weeks after the show, says Barbara, while strangers came up to her on the street, at the supermarket, in the post office, to speak about the broadcast. One straight woman commented to her, 'Why, you homosexuals love each other just the way Arnold and I do!' Many gay people reported they had watched with parents. One gay man wrote: 'It was a very strange experience … such a fantastic feeling for me to sit there and watch all of you on the screen, speaking *for me,* while I sat in silence, grinning inside, aglow really.'"

There were some negatives. "Well, one woman called up to say I was absolutely disgusting! And there's a man who keeps sending me Playmate photos from *Playboy* with notes like, 'Whatever turns you on.' Otherwise the response was intelligent and encouraging," Gittings said.

"When I agreed to appear on the nationally televised *David Susskind Show* in 1971, I knew that I had to reveal my lifestyle to my mother," Gittings told Perry and Swicegood. "I couldn't just let somebody call her on the telephone and say, 'Have you seen your daughter—the lesbian!—on television?' So my mother was told in advance, although she was not comfortable with the information. The jolt came years later when she surprised me by revealing that following the *Susskind* program, a friend of hers had indeed called—to make negative comments about my being on the show.

"'At least Barbara's doing something to help others!' she replied.

"My lover was present as Mother related the incident. 'Did that "friend" ever raise the subject again?' asked Kay.

"'She did not!' said my mother."

Susskind continued the dialogue on the topic during a January 1972 panel titled "Sex in the '70s" with Gittings and others. The event was at the Golden Slipper Club in Philadelphia.

"As I grew older," admitted Barbara, "I found I cared less about what people thought. When the first invitations came to go on radio, I was scared, but I accepted. As it turned out, I enjoyed it. I was always ready to do something different, and I haven't had any regrets.

"Good times were part of the early years, even though you never knew what was going to happen. This was particularly true of some of the first gay conferences. How were hotel people going to treat you? Were they going to give you a hassle? Was there going to be a disruption from outside? Would police arrive and trump up some kind of stupid charge against us? All those things happened on occasion.

"But we had to take the chance. That's how I always felt. Every time I had to make a decision to put myself forward or stay back, to use my real name or not, to go on television or decline, to get out on some of the earliest picket lines or remain behind, I usually took the public position because there weren't many of us yet that could afford the risk."

Getting Out There

Gittings was a popular speaker across the country. "It's important to know just what their most basic resistance to our message is," Gittings said in *Crusaders*. "I've found that even an ordinary effort by gays to get something across in an educational way immediately rouses all kinds of myths and fears people have about us. They think we're out to 'recruit.' Or they think that we're sex-crazed people who want more sexual freedom than is permitted everyone else. You get this even from sophisticated audiences."

According to a fall 2001 article in Maryland's *Visions Today* magazine, Gittings and Jack Nichols were among the first movement speakers at a college campus, at Bucknell University in 1967. "There were just a few of us at the beginning of the movement, but we were all people who were not particularly impressed by authorities. I don't think we were militants—we were just sensible," she said.

Gittings relayed one speaking incident to Perry and Swicegood that shaped her views on community building:

"There are millions of homosexuals out there in the world who have no connection with the gay movement, who are running scared, wearing a mask. I met one while I was the invited gay speaker at a local divinity school that was having a conference on religion and homosexuality. When I was finished speaking, I remained to answer questions. The hostility in the room was palpable. The questions were harsh in the beginning, and got worse. I was holding my own, because over the years I've developed a tough hide. I can handle abuse if necessary. So I was fielding questions that were coming hot and heavy in my direction from those preachers-to-be when, without warning, a divinity student jumped up. 'Stop this!' he protested. 'Stop attacking this woman! Because you invited her and you know who she is, you think she's the only homosexual in this room. Well, you're wrong about that! She's not the only homosexual here! I've lived with you, and I've worked with you, and I've prayed and studied with you for three years, but none of you know that I'm a homosexual too!'

"You could have heard a pin drop in that room. That young divinity student was so upset about how I was treated. I was used to a horrible reaction, but he wasn't. He told me afterward that he never expected to do what he did. He was simply galvanized into action. And it really changed the whole atmosphere. That took a lot of courage. It shook up the divinity school, and it shook up his career. He wound up doing something else. Some years later he told me that he never regretted blowing his cover.

"Nowadays there's a change in public awareness. Nearly everybody concedes that he or she knows somebody, a man or woman, who's gay. That's important, because there's nothing that overcomes prejudice faster than learning someone you're close to, or admire, is homosexual. It forces people to reevaluate their thinking.

"If every gay person came out, that might, by sheer numbers, instantly end discrimination. But in the meantime, those of us who are visible have to concern ourselves with establishing gay rights in law. I hope the time will come when none of us will need to hide anymore, that eventually we can be treated as individuals, on our own merits.

"It's not pleasant when you're dealing with nongay people, and you're on their wavelength with strong mutual interests when, somehow, it becomes apparent you're gay. Suddenly, an invisible wall goes up! You can feel the barrier! Things are never quite the same again. The relationship changes because sexuality becomes the overriding issue, and all the good things that were going on before become incidental. That's something I would like to change. The problem is, a lot of heterosexuals can't make the leap beyond seeing us as homosexual, and therefore different.

"Remember the painted bird story? They took a bird from its flock and they painted it, then released it back among its own, and the flock pecked it to death. It was the same bird, but with slightly different plumage. The flock couldn't accept it. Yet it was their kind. There was nothing wrong with the bird. Sometimes I have a feeling, if we don't keep up our guard, they're going to peck us to death. Some are trying. It's wrong that we have to be afraid, but as vigilant defenders of our liberty, we must be ever watchful."

Behind Every Good Woman ...

While the contributions of Gittings have often won awards and been documented, Lahusen, the first out LGBT photojournalist in the U.S., was the woman behind the lens, making Gittings' work all the more visible.

Gittings would credit Lahusen at every chance she could get. "It was Kay's campaign to move *The Ladder* from mediocre illustrations to good images. Images were important to us and we thought that we ought to make lesbians and the world in general see that lesbians were happy, healthy, wholesome, good-looking people. The only way to do this was to have [photographs of] live women as the cover subjects of the magazine. This wasn't easy to do. Hardly any lesbians were openly gay in the mid-1960s," Gittings said in a short profile written about Lahusen.

Lahusen, who had a box camera as a child, said she was always interested in photography: "We were interested in 'living propaganda,' trying to bring the lesbian out of the closet and into the light of day. The problem was we couldn't find people who were willing." Lahusen's first cover photo was for the July 1964 issue of *The Ladder*, a photo of a sculpture of a nude woman.

"I wanted to show our great diversity and to give viewers someone they could identify with, some positive role models. After all, role models were badly needed in the 1960s when most gay people were afraid to be photographed," Lahusen said in a 2012 interview with *Philadelphia Gay News* writer Jen Colletta. "It's been said that I'm the first gay photojournalist, since I kept at it sporadically over decades. There was no way I could be at every event, every time, but I believed it was a way of preserving gay history."

Of those early protests, Lahusen told Colletta: "Some participants were fearful, some were proud, others were simply marching in the belief that they had to come out if things were going to change. It's been said that all social-change movements find they ultimately have to take to the streets. Think of the early suffragettes, for example. Of course, when you're marching, you have no crystal ball to tell if you're helping make changes but you hope so, even believe so. I certainly believed we were doing something historically significant, something to help lift GLBT people as a class in our society."

In their activism work, Lahusen told Colletta, she and Gittings always came to agreement on the right approach, sometimes "after long hours of discussion." And they worked as a complementary team, she said, with Gittings possessing the "higher profile" and Lahusen working in a "support role."

"We brought different talents," Lahusen said. "Barbara was a terrific public speaker, she could always rally the troops. I especially loved photography, making exhibits and doing what you might call promotion work. Barbara was a terrific editor, and I was a pretty good reporter. The ideas we advanced were generally the same and summed up in our friend Frank Kameny's simple, but inspired, motto,

'Gay is good.'"

Lahusen continued to be a journalist, photographer, and activist in the movement, sometimes alongside Gittings, and sometimes independently. While she was content to let Gittings be the one in the spotlight, Lahusen was herself not in the closet. She worked for *GAY* newspaper and in the first gay bookstore in the U.S., the Oscar Wilde Memorial Bookshop in New York City, founded by Craig Rodwell.

Barbara Gittings on *The David Susskind Show*, **1971.**
Publicity photo

Guests on the lesbian episode of *The David Susskind Show*, 1971. Above right: Gittings, Susskind and Lyn Kupferman.
Publicity photo

Left, from top: Gittings, Susskind with Kupferman, Lilli Vincenz. Below: The Reverend Magora Kennedy (left) and Anna Salvato.

7 GAY WOMEN

SPEAK WITH

DAVID SUSSKIND

FRIDAY, DEC. 10 - 8:30 P.M.
SATURDAY, DEC. 11 - 8:00 P.M.

WHYY-TV, CHANNEL 12

DISCUSSION INCLUDES:
WHY GAY PEOPLE ARE COMING OUT OF THE CLOSET
GAY LOVE RELATIONSHIPS
GAYS AND THEIR PARENTS
GAY PRIDE VERSUS PSYCHIATRIC PROPAGANDA
THE GAY LIBERATION MOVEMENT
THE GAY SUBCULTURE IN A PERIOD OF CHANGE
GAYS WHO ARE MARRIED

SPECIAL INVITATION:
COFFEE HOUR AND DISCUSSION
OF THE DAVID SUSSKIND SHOW
TUESDAY,   DEC. 14 - 8:00 P.M.

GAY ACTIVISTS ALLIANCE
PHILADELPHIA

AT THE CHRISTIAN ASSOCIATION

36TH AND LOCUST WALK

UNIVERSITY OF PENNSYLVANIA

A flier promoting a discussion related to the 1971 Susskind TV episode on lesbians.

A discussion in Philadelphia about "Sex in the '70s" in January 1972. Gittings is pictured in these two photos debating with David Susskind.
Photos by Kay Tobin Lahusen. Copyright Manuscripts and Archives Division, The New York Public Library

The Mayor of the City of New York

Edward I. Koch

in cooperation with Heritage of Pride Inc.
and the Lesbian & Gay History Month Committee

cordially invite you to celebrate the

20th Anniversary of Stonewall

with the dedication of Stonewall Place and
the Proclamation of Lesbian & Gay Pride and History Month

Thursday, June 1, 1989

at 6:00 p.m.

Christopher Street and Waverly Place off 7th Avenue

1989, Stonewall reunion, New York City. Gittings and Lahusen were invited to be among the participants. From Kay Tobin Lahusen

Gittings editing a manuscript.
Photo by Kay Tobin Lahusen. Copyright Manuscripts and Archives Division, The New York Public Library

Gittings always marched with a big smile.
Photo by Kay Tobin Lahusen. Copyright Manuscripts and Archives Division, The New York Public Library

Chapter 7
Love and Partnership

The work-and-love partnership between Barbara Gittings and Kay Tobin Lahusen lasted from 1961 until almost 46 years later, when Gittings died four days after Valentine's Day 2007.

There were very few movement partnerships that proved so mutually productive. They collaborated on projects and also worked independently. They lived together during most of their relationship, but sometimes were separated between Philadelphia (Gittings) and New York City (Lahusen).

They also struggled financially for much of their activist careers. Correspondence in their files shows how they often relied on the support of friends, or on Gittings' aunt, Tante Kay (who helped them pay off their mortgage, among other gifts over the years). The couple also lent friends money in times of need. Gittings spent a lot of energy and time focused on her mother's push-and-pull concerning support and finances.

But even with the financial sacrifices they would make for the movement, their partnership remained solid from the beginning.

"When I met Barbara at the [1961 DOB] picnic, I thought she was a very interesting person. I was quite taken with her," Lahusen told Marcus for *Making History*.

"And I was quite taken with Kay," Gittings said. "We started jabbering away and, as I recall, after the picnic we went somewhere, and then we started long-distance courting."

"Barbara expected some mousy little old lady to turn up."

"That's because I knew Kay worked for *The Christian Science Monitor*. My stereotypes were such that I expected this rather dour type of person. And Kay was anything but that. She dressed in bright, cheerful colors. Red hair. Just awfully attractive."

"It was a pretty motley crew that showed up at the picnic," Lahusen told Marcus. "I don't think we even had 10 people. There was Marge and her hopeless love for Jan. There was an older woman who wasn't with anyone. And I think because of her age she felt out of it. But she told Barbara that I was a 'cute little package' and that she should go after me. That really ticked me off."

"It's been a standing joke with us ever since—'cute little package.'"

Gittings, in an interview with David Warner of Philadelphia's *City Paper*, recalled: "I flew to Boston [to see her] and got off the plane with a big bunch of flowers in my hand. I couldn't resist. I did not care what the world thought. I dropped the flowers, grabbed her and kissed her. That was not being done in 1961."

"Frankly, in the beginning days of the movement, the people who turned up were, by and large, pretty oddball," Lahusen said to Marcus. "It's only from the most oddball fringy-type gay people that we have worked our way into the mainstream of the gay minority. You see, in the early days, getting involved in the movement was such an unpopular thing to do. It was nonconformist at a time when most gay people were trying to blend in and pass. And you had to have some reason to want to crusade, in spite of whatever it might cost you. Because back then it could cost you a lot, including your job. …

"Let me leave you with one thought. The driving force and the reason I am so passionate about this is because it's so wrong that a good gay relationship had to break up because it was felt at the time that this [being gay] was no kind of life to be lived. I just want to turn that around in this world. This is what drove me then, and still drives me now."

Concerns about money started to enter their minds in later years, so by the 1990s they were focused on economics, while they still did work for the movement.

"During the 15 years that I was running the Gay Task Force in the ALA, I spent more than 50 percent of my time answering correspondence and helping set up our programs at conventions. It was all volunteer work," Gittings told Marcus. "I have never received a cent, except occasionally for a speaking engagement. Even then I would tell people, 'If you're going to give me money, fine, but it's going back into the movement.' I make my living as a freelance clerk-typist, working mainly for a small tax-accounting firm . ...."

"For many years after we met in 1961, Barbara and I lived in small apartments, cramped by stacks of materials from our movement activities," Lahusen wrote in the Bullough book. "We lived frugally; Barbara scraped by on low-paid clerical jobs so she could put her main energy into activism. Finally in 1980 we bought a house, a small row home in Philadelphia's University City, and for 18 years enjoyed a succession of friends, gay activists, writers, historians, and documentary filmmakers who came to call."

"We've never been rich," Lahusen said to Marcus. "We've always scrimped along. A lot of this furniture is secondhand and thrown together higgledy-piggledy from assorted places. Now that I sell real estate, I try to get something from every house I sell. Eighty percent of my real estate business is gay. My latest crusade is to try to organize gay realtors in this area, the Delaware Valley. I've organized a little network within my own chain, and I've been the one gay realtor in the New York Gay Pride Parade for the last three years. There are other realtors in the parade, but they march with other contingents. I'm going to try to get a group behind me this year [1990] who march as realtors. But I told Barbara recently that I feel the life going out of me. Getting the realtors organized is my last crusade."

That was far from their last crusade, but with the movement growing at such a quick pace, Gittings and Lahusen were no longer pressured with being among the few go-to presenters and speakers on what was becoming the LGBTQ equality movement.

Music as Fuel

Gittings was always much more than the pickets and speeches. In fact, her top love was probably music, especially Baroque and Renaissance. She sang in glee clubs at school and in choirs throughout her adult life, and she always enjoyed attending classical music concerts.

"Immersed though she is in gay liberation, Barbara is no gay separatist in her personal life," Lahusen wrote about her partner for her 1972 *Crusaders* book. "Now she picks up her music folder. Tonight her chorus is rehearsing Bach's *St. John Passion.* 'If I were offered a prime speaking date or TV appearance that conflicted with one of our concerts, it would be a hard decision, but I think I'd choose the concert. Singing is a form of personal liberation I can't do without.'"

She performed for more than 50 years with the Philadelphia Chamber Chorus.

"A key event for [Gittings] was a concert during the 1987 March on Washington when more than 500 gay men and women from all over the country sang and played at Constitution Hall, the very auditorium from which the great American singer Marian Anderson was excluded in 1939 because she was black," Lahusen wrote in the chapter on Gittings for Bullough's book. "In summer 2000, Barbara spent an entire week hearing over 5,000 singers at the GALA international festival of gay and lesbian choruses ... . [In] Barbara's view, gay music groups are not only fun for their members and fans, they're an important part of the drive for gay rights. 'Amateur choruses and bands are a great tradition in this country,' she points out, 'and it'll be harder and harder to deny us a place in the parade.'"

"Just don't make me out to be a movement grind," Gittings told Lahusen. Lahusen then added:

"Her mother called her character 'golden,' and I agree. Plus, she has the disposition of an angel—until she's crossed. She's mad about music and music comedians such as Anna Russell and Victor Borge. She loves reading mystery novels and *The New Yorker* and stories of whimsy such as *Ferdinand* and *Wind in the Willows.* She loves old movies and gay film festivals, rare books and prints, museums, theater, cartoons, ice cream, aerobic walks, sunsets, wilderness, parades, political satire. She loves to laugh, eat heartily, sip a little wine, and be merry with friends. She loves the gay cause and promoting it. She loves life, she loves her people, and thank heavens she loves me."

In addition to the love the two women had for each other, they maintained lifelong friendships with people both inside and outside the movement. Those friends were key to their support as they aged, coming to help in times of need.

On a personal level, "Barbara was good company," said friend Marie J. Kuda. "She believed working for gay liberation was serious business, but didn't have to be grim. She believed in doing things 'frugally but with flair.' She had great good humor."

"They're quite a team," their friend John Cunningham said in a 2001 interview with Maryland's *Visions Today* magazine writer Kevin Riordan. "Together, they've dedicated their lives to civil-rights issues. The movement is their life."

A Final Closet Opened

Perhaps their final "coming out" was in an article in the newsletter for the Pennsylvania retirement community they moved into in January 2007. "Sadly, Barbara was to fight her last bout with breast cancer with the loving care of Kay and the personnel of Cumberland [part of the Kendal community] and hospice," the newsletter said. The article went on to note Gittings' critical role in the gay-rights movement, and the work she and Lahusen did side by side to make change.

Since Gittings' death, Lahusen has made sure to keep Barbara's spirit alive. Kay's room is decorated with the photos of their life together and with photos from the movement. There are the many awards, paintings, posters, magazine covers, editorial cartoons, buttons, and coffee mugs with their images screened on. Books are everywhere—on the floor, on shelves, a chair, and on the tops of boxes. Even the shower serves as storage. As she guided a guest through this rich history, Lahusen smiled a lot, and frequently said, "I love this photo." But some are special. "One of my favorite photos is at Frank's house, with Barb, Frank and I on his front steps." Picking up another image of Gittings in a red shirt, one hand raised with fingers making a victory sign, she said, "This is so typical Barbara." A "great favorite" photo of Lahusen's is one with Gittings in a T-shirt that reads I CANNOT LIVE WITHOUT BOOKS, a Thomas Jefferson quote.

As she looked through the hundreds of photos, Lahusen added, "We laughed all the time."

There is a bench that marks Gittings' final resting place, in Washington's Congressional Cemetery, near what will likely be the final resting place for Frank Kameny (there is a legal battle over his remains). "This is where we will be buried together, our ashes will be together in this bench," Lahusen said. On the top it reads "GAY PIONEERS who spoke truth to power. GAY IS GOOD."

The front of the bench reads: "Partners in life. Married in our hearts." They were never legally married.

Gittings at home, circa 1962 in Philadelphia.
Photo by Kay Tobin Lahusen. Copyright Manuscripts and Archives Division, The New York Public Library

**Gittings working and
relaxing at home in
Philadelphia, circa
early 1960s.**
Photos by Kay Tobin
Lahusen. Copyright
Manuscripts and Archives
Division, The New York
Public Library

Right: Lahusen holding an artful turtle, early 1960s at home in Philadelphia.
Photo by Barbara Gittings

Bottom: Gittings prepares for a party at home in Philadelphia.
Photo by Kay Tobin Lahusen. Copyright Manuscripts and Archives Division, The New York Public Library

Gittings, circa mid-1960s.
Photo by Kay Tobin Lahusen. Copyright Manuscripts and Archives Division, The New York Public Library

Gittings, circa mid-1960s.
Photo by Kay Tobin Lahusen. Copyright Manuscripts and Archives Division, The New York Public Library

Below: Kay Lahusen at home.
Photo by Jack Nichols

This page: Gittings, reading and writing, circa late 1960s and early 1970s. Top photo taken in Fire Island, bottom photos in Philadelphia.
Photos by Kay Tobin Lahusen. Copyright Manuscripts and Archives Division, The New York Public Library

Gittings always seemed adaptable to any location, and to always have a smile. These photos all taken in Philadelphia.
Photos by Kay Tobin Lahusen. Copyright Manuscripts and Archives Division, The New York Public Library

**Other candid photos
of Gittings taken by
Lahusen, and a posed
photo of Lahusen
(photographer
unknown).**
Copyright Manuscripts and
Archives Division, The New
York Public Library

Why are these women smiling?

At last we've acquired a house! No time to draw up a long and chatty holiday letter. Just a brief announcement that yes, we now are homeowners. After years of living in far-too-small apartments, we finally found a two-story row house that exactly suited our needs. We moved into it in August 1980, thanks to a lot of help from several good friends. And we love it, mortgage and all!

So if you don't hear further from us for a while, you'll know we're busy nesting. Meanwhile, this is what our little house looks like. We hope you all will visit us one day--but not all at once! Love to all our friends and special holiday greetings from us on this our first Christmas/New Year in our first house.

Barbara and Kay

Chez Barbara Gittings and Kay Tobin

They've moved!

Please continue to send mail to our postal box 2383, Philadelphia, PA 19103

Our new phone number is (215) 471-3322

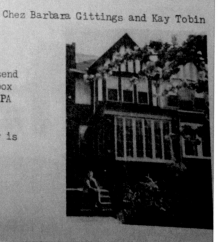

A flier from 1980 noting the home Gittings and Lahusen purchased.
Flier composed by Lahusen.

Lahusen and Gittings at home in Philadelphia, circa 1990s.
Photo by Ed Hermance

**Gittings and Lahusen
in Philadelphia, in the
2000s.**
Photo by John Cunningham

Gittings and Lahusen sorting files in 2003 in Wilmington, Delaware. They had a condo across the hall from the condo they lived in— to store their archives.
Photos by Steven Capsuto

**Gittings and Lahusen in 2006,
holding items from their archives.**
Photos by Patsy Lynch

Two of the last photos taken of Gittings and Lahusen together, December 29, 2006. The next month, they moved to their retirement community, in Kennett Square, Pennsylvania, just weeks before Gittings died.
Photos by Patsy Lynch

Chapter 8
The Final Years

Gittings died in 2007 of breast cancer at age 74, but not before she fought valiantly against the disease—multiple times.

In an August 22, 2001, email to professor and Episcopal activist Louie Crew, Gittings wrote: "At this time I need all the cheer I can get because I've crossed a divide. Five years ago I was diagnosed with breast cancer. At the time all the signs were favorable for long-term survival. Then three years later, we found the cancer had metastasized—it's in my liver and my bones. The bones don't worry me, but the liver tumors are life-threatening. There is no cure, and the best treatment can only subdue the tumors for a while, give me a bit more time. I'm only 69, and with the long-life genes in my family, I should have another twenty years; that won't happen.

"It's devastating to be facing early death. Still, I do what I can and enjoy what I can, and try not to think about the elephant in the living room. I've even set up speaking engagements for the fall, to give my show-and-tell history of our gay rights movement with emphasis on the first three decades, the 1950s, '60s, and '70s, which most people know little about. …

"But [Kay and I] tap humor and music as much as we can to counter the stresses in our lives. And of course friends are important!" She signed the letter "In gay spirits."

In a July 23, 2005, letter to Marie Kuda, she wrote via email:

"I'm now in my third year—yes, 25 months—of continuous chemotherapy with no remission. Having toxic drugs every week (at first) or every other week (as now) is really hard on me. The tumor markers have gone down some but are still way too high, so we have to persist. The main toll of chemotherapy is fatigue. Chemo fatigue is indescribable, it's beyond being tired. Also I have pain to cope with, some from cancer, but some from arthritis and some of unknown cause … .

"Despite my great fatigue, I've had a hectic year of travel for speaking engagements, especially with showings of the film *Gay Pioneers*. Plus, much time devoted to obliging people who want old photos from Kay, materials and information from me, and interviews with both of us, for their projects, their books or articles or documentary films or whatever. We're so busy helping everyone else with their projects, we can't get our own!

"Our own? Kay wants to do a gay photo-history book. … We're sitting on a gold mine of over 45 years of incredibly diverse gay movement material and it's full of surprises."

In a letter to Kuda on March 14, 2006, Gittings wrote: "Still in chemotherapy, now 33 months continuous, no remission in sight. One bad side effect—besides the chronic fatigue which really drains me—is lesions on my fingers and feet. It's as though I took a knife and made cuts and scrapes on my hands and feet, only these cuts come from inside, from the chemo drug. They hurt worse when healing than when the wounds first erupt. Walking is uncomfortable, and anything requiring use of hands is really painful! Kay can't help. She's out of commission with her arthritis, so it falls to me to do almost everything: all our errands, shopping, cooking, clean up, daily household chores, driving. The only task Kay can handle is our outgoing phone calls; she can't even struggle to the phone in time to answer incoming calls. … Don't get old—it's a killer!"

Awards and Recognition

It is estimated that Gittings addressed more than 500 audiences during her career. In 1973, she was a founding member of the National Gay Task Force. She was a charter member of the board of the Gay Rights National Lobby, which later merged with the Human Rights Campaign, where Gittings was on the advisory committee. She served on the first board of the Delaware Valley Legacy Fund. From 1998 to 2002 she served on the Endowment Committee for the James C. Hormel Gay & Lesbian Center at the San Francisco Public Library. She was a member of most major national and Philadelphia-area LGBT groups.

During the 1989 New York pride celebrations, Gittings was among the pioneers invited by Mayor Ed Koch to a special 20th Anniversary of Stonewall event, at a dedication of Stonewall Place, on June 1. Gittings served as co-grand marshal with U.S. Representative Barney Frank at the 1997 New York City Gay and Lesbian Pride March, where Gittings was declared the "Grand Mother of Lesbian and Gay Liberation" by Jack Nichols ("Grand Mother," not "Grandmother"). That same year, the couple pushed the American Association of Retired Persons to grant a couple's membership to them.

Gittings received dozens of major awards during her life. Some came early, such as a 1977 award from Mattachine Midwest in Chicago. She and the Reverend Peggy Way received the group's annual Pearl M. Hart Award. "Oh, lucky, lucky city to have had Pearl Hart," Gittings said at the event, as reported in the April 1, 1977, *GayLife* newspaper. Of anti-gay attitudes, Gittings said that night, "we're seeing the dying dragon lashing its tail."

Gittings was honored for her life of activism by the Statewide Pennsylvania Rights Coalition (SPARC) on September 16, 2000.

The Independence Branch of the Free Library of Philadelphia named a gay and lesbian collection of books in Gittings' honor in 2001. Gittings told the *Philadelphia Gay News* she was "deeply touched" by the honor, adding, "It will be an honor to have my name linked to a first-rate collection of gay and lesbian books and other materials—right in the shadow of Independence Hall." In the Bullough book, she said: "This prominent special collection means that our work is bearing fruit. How exciting to see results! For me it's like a bit of heaven brought to earth."

The Gay and Lesbian Alliance Against Defamation presented her with the first Barbara Gittings Award in 2001.

The Gay, Lesbian, Bisexual, and Transgender Round Table of the ALA renamed one of its book awards the Stonewall Book Award–Barbara Gittings Literature Award in 2002. In 2003, the American Library Association itself rewarded her with a lifetime honorary membership. She received the first John E. Fryer Award from the American Psychiatric Association in 2006 with Frank Kameny.

Her adopted hometown of Philadelphia gave her a posthumous special tribute on October 1, 2012, when the city named a section of Locust Street "Barbara Gittings Way." That same year, Chicago's Legacy Walk, an outdoor public display that celebrates LGBT history and people, dedicated a plaque to Gittings.

She is also featured in the documentaries *Gay Pioneers*, *Before Stonewall*, *After Stonewall*, *Out of the Past*, and *Pride Divide*.

The sign Gittings carried in the 1965 Independence Hall picket, which was in Kameny's collection, was donated to the Smithsonian Institution's Museum of American History in 2006. The sign reads: SEXUAL PREFERENCE IS IRRELEVANT TO FEDERAL EMPLOYMENT. Kameny died in 2011.

Gittings was also among those featured in a 2008 calendar by the Lambda Literary Foundation, *LGBT Literary Pioneers*.

Meanwhile, Lahusen's photos have been featured in numerous exhibits. In 2001, Delaware's Wilmington Public Library, in the city where Lahusen and Gittings spent some of Gittings' last years, showcased her work in "Opening the Closet Doors: Photos of the Early Gay Civil Rights Movement." For the exhibit, she described photography as "an indispensable tool in the struggle for social change, for un-demonizing people and for saving our history."

The summer of 2015 will mark the 50th anniversary of the original Reminder Day demonstrations in front of Independence Hall and the Liberty Bell. There will be major celebrations.

While their photos and most archives are in the New York Public Library's Manuscripts and Archives Division, the couple also donated more than 1,000 of their books to the University of Massachusetts Amherst Libraries' Department of Special Collections and University Archives.

"People like Kay and Barbara deserve all the recognition they can get," 1960s activist Randy Wicker said. "Barbara was really the movement's most important 'builder.' They're the worker bees in the movement. Every movement has a few stars, and I'm great at getting publicity, but people that really stick their nose to the grindstone, and meet monthly deadlines, and organize all these details, figure out the homophile coalition events, etc., they deserve the recognition. They always made me feel more of a part of the movement than any other activist did."

A Lasting Legacy

While Gittings was still alive, she and Lahusen decided on the New York Public Library as the recipient of the majority of their archives, including Lahusen's treasure trove of movement photographs.

Melanie Yolles from the library was among the speakers at Gittings' memorial. "Barbara Gittings and her partner Kay Lahusen didn't have just one, two or even three boxes, they had more than 300 boxes," Yolles said, "filled not just with private memories but with history. That's fitting; after all, Barbara and Kay helped make that history. … At some point the temptation to pitch it all must have been overwhelming, but they didn't. Instead they bought a condo for it. And it became their next-door neighbor."

Yolles emphasized that the women donated their archives; they did not sell them. They wanted it to be a prominent collection, and open to the public, sharing space with the papers of other movement people such as Vito Russo, Karla Jay and Morty Manford—plus George Washington, Thomas Jefferson, Emma Goldman and other legends.

The 50 years of correspondence with the community's most accomplished activists, plus everyday LGBTQ people, provides an intimate connection to the development of the movement. There are files on Russo, Wicker, Kameny, John Fryer, Foster Gunnison, Jack Nichols, Del Martin and Phyllis Lyon, Ros Regelson, Jim Carmichael, Tee Corinne, Louie Crew, John Cunningham, Lisa Ben, Jeannette Foster, Pearl Hart, Leslie Feinberg, Jewelle Gomez, Marie Kuda, and Lilli Vincenz, among others.

The New York Public Library described the collection in part:

"This collection chronicles Barbara Gittings and Kay Tobin Lahusen's careers as activists as well as their efforts to document the gay rights movement from the 1960s to 2007. The breadth of material compiled is impressive not only in content, but in its scope: it spans the gay rights movement from the first sustainable homophile organizations to the twenty-first century's debates on gay marriage. According to Barbara Gittings, the homophile movement she joined in 1956 consisted of a club of 200 people spread across the United States. This collection documents how that scattered group of 200 grew into a highly visible socio-political movement by tracing the donors' activities in pre- and post-Stonewall America. …

"Interviews, film appearances, and speaking engagements would later become a second career for Gittings: her post-Stonewall activities were dominated by lecture schedules. Although she often acted as a cheerful ambassador to gay life, Gittings' passion was educating people on gay history. Due to the lack of information available in libraries when they were young, Gittings and Lahusen felt a responsibility to document the history they shaped. Gay-themed materials were consciously assembled and incorporated into their personal papers to create the most comprehensive collection possible."

The collection includes materials from the many organizations the couple were involved with, some as founders, some as board members, some as key volunteers and supporters, arranged under these headings:

— American Library Association's Gay Task Force
— American Psychiatric Association
— Daughters of Bilitis
— East Coast Homophile Organizations
— Eastern Regional Conference of Homophile Organizations
— Gay Activists Alliance
— Gay Rights National Lobby and the Human Rights Campaign
— Homophile Action League
— Mattachine Society
— National Gay Archives and Library Committee
— National Gay Task Force
— National Planning Conference of Homophile Organizations
— North American Conference [of] Homophile Organizations
— Pennsylvania Council for Sexual Minorities
— Plus other organizations including the ACLU, American Medical Association, Gay Nurses Alliance, Gay Teachers Association, Janus Society, National Organization for Women, and PFLAG.

There is also a collection of exhibits curated by Lahusen, plus an informal exhibit by Wicker that was displayed in the storefront window of his New York City button shop in 1994.

As part of their dedication to history, Gittings and Lahusen were part of the National Gay Archives and Library Committee, which tried to form a national gay archive. The New York Public Library states: "The committee was formed in February 1975 and initially conceived by Dr. Howard Brown. According to its initial press release, the committee 'intended to bring together gay-related personal papers of prominent homosexual women and men, as well as books with homosexual themes and every kind of gay movement material.' Notably, the committee was in talks with the New York Public Library with the intention of creating such an archive there in the late 1970s.

"In the course of her work for the committee, Gittings gathered records from the following organizations: Gay Support and Action Group (Maine), Detroit *Gay Liberator*, and the National Gay Task Force. The National Gay Archives and Library Committee folded by 1981, when its bank account closed. When it failed to establish a gay archive, Gittings and Lahusen absorbed the records they had collected on behalf of the committee into their personal collection and continued to collect materials to document gay history."

The couple also kept extensive subject files on a wide range of topics, including AIDS, the Briggs Initiative, Anita Bryant, theater, youth, hate crimes, immigration, and even gay stamps.

A dizzying array of speaking engagements is listed in the files. Gittings spoke at universities but also at many professional association meetings, church events, conferences, donor forums, pride rallies, film festivals, youth groups, community centers and employee groups.

Reflections on Change

In the midst of their early years of activism, Gittings reflected on how far they had come, as well as on the necessary future steps for progress.

For Lahusen's 1972 *Crusaders* book, Gittings said: "The movement we have today could not have developed if there hadn't been this earlier effort to get over the really severe feelings of inadequacy about being gay that most of our people had.

"Also we talked about doing something, such as getting laws changed, to ease things a little. Later we began to claim we were entitled to some rights. I recall that a homosexual bill of rights was the subject of an early gay group conference on the West Coast, and the bill of rights proved so controversial the delegates from one group walked out of the meeting. There was still a strong feeling that if we spoke nicely and reasonably and played by the rules of the game, we could persuade heterosexuals that homosexuals were all right as human beings.

"Later yet we came to the position that the 'problem' of homosexuality isn't ours at all—it's society's, and society should change to accommodate us, not try to change us. This was the era of 'Gay Is Good.'"

In 1974, Gittings spoke to Jonathan Ned Katz about the newest changes in the movement:

"Now we have several thousand people in the movement instead of a few dozen as at the beginning. It used to be that everyone in the movement literally knew every other person active in the movement. I suppose, for some people, the pleasures of being in a little club disappeared when the movement grew. But I think this is a great improvement, because not only are many more people coming in to do the work, but many more kinds of work can be taken up. The existence of gay professional organizations is something that we wouldn't have dreamed of 10 years ago.

"Despite the progress, the vast majority of gay people are still living masked and closeted lives, and do have to be concerned with what the straight world thinks. In my view, the purpose of gay liberation is to change this. I feel the purpose of the movement is to get all those closet doors opened. It should be possible for gay people to live their lives, feeling good about themselves, without having special problems of self-image. This is what I look forward to. Those of us who are lucky enough to be able to be out and active in gay liberation have a special responsibility to those who cannot afford to come out yet. What we're saying to them is: 'Hang in there, people, because those of us who are out are oiling the closet hinges just as fast as we can.'

"Having gone through many years of unhappiness, uncertainty, and negative feelings about myself, I want to see to it that younger gay people don't have to go through the same thing. Those years of worrying and wondering were, in a way, productive for me. I'm assertive and I kept grappling with it until I finally evolved a positive view of my gayness. But it was a long, hard journey, which might have broken someone else. People shouldn't have to go through that."

"It's easier for young gay people today," Gittings said to Perry and Swicegood for their 1991 book. "They don't have to start from scratch to learn how to survive. The veil of silence has been lifted. It isn't necessary to be like people of my generation who grew up thinking, 'I'm the only one of this kind in the whole wide world!'

"There are still people hiding in the closet, fearful, trembling about what will happen to them if they're found out, or if they reveal themselves. But today's homosexuals don't start out thinking there is nobody on earth like them, which was true of most gay people not too many years ago. At least now it's obvious they have plenty of good company. ...

"Every group, big or little, in the gay movement that reaches out to involve gay individuals is engaged in important work. The beauty of our community is that we are doing a great variety of things. We have outdoors groups, athletes, naturalists, gay choruses and gay marching bands, political groups all along a full spectrum, groups in the professions and in business, campus groups, social groups, and hundreds of miscellaneous special-interest nooks and crannies. I'm delighted that as more and more gay people come along with their own varied interests, they are finding and filling the niches.

"Among the things that keep me going are the responses I receive. I owe a great debt to those gay people who've telephoned and written, telling me their stories that are sometimes sad, sometimes funny. The simple truth is, they are the people we do this for. ...

"The gay community has put me in touch with proud and marvelous people. I know thousands who've come out, who've come into our movement—and the number keeps expanding."

"Things have changed much more than I dreamed possible!" Gittings told Marcus for his 1992 book. "The sheer growth of the movement in size and the variety of organizations is something I wouldn't have thought possible when I first joined the movement in 1958. I'm just thrilled that we have gay marching bands, gay choruses, gay outdoor groups, the Gay Games, and gay rodeos in addition to the standard political-action groups and legislative efforts. ... These groups bring gay people together who start talking about their problems and eventually start talking about how they might solve them. It was how the movement got started in the first place.

"You know, it's been a ball. I love being part of a special people. I think gays are a special people. However much we may now blend into the woodwork, and however desirable it may be for us to have as few barriers and obstacles as possible so that we are more like other people, we will always be a special people. There is something innately different about us. I prize it. I value it. I think in our hearts most of us do. And I think it gives us that special bond that's very enriching to me. I just don't feel that same sense of community with straight people. Oh, sure, there are straight people I like, but I can't imagine not being gay. What would life have been like? Dull? Dismal? Decrepit?"

"Come to think of it, there is something important still to be done," Lahusen said. "The gay retirement homes. We're not actively working on that, but it is a twinkle in our eye."

Gittings added: "I want a place where I can sit back in the rocker and say, 'Do you remember when we picketed the White House in 1965?'"

In an interview for the August 1999 edition of *Pride* magazine, Gittings gave advice to young activists: "A) Don't be daunted. Over the long haul, for every setback, we've made four or five giant strides forward. Be persistent, be patient, be persuasive. You'll see results. B) Keep and use your sense of humor. Gay rights is a serious business but it doesn't always have to be grim. And a light touch often helps to push our message." She also pointed out, "Progress on paper is fine but we can't stop there. The struggle for equal treatment has to be won in people's hearts and minds where it really counts."

One concern Gittings had was errors that were creeping into newer accounts of gay history. She told Kuda at one point she was wary of the new generation of "historians" who weren't around when activists were doing the "scut work and risk-running" and now were playing "safe academic games." She wrote: "Kay and I are too constantly having to correct other people's 'history' from wrong-slant emphasis to major factual goofs. And we can only correct it if we're asked before the damn stuff is published. It's frustrating, sometimes infuriating." Kuda added in a 2007 piece she wrote in tribute to Gittings, "Going through thirty-five years of correspondence these last few weeks has reminded me of what a truly remarkable woman she was and how much she influenced my life and work."

Gittings told Lahusen in the 2002 Bullough book: "I'd like to see us out of business as a social change movement. Then we can be ourselves without special effort. Meantime, it's a wonderful experience, working with thousands of gay women and men to get the bigots off our backs and to show that gay love is good for us and for the rest of the world too!'"

"It was something that needed to be done," Gittings said in *Visions Today*. "We thought, 'It doesn't matter what the world thinks. We have to do this.'"

"I believe most Americans have come to accept the fact that 'black is beautiful' and most are coming to accept the fact that 'gay is good,'" Lahusen said in her 2012 *Philadelphia Gay News* interview. "I believe our movement is on the right side of history. Meanwhile, let's keep on marching for gay equality."

Remembrances

When Gittings died February 18, 2007, at age 74, there was an immediate outpouring of love from around the country. Author Katherine V. Forrest, then head of the Lambda Literary Foundation, said Gittings "will live forever in our hearts and our memory. In the history of LGBT people, she will stand forever among our giants." Gittings was also recognized during a tribute at the Lambda Literary Awards that May, among 11 LGBT literary heroes who had died in the previous 18 months.

Lahusen asked that memorial donations be given to Lambda Legal, the national LGBT legal organization.

About 200 people attended the April 28, 2007, memorial gathering for Gittings at the National Constitution Center in Philadelphia. The carefully crafted program featured speakers and music, as listed here from the DVD of the event (job titles as of 2007):
— Musical interludes by the Philadelphia Voices of Pride
— A tribute by Frank Kameny, pioneer gay activist
— Dorothy Wax, who was vice president, Delaware Valley Legacy Fund
— Joe Solmonese, at the time president, Human Rights Campaign
— Jan Weatherford, friend and breast cancer survivor

— Matt Foreman, at the time executive director, National Gay and Lesbian Task Force

— Marcia M. Gallo, author, *Different Daughters: A History of the Daughters of Bilitis and the Rise of the Lesbian Rights Movement*

—Dr. Jack Drescher, past chair (2000–2006), Committee on Gay, Lesbian, and Bisexual Issues, American Psychiatric Association

— Melanie Yolles, Manuscripts and Archives Division, New York Public Library

— Kevin Jennings, founder and then–executive director, Gay, Lesbian and Straight Education Network

— John Cunningham, friend and colleague

— Anne L. Moore, past co-chair (2002–2006), Gay, Lesbian, Bisexual and Transgender Round Table, American Library Association

— Karen Faulkner, from the Philadelphia Chamber Chorus

— Concluding remarks by the Reverend Elder Troy D. Perry, founder, Metropolitan Community Churches

Philadelphia Gay News publisher Mark Segal and Debra D'Alessandro, host of WXPN's *Amazon Country*, served as masters of ceremonies for the memorial.

"The gay movement is some 56 years old," Kameny said. "Over that period of time we have had our share of movement luminaries. Almost all of them are now gone ... only a tiny few are left. We are here today [for] one of the most luminous of those luminaries, and to pay her the tribute which she deserves far more richly than can easily be articulated. I knew her well, and worked closely with her for some 45 of those 56 years. And so I speak with the greatest of sadness in tribute to and in the fondest of memory of a valued, longtime colleague and associate, and a truly cherished friend, with whom I worked closely and productively for all those years."

For the gay movement, he said she ultimately became "one of its founding mothers. ... She was a force to be reckoned with. ... With an ineffable sense of loss, I say goodbye to Barbara, goodbye, goodbye, goodbye. We are all the less for her departure. ... I will always remember her fondly as one of the more important players in my gay activist life, and in the incredible progress of the gay community over the past half century."

"What do lesbian, gay, bisexual and transgender Americans owe to Barbara and Kay? Everything. Literally, everything," said Matt Foreman at the memorial. "Some would say, Isn't that giving one person too much credit? The answer is actually 'no.' Because contrary to those who think that being gay, or the gay community, is something that's transitory and it's going to fall out of fashion soon, I believe we have always been there both as individuals and as a community. But we were tortured, beaten down, terrified, isolated for centuries. It took a handful of audacious and courageous men and women to step forward, to never retreat and never give up. And it was indeed only a handful of people that did that. They persevered, endured, and Barbara Gittings was one of them. But was more than ... one of those in that handful, she was the essential ingredient holding it together—that 'it' was our fragile, embryonic movement. Others came and went, Barbara stayed."

Foreman reminisced about Gittings' time on his organization's board and her efforts to build a national gay-rights movement. Foreman told of the Task Force's early days, from deciding "What did we want?" to dealing with anxieties about money and paying for health insurance. Foreman called Gittings an anchor who was "the epitome of a public-minded activist" and "unfailingly kind and considerate." He added: "One did not even think of telling Barbara 'no.'"

Reading the minutes of the board in those early years, "throughout every meeting, you hear Barbara's measured, calm voice," he said. "I know without a doubt that without Barbara serving as that anchor for us at the Task Force, and so many other institutions, we would have spun out of control, and we, collectively, would not be where we are today."

Foreman also quoted Elaine Noble, the first openly gay person elected to a state office in the U.S., as saying Barbara was our "stellar leader." Noble said Gittings was always on the phone urging the community to support those in need, including doing so during tragic times. "I know she will be up there in heaven, and I know she's already organizing the angels."

Chicago's William B. Kelley, who was also on the NGTF board with Gittings, could not be at the memorial because of a recent heart attack, so Foreman read his comments: "Barbara was the epitome of a public-minded activist in the best sense. She always exemplified a regard for how to make her message the most effective. She eschewed jargon and infighting. She concentrated on clear, vivid, honest and cheerful expression. She was one of a kind."

Dorothy Wax emphasized that Gittings and Lahusen are both advocates of "checkbook activism," and they practiced what they preached, including doing so in their wills.

Marcia Gallo spoke about what she learned from Gittings and Lahusen when writing her *Different Daughters* book: "She had a phenomenal sense of humor. You never left a conversation with Barbara without having at least one good belly laugh. ... She was one of the most generous people I have ever known."

Gallo interviewed DOB co-founder Phyllis Lyon for the book, and Lyon said of meeting Gittings in 1956: "We met her plane. She was a cute, curly-haired young woman wearing a shift and sandals. I remember she had this satchel, this backpack, I'd never seen anything like it, or her."

In 1962, when Gittings became editor of the DOB magazine, *The Ladder,* "it would never be the same," Gallo said. "She revolutionized not only that magazine, but the ways in which lesbians were portrayed in the media. For the first time, a woman or a man, or a questioning anybody, could go to a newsstand, and there would be a magazine that not only had a photo of usually a beautiful young woman on the cover, but said in big, bold letters, 'A Lesbian Review.' This had never happened before. And Barbara, and Kay, made sure that it did.

"She was one of the most brilliant propagandists of our movement. ... She claimed the importance of visibility, of public relations, dare I say marketing, at a time when our movement was just struggling to have a face. She took that face and made sure that it was writ large.

"Her generosity to researchers, to writers, to historians, media makers, politicians, students, friends of friends, even when she battled the devastating effects of cancer, won my heart forever. Barbara was much more than one of the most important sources of information, she also took her time to go through my manuscript many times, and not only do suggestions, but do line edits.

"Her last public appearance was on December 1, 2006, at the Ninth Street Book Shop in Wilmington, Delaware. She appeared there as the honored guest at the party celebrating my book's release. ... She was there even though that afternoon she had undergone chemotherapy, and was in a great deal of pain. She not only got to the event and charmed everyone there, and posed for photographs, and had a lot to say about the future of the gay movement, of course, she [even] refused the wheelchair that we offered. ...

"[Gittings] left not only her valuable collection of gay movement materials [to the New York Public Library], but a legacy of lesbian visibility, leadership, collegiality and love."

Dr. Drescher said the efforts of Gittings and Kameny at the APA conferences had a profound effect on individuals and society. Eventually, international psychiatry followed, though it took almost 20 years. "In 1992, the World Health Organization removed homosexuality from the international classification of diseases," he said.

"The activists had been correct," Drescher said. "Their actions eventually deprived the media, religious, government, military and educational institutions of their medical and scientific rationalizations for discrimination. So what followed was a gradual increase in social acceptance of gay men and women as people began to realize that if being gay is not an illness, and if one doesn't literally accept Biblical prohibitions against homosexuality, and if secular democracy separates church and state, and if openly gay people are productive citizens, then what's wrong with being gay? We know how much things have changed since '73. In my own profession the change has been enormous."

Weatherford summarized Gittings' attitude toward cancer this way: "It is not about the dying; at the end dying will take care of itself. It is about the living." She also said Gittings "never stopped being passionate about gay civil rights; cancer never took that away from her."

Cunningham, who said he "entered the movement through the women's door," because he was so influenced by the lesbians in the movement, said watching Gittings on the *Susskind Show* changed his life. "Throughout her life, Barbara threw a lifeline to thousands of people like me and you, offering hope, and courage, with her characteristic enthusiasm, eloquence, good humor, and most importantly, her impeccable diction. I'll be forever grateful for Barbara ... for how she helped change the world."

Jennings pointed to the impact Gittings had on youth. GLSEN produced a film, *Out of the Past*, to look at gay figures from the 17th century until modern times, with Gittings featured in a prominent role. The film won the 1998 Sundance Film Festival's Audience Award for Best Documentary.

"I did joint appearances with Barbara, and to see her interact with young people, who simply flocked to her, these 14-, 15-year old, really dykelings and little baby fags, they were all flocking to Barbara, who simply radiated love and warmth and inspiration to these children, who at that point were young enough to be her grandchildren—and in ways they will never understand, are [her grandchildren]," Jennings said. "Perhaps the single most moving opportunity I had to show the film with Barbara was in June 1998, when it was chosen to be the centerpiece of the first-ever White House recognition of Pride Month [it was screened at the State Department]. And Barbara, Kay, I and 10 high school students went together to the White House to watch the film be shown. Kay was carefully documenting it with her trusty camera, making sure there would be a record in history.

"My last chance to speak together with Barbara was in 2001 in Anchorage, Alaska, when we were speaking together at a conference for high school gay/straight alliances ... . It was less than three weeks after 9/11, when most people were still terrified to get on planes. But not Barbara; cancer or no, she had gotten on a plane; terrorists or no, she had flown to Alaska; and as she had done countless times before, she inspired young people, and LGBT people of all places and all sizes, in this most remote corner of America, to believe that they too could make history, just as Barbara had.

"I am deeply aware that the freedom I possess today is thanks to Barbara and Kay. And the only way I can ever truly say thank you is to make sure the next generation is freer than I am."

Faulkner of the Philadelphia Chamber Chorus said Gittings told her that "singing was essential for her mental health, and it fueled her for her work in the world." A few days after the memorial, the chorus performed a special Gittings tribute concert.

Troy Perry concluded the official program, before audience members were given time to tell their own stories. Perry spoke about three things for which history will remember Gittings: the fact that in doing the work she would use her real name—she wanted to have hope in her life, and nobody could take that away from her; her belief that the community needed healing, getting gays all healed on the same day (when the APA changed its designation of homosexuality); and her secular belief in heaven: Though not religious, she was spiritual and believed in getting a helping of heaven on earth.

"I loved Barbara, because Barbara was always herself," Perry said. "Sometimes we have a face for one part of the community, and a face over here for something else. Barbara was the same no matter where you met her. She was my role model. ... She said, 'We can have hope.'"

Windy City Times included quotes from colleagues and friends of Gittings in its February 21, 2007, edition.

"Gittings was, to my great fortune, the first lesbian I ever saw," said Toni Armstrong Jr., a longtime Chicago teacher and activist now living in Florida. "This was in 1971, when I was still in high school and had never yet heard a good word about gay people. I happened to tune into *The David Susskind Show*, during a segment on 'Women Who Love Women.' Barbara made her famous statement: 'Homosexuals today are taking it for granted that their homosexuality is not at all something dreadful—it's good, it's right, it's natural, it's moral, and this is the way they are going to be!' I completely believed her, and she has been my role model and guiding light since I was 17 years old. In later years we became friends, but she continued to be high on a pedestal for me, as an activist. As the editor of *HOT WIRE* lesbian magazine, I was further inspired by her work with the pioneering lesbian publication *The Ladder*. All that I wanted to do, she had done decades earlier—when it was so much scarier. I think in later years the two most important lessons she taught me directly were that LGBT activists need to work on many, many issues all at once—that way those who oppose us can't ever stop us all—and that you can have a lot of *fun* the whole time you're being an activist.

"Whether they know it or not, whether they have heard of her or not, I believe every single gay person on the planet's life is better because Barbara Gittings was here. Whenever someone dies, the word 'beloved' gets thrown about, but in this case, it truly applies. She was as nice, generous, and upbeat as she was formidable, courageous, and effective. Legacies don't get much better than that."

"She exuded this incredible warmth and friendliness; she was the glue that helped keep together often contentious organizations during the early phase of the movement," said Ken Sherrill, professor of political science at Hunter College. He first met Gittings through the founding of the short-lived Gay Academic Union in 1973. "She was a deeply principled, highly courageous person, but also warm and focused. If she had any enemies, I never met them."

Mark Meinke posted many memorial responses on the Rainbow History Pages website he founded, including this from Kameny: "I will miss Barbara keenly. She was a truly valued and cherished colleague, associate, and friend—one-of-a-kind in my own life. We were in close, continuing, and cooperative contact, mutually supportively and enormously productively for both of us individually and for the world around us, from the early 1960s until the very present."

"I first met Barbara through a full-page picture of her in Ginny Vida's book *Our Right to Love.* Late '70s I think that was," said Peg Cruikshank. "Later we had some contact through her work with the American Library Association. Sometime in the '80s, I stayed overnight with Barbara and Kay, and they took me around Philadelphia showing me the sights. I have a vivid picture of a dinner at their house. Barbara went out on the porch to dry the lettuce, swinging the container over her head with wonderful vigor and determination. I think that same spirit shows through all her work for the movement. I saw Barbara and Kay again in '05 at a meeting of gay and lesbian elders in Philadelphia, part of the American Society on Aging national convention, I believe, our first meeting in many years. Barbara's talk was animated, informative, and humorous. We will not see her like again."

"She was one of the most decent people I've ever known," gay activist and writer Arthur Evans said of Gittings. "She brought out the best in everyone."

**Above: Gittings with a
rainbow. Right: Gittings with
just some of her many awards.**
Photos by Kay Tobin Lahusen.
Copyright Manuscripts and Archives
Division, The New York Public Library

Gittings with Elliot Shelkrot (left) and
Steven Jay at the presentation of gay
books to the Free Library of Philadelphia,
1991. The collection was a circulating
collection of the Free Library of
Philadelphia. Below: John Cunningham,
Gittings and Ada Bello in front of the
Barbara Gittings Gay/Lesbian Collection
at the Free Library of Philadelphia,
1990s. Bello was one of the participants
in the Annual Reminder Days at
Independence Hall.
Photos by Kay Tobin Lahusen. Copyright
Manuscripts and Archives Division, The New York
Public Library

Left: GLSEN Philadelphia representatives with Gittings, 1990s.
Photo by Kay Tobin Lahusen. Copyright Manuscripts and Archives Division, The New York Public Library

Gittings was a frequent visitor to the Chicago area. She's pictured at right with youth advocate Toni Armstrong Jr., and below with others at the same 2002 event, which was for the Gay, Lesbian and Straight Education Network, as covered by *Windy City Times*.
Photos by Tracy Baim

GITTINGS IN CHICAGO

Barbara Gittings, a key activist in the lesbian and gay community for nearly 50 years, gave two lectures in the area last week. The Gay, Lesbian and Straight Education Network hosted her at DePaul, and the Berwyn United Neighborhood Gay and Lesbian Organization also hosted her. The informative and humorous slide shows were attended by people of all ages. Gittings is pictured top, left, with

GLSEN's Toni Armstrong Jr. (left) and Miranda Stevens-Miller (right), as well as with some of the teens who attended the DePaul event (above). Photos by Tracy Baim

Gittings and Lahusen at the 1994 Stonewall celebrations in New York City.
Photos by Wayne Marquardt

In 2001, these four lesbian publishing pioneers were together in San Francisco. The event was at the Harvey Milk Branch of the San Francisco Public Library. Back row: Lahusen and Gittings. Front: Phyllis Lyon and Del Martin. The event celebrated Gittings' work with the American Library Association.
Photo by Jim Mitulski

David Carter visiting Lahusen in 2010. Among Carter's books is *Stonewall: The Riots That Sparked the Gay Revolution*.
Photo by Kay Tobin Lahusen. Copyright Manuscripts and Archives Division, The New York Public Library

Gittings and Kameny, relaxing on the second floor of the Independence Visitor Center in Philadelphia.
Photo by Rachelle Lee Smith, courtesy of Equality Forum.

Gittings and Lahusen with Frank Kameny. They are in front of Kameny's house at 5020 Cathedral Avenue, N.W., in Washington, D.C., now on the D.C. Register of Historic Places. It is a candidate for the National Register of Historic Places.
Photo by Jim Oakes

Lahusen said Gittings loved music and singing with choirs as much as she loved her gay movement work. The National Gay Task Force used her image in a promotional flier, lower left. Photo below right is Gittings performing in her later years, with the Philadelphia Chamber Chorus.
Photos by Kay Tobin Lahusen. Copyright Manuscripts and Archives Division, The New York Public Library

Left: Gittings relaxing at home in Philadelphia in the 1990s.

Below: Gittings in Philadelphia, 2000s.
Photos by Kay Tobin Lahusen. Copyright Manuscripts and Archives Division, The New York Public Library

Left: Gittings holding publications that represented great progress on gay rights.

Bottom: Gittings outside the Human Rights Campaign headquarters in Washington, D.C.
Photos by Kay Tobin Lahusen. Copyright Manuscripts and Archives Division, The New York Public Library

WINDY CITY TIMES May 4, 2005 PAGE 21

Philadelphia Marks 40th Anniversary of Protests

Several hundred people turned out to watch the honoring of 40 GLBT pioneers and allies during the National Celebration on Independence Mall Sunday in Philadelphia. Thousands more turned out for concerts, a street fair, workshops, film screenings, and interfaith service, and other events.

The Gay Pioneers & 40 Heroes Tribute was the centerpiece of the 16-hour National Celebration of the 40th Anniversary of the Philly demonstrations. There has been controversy about the date for months. Even many of those original 40 who marched in 1965 want to make sure that prior activism is not forgotten. And still others are planning a big Philadelphia Freedom concert in the town on the actual July 4 date—including the unveiling of a plaque to honor the original protests, and a concert by Elton John, Patti LaBelle and others.

Regardless of the controversy, many of those selected came to be honored, including pioneers Frank Kameny and Barbara Gittings (who spoke at a panel earlier that day but had to leave for another event). Chicagoan William Kelley travelled to Philadelphia to remember his own participation four decades ago.

"Through the efforts of 40 heroes, many organizations, and individuals coming out, we are at a tipping point. Forty years ago, we were in a debilitating closet. In 2005, we have a lot to celebrate, and we reaffirm our commitment to ensuring equality," said Malcolm Lazin, executive director of Equality Forum.

Kameny and Gittings were among those who staged the first annual and organized gay and lesbian civil-rights demonstration at Independence Hall and the Liberty Bell July 4, 1965.

Joining those two among the 40 honored were people from the a wide range of backgrounds, from activists to lawyers, politicians to business people. The 40 heroes honored included Rep. Barney Frank, Rep. Tammy Baldwin, Jim Hormel, Judy Shepard, Larry Kramer, Bishop Gene Robinson, Phill Wilson, Germany's Volker Beck, Tony Kushner, Col. Margarethe Cammermeyer, Kate Kendell, Evan Wolfson, Olga Orraca Paredes, Kevin Jennings, Matt Foreman, Ambassador Jim Hormel, Del Martin and Phyllis Lyon, Martina Navratilova, Melissa Etheridge, Ellen DeGeneres, Faisal Alam, Olga Orraca-Paredes, Jarrett Barrios, Kevin Bourassa & Joe Varnel, David Mixner, Kevin Jennings, Matt Foreman, Tim Gill, Rev. Troy Perry, Andrew Sullivan, Riki Wilchins, Evan Wolfson, and Supreme Court Justice Anthony Kennedy.

Many of the 40 have died—including Bayard Rustin, Harvey Milk, Randy Shilts, Audre Lorde, Essex Hemphill, Tom Stoddard, Vito Russo, Leonard Matlovich, Storme DeLarveri, Evelyn Hooker, and Marlon Riggs.

About a dozen anti-gays protested—as promised by Fred Phelps' Westboro Baptist Church of Kansas. But dozens of pro-gay marchers, spearheaded by the Metropolitan Community Church, surrounded the anti-gays wherever they marched and stood.

See www.equalityforum.com.
— *Text and photos by Tracy Baim*

TOP: Lavender Light Gospel Choir of NYC; Col Cammermeyer. **RIGHT:** Bishop Robinson, and MCC counters the protesters. **BELOW:** A few of the original marchers from 1965, and the Liberty Bell.

Barbara Gittings addresses a workshop on the movement, and, left, pictured with fellow original marcher Chicagoan William Kelley.

In May 2005, Gittings, Kameny and Lahusen were part of the 40th-anniversary celebrations of the Philadelphia demonstrations for homosexual rights. Longtime Chicago activist William B. Kelley is pictured with Gittings, (bottom left of layout), during the celebrations. He was among the few dozen who marched in Philadelphia in the 1960s.
Coverage in *Windy City Times* at right, featuring photos by Tracy Baim

Gittings on her porch in the early 2000s.
Photo by Kay Tobin Lahusen. Copyright Manuscripts and Archives Division, The New York Public Library

Below and left: Lahusen with two exhibits of her photographic documentation of the gay movement, 2000s.
Photos by Judith Armstrong

Above: Gittings in 2000, during her cancer treatments.

Bottom: In the mid-2000s, facing further cancer struggles.
Photos of Gittings by Kay Lahusen. Bottom photos, photographers unknown

Gittings died February 18, 2007, at age 74. Above is the photo display at her April 28, 2007, memorial, held at the National Constitution Center in Philadelphia. Right: Lahusen at that memorial, surrounded by longtime friends Eva Freund, Paul Kuntzler, Frank Kameny and the Reverend Troy Perry.
Photos by Patsy Lynch

Above: Friends gather around Lahusen at the 2007 memorial for Gittings.
Photo by Patsy Lynch

Below: The Philadelphia Chamber Chorus held a special tribute concert May 6, 2007.

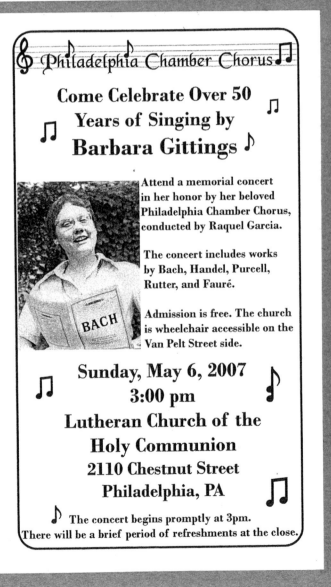

Philadelphia Chamber Chorus

Come Celebrate Over 50 Years of Singing by Barbara Gittings

Attend a memorial concert in her honor by her beloved Philadelphia Chamber Chorus, conducted by Raquel Garcia.

The concert includes works by Bach, Handel, Purcell, Rutter, and Fauré.

Admission is free. The church is wheelchair accessible on the Van Pelt Street side.

Sunday, May 6, 2007
3:00 pm
Lutheran Church of the Holy Communion
2110 Chestnut Street
Philadelphia, PA

The concert begins promptly at 3pm. There will be a brief period of refreshments at the close.

At right: Lahusen in her retirement home in Pennsylvania in 2013. In the top photo, she is holding a photo taken in 2012 by Hal Baim at the dedication of a street plaque in Gittings' honor as part of The Legacy Project's Legacy Walk in Chicago.
Photos by Tracy Baim

Barbara Gittings Way was dedicated in Philadelphia in 2012.
Photo by M. Fischetti, courtesy of Visit Philadelphia

Below: Gittings' final resting place in the Congressional Cemetery in Washington, D.C., where she will be joined by Lahusen. The monument fittingly reads: "GAY PIONEERS who spoke truth to power." The bench is inscribed, "Partners in Life, Married in their Hearts."
Photo from the Congressional Cemetery

Kay Lahusen and Barbara Gittings in the mid-1980s on the steps of Barbara's mother's house in Wilmington, Delaware. They are holding two stuffed dinosaurs, props they brought around to many gay community meetings and events starting in the early 1970s. They were making light of the time they were called "dinosaurs" by younger activists at a meeting of the Gay Liberation Front, a short-lived post-Stonewall group.
Photo Courtesy of Kay Tobin Lahusen. Copyright Manuscripts and Archives Division, The New York Public Library

Appendix

Writings and Speeches

Following are writings and speeches by Barbara Gittings. Some of these appear in *Historic Speeches and Rhetoric for Gay and Lesbian Rights* (1892–2000), edited by Robert B. Ridinger for Routledge.

The Homosexual and the Church

This chapter by Gittings, with assistance from Kameny, ran in the 1969 book The Same Sex: An Appraisal of Homosexuality, *published by United Church Press. The impetus for the book, according to the introduction by its editor, Ralph W. Weltge, was a United Church of Christ staff consultation on homosexuality, with six of the authors at that meeting. Frank Kameny was among those contributing to the book, as were Evelyn Hooker, Wardell B. Pomeroy, Foster Gunnison Jr., William Simon and several more.*

The traditional attitudes of the churches toward the homosexual have been ones of condemnation, hostility, antipathy, denigration, and total rejection. These attitudes are completely and almost uniquely at odds with the approach which is the very essence of Christianity: that *all* human beings are children of God. That the churches have generally considered the homosexual as something not acceptable, and even not quite human, is too well known and still too widely accepted to need to be described here.

The very existence of this book is indicative of a long-overdue reexamination of those ancient attitudes, a reexamination that is bound to lead to a discarding of the old and the adoption of new. So a detailed review of the old attitudes is less important than consideration of what might replace them. What does the homosexual want of the churches, and what does he feel that he should expect?

Of course "the homosexual" is not a name which identifies a group any more than is "the Negro" or "the Jew." Each of these groups, and every minority, has in common its single minority characteristic— affectional preference, skin color, religion—and that alone, and is in all other respects as diversified as, for instance, heterosexuals, whites, and Protestants. It is therefore impossible to speak for the homosexual. However, any group subjected to severe, extended, unrelenting prejudice and hostility in a particular context will develop certain desires about which generalizations can be made, provided they are recognized as generalizations, with some of which different individuals in the group may well disagree.

Therefore the question of what the homosexual wants of the churches and what he feels he should expect will be answered in terms of generalizations about the wishes of the homosexual community, plus the personal ideas of this writer, as a homosexual, about how the churches should respond to these wishes.

In their treatment of the homosexual, the churches should begin working in two areas: *supportive* and *integrative*. (These have a tendency to merge and overlap at times.) Each of these areas in turn has two faces. Let us briefly define these two areas and the two faces of each, before expanding them.

Supportive: the homosexual should expect to receive from his church (and he should indeed be able to consider it *his* church—as he cannot now do) *individual* support in terms of constructive assistance in coping with his personal problems, and *minority* support in coping with the discrimination and other problems thrust upon homosexuals by an unaccepting society.

Integrative: the homosexual should expect active efforts by the churches at what might be called *congregational integration*—that is, integration of the homosexual *as a homosexual* with the church congregation in its many aspects; and *community integration*—that is, active intervention by the churches to assist the homosexual in integrating with the community at large, outside the narrow confines of the church congregation itself.

In each of these areas it cannot be overemphasized, first, that these efforts must be directed at support and integration of the homosexual as a homosexual, not as a candidate for conversion to heterosexuality; and second, that in the majority of cases, the efforts must be directed not at the homosexual but at the heterosexual portion of the general community. It is aspects of the heterosexual community, not anything about the homosexual himself, which stand in the way of integration and which are the total source of the homosexual's problem as a homosexual.

Above all, there must not be the patronizing attitude so often found, that "we must help these poor, sinful, afflicted, emotionally crippled people, and perhaps someday they can be 'cured' and returned to the ranks of 'healthy' heterosexuality." This condescension is often cloaked in pious references to expressing "Christian love and charity" toward homosexuals.

Homosexuality is not a sickness, not an impairment, not a failure, not an arrested development, not a flaw, not an incompleteness, not a distortion, not a sin or a sinful condition. It is not something to be regretted in any way; it is not something to be resigned to or endured.

The majority of homosexuals would not change even if they could. More important, they *should* not change even if they could. What the homosexual wants—and here he is neither willing to compromise nor morally required to compromise—is acceptance of homosexuality as a way of life fully on par with heterosexuality, acceptance of the homosexual as a person on par with the heterosexual, and acceptance of homosexuals as children of God on an equal basis with heterosexuals.

Therefore we are not interested in compassion, or in sympathy as unfortunates. We do not wish to be looked down upon. Our homosexuality is a way of life as good in its every respect as heterosexuality. We are prepared to address the world as equals, and to be accepted as such.

Now let us consider the ways in which the church should operate in its treatment of the homosexual. First, in the supportive area, there is the matter of individual support.

In general, at present the homosexual who has personal problems of the kind that the heterosexual can and should and routinely does take to his clergyman, cannot and does not do so. He expects, with ample justification, to be condemned or rejected, or at the very least to be pressured into trying to change to heterosexuality. Far more often than not, his legitimate personal problem will be shunted aside and his homosexuality will become the issue.

How many homosexual couples having problems within the relationship can go to a minister for counsel and receive meaningful counsel rather than an attack upon their homosexuality?

Similarly, while the churches provide a great variety of social activities for their heterosexual younger people, as well as for those who are single but not so young, it has apparently not occurred to those running such activities that homosexuals need, desire, and can benefit from such activities quite as much as the heterosexuals. We like to dance too. Why should we not expect our churches to minister to the social needs of their homosexual members quite as fully as to those of their heterosexual members? We do.

A particular concern for many homosexuals is their relationship with a family that is strongly disapproving and hostile. Very rarely can a homosexual expect constructive intercession by his clergyman, of the kind that a heterosexual could expect were he in serious conflict with his family.

Another special area of concern is the troubled homosexual teen-ager. In general, he is just not going to go for assistance to those who are going to denounce his homosexuality, or to those who will try to "save" him "before it is too late." He wants guidance in making a comfortable adjustment to his homosexuality, and assistance in creating for himself the homosexual equivalent of the full, active social life that his heterosexual peers are enjoying and that he, too, deserves to have and to enjoy. He ought to be able to go to his clergyman. At present, the wise homosexual teen-ager with these problems will stay as far away from the church as he can—to the loss of both. This should not be.

In short, we feel that we should expect from our churches all of the forms of spiritual, emotional, personal, and social support which they supply as a matter of course to heterosexuals, and that these should be supplied to us in a spirit of acceptance of us as homosexuals, not in a spirit of missionary zeal to convert us to heterosexuality.

Before this can occur, of course, there is going to have to be a great deal of rethinking and special training on the part of the clergy. We in the homophile organizations know of very few clergymen whom we would trust, at present, to provide adequate guidance for homosexuals, and we seldom refer troubled homosexuals to the clergy.

In the area of minority support, the role of the churches is rather different, but just as vital. Homosexuals are subjected to constant and pervasive prejudice and to the discrimination which flows from that prejudice. This comes from private individuals, from industry and institutions, and from all levels of government. It is just as much the proper role of the churches to attempt to change attitudes and to dispel prejudice and discrimination directed toward homosexuals as toward others of our various minority groups.

It has been pointed out in another essay in this book that if homosexuals had the visibility of the Negro, there would be many millions of unemployed homosexuals in the country. Young persons known to be homosexuals may well find it impossible to get an education at any level—in elementary school, high school, or college—in the United States. Homosexuals are denied government employment—federal, state, and local—for reasons of bigotry in no way different from those for which Negroes and other minority group members are denied private employment. Regardless of the quality and merit of their service, homosexuals found in the military service are given less-than-fully-honorable discharges, which can be permanently destructive of their future productivity in society. Without proper consideration as individuals in regard to personal character and integrity, homosexuals are denied security clearances—and it should be noted that one fifth of all jobs in private industry today require security clearance.

In short, there exist very real problems of civil liberties and human rights which are no less significant for homosexuals than for others. The churches not only should be in the forefront of efforts to resolve the manifest problems (such as those described, as well as the critically important one of repeal of criminal laws in regard to private, consensual, adult homosexual—and heterosexual—acts); but also the churches, as one of the more effective forces for shaping attitudes, should be leaders in efforts to remold the attitudes which underlie these problems.

It is a sad reflection upon our churches that they have not thrown their weight behind efforts to remedy the civil and social injustices from which homosexuals suffer. But that the churches themselves have been one of the primary sources of problems of prejudice and discrimination for the homosexual, is grounds for the severest possible castigation of the churches.

While the supportive role of the churches is probably the one of more immediate importance to the individual homosexual, the integrative role is certainly of greater long-range importance, since the homosexual's need for support will recede to the same level as those of the heterosexual, when he has been fully accepted by and integrated into the larger society.

The homosexual in general is not asking for a separatist or segregationist society. He does not want to be placed into a "separate but equal" ghetto of his own. And so within the church community he should find what has been called here congregational integration. There is no reason why, as a known homosexual—that is, with general knowledge of his homosexuality, and without the need for covertness and secrecy—he should not participate in the congregational activities of the church, along with all other church members, homosexual and heterosexual human beings alike; or why, in the various church social activities, he and his fellow homosexuals should not participate as homosexuals. The only way to break down misunderstanding and prejudice is by meeting and working with and learning to understand people.

The churches should be in the forefront in setting actual examples of congregational integration. Putting aside theological questions of the formal or ceremonial marriage of homosexuals, there is no reason, for instance, why de facto homosexual "married" couples should not enter, on that basis, where relevant, into those of the churches' activities being conducted for the heterosexual married couples.

Finally, the churches should be actively supporting and assisting the homosexual in the logical outgrowth of both congregational integration and minority support: community integration. That is, efforts should be made by the churches to change attitudes in the general community so that the homosexual can be a full member of the larger community—as a homosexual and without concealment. The churches, as the moral leaders of the larger community, are uniquely suited for this task. They have defaulted totally in the past.

The entire program set forth above represents a radical break with traditional viewpoints and practices—a break that will not come quickly or easily. But it is a break which is very long overdue, and which must be begun promptly.

There is no fundamental inconsistency between full Christianity and full practicing homosexuality. There need not be any compromise on either side in order to achieve the goals outlined here. There need be no change in *fundamental* theology—although a great deal of excess intellectual baggage will have to be discarded, and a thick growth of underbrush of tradition cleared away. There will need to be, however, a willingness to look anew at the old, basic ideas. But of course this is merely part of the fresh look being taken by the churches at the whole question of sex in all its many aspects and guises.

Above all, the homosexual himself—and of course, herself—must play an active role in the changes occurring. Otherwise the process of change will quickly go astray. This chapter and other chapters in this book represent part of the opening of dialogue between the churches and the homosexual. That dialogue must continue and be expanded.

D.S. Bailey, in his book *Homosexuality and the Western Christian Tradition,* states in his introduction that he did not carry his account of the development of the Christian attitude toward the homosexual beyond the Middle Ages "because it does not appear that the tradition has undergone any significant alteration since that time." This is indeed a sad commentary upon a living church. Were this true with regard to some abstract doctrine, it would be bad enough; when the truth of this is responsible for the utter rejection of an entire class of people, and for the totally unnecessary creation of incredible amounts of human misery, it is unforgivable. It is time for a long overdue reassessment in the light of modern knowledge and of modern ideas of the expanded extent of the proper exercise of human freedom. Any institution that allows itself to become intellectually fossilized soon becomes totally fossilized and vanishes from the scene.

Where should the churches start? In chapter 8 Lewis Maddocks sets forth an action program.

Some start has already been made in the directions that list suggests. There are growing up, around the country, organizations composed of homosexuals as such and of clergymen and laymen of a variety of faiths and denominations. At the minimum, these groups are devoted to establishing dialogue between the churches and the homosexual. Often they are devoted not merely to dialogue alone, but also to action to implement some of the specific proposals outlined in Dr. Maddocks' program mentioned above.

Following the lead of the first of these organizations in San Francisco, they all include in their name the phrase "Council on Religion and the Homosexual" (except one which uses "homophile" instead of "homosexual"). They exist—to a greater or lesser degree—at present in San Francisco, Los Angeles, Washington, D.C., Dallas, Philadelphia, New York, and Omaha-Lincoln, Nebraska. These are all independent organizations, and each has its particular organizational structure and personality. Some are relatively closed, open to selected clergy and representatives of homophile organizations; others are open to anyone in either of the two communities who wishes to participate.

The primary purpose of these organizations is the accomplishment of the aims and goals—the changes of attitude, the dialogue, rapprochement, and integration—which are the fundamental theme of this essay.

Most of these groups are fairly new and not much can be said about them. However, the pioneer Council on Religion and the Homosexual of San Francisco, launched in 1964, is well-known and has had a significant impact upon community attitudes and upon local police practices. It represents a manifestation in the best possible sense and tradition of the church taking a lead in changing community attitudes and remedying social injustices, of the church acting as an effective instrument for necessary social change.

The activities of this council have ranged from discussions between churchmen and homosexuals, to retreats involving churchmen and homosexuals, to visits by churchmen to homosexual bars and other gathering places, to sponsorship of dances—both in churches and elsewhere—and other wholesome activities for homosexuals, to initiation and support of court actions testing civil liberties issues, to pressure for fair employment practices for homosexuals, to public speaking appearances, to confrontations with police and other public officials in regard to harassment and other abuses of homosexuals, to publication of a variety of materials to advance the achievement of its aims and goals.

In addition to organizations on the model of the councils on religion and the homosexual, particular problems suggest other models for cooperative endeavor.

For example, there is the area of counseling the homosexual teen-ager. With rare exceptions, social agencies of any sort will not give and are not capable of giving competent and constructive advice. Without guidance, the churches themselves are at present not capable of handling this problem. Yet adult homosexuals cannot undertake to counsel or otherwise deal with younger homosexuals without risking a great deal of social "static." (Out of caution, the homophile organizations have set their minimum age limits for membership at twenty-one, or, in a few cases, after much careful consideration, at eighteen.)

In short, those who may, cannot, while those who can, may not. Therefore there should be a combined effort. Two ways in which homosexuals and clergymen can work together to help the younger homosexual are (and these can be complementary): (1) have thoughtful and knowledgeable homosexuals work directly with the clergy in counseling situations, (2) set up training programs conducted by homosexuals for the clergy.

Similarly, in the area of the general training of the clergy to deal with homosexuality, homosexuals can serve as consultants or as teachers or both. To help equip the clergy to handle matters of homosexuality, the churches should (1) have homosexuals actually do the teaching on the subject in seminaries, (2) have homosexuals provide special training for the teachers in seminaries.

Not all cooperative endeavors need to be in new forms such as those outlined above. For instance, the homosexual should be integrated into the existing administrative life of individual local churches. Just as we expect to find Negroes on governing bodies of churches which have Negroes in their congregations, so we should expect to find homosexuals on boards of trustees, vestries, and other bodies responsible for governing and administration of churches.

Homosexuals are being brought in—as "resource" persons on a temporary, consultative basis—at higher levels in the United Church of Christ, the National Council of Churches, and elsewhere. But there are no homosexuals as such permanently on appropriate boards and committees at the higher levels.

At lower levels, there is not even the beginning of a pattern of consultation with homosexuals by church governing and administrative bodies, much less ongoing participation by homosexual church members in these bodies. This is not as it should be, in view of the number of homosexuals in congregations (probably close to 10 percent on the average, as in the general population), and of the even larger number of church members who have been involved in homosexuality in at least some way and at some time in their lives (see Kinsey), and of the fact that homosexuality and homosexual involvement are not at present considered trivial matters by most people.

Of course, before any such active participation in church administration is possible, the homosexuals in the congregations must be made to feel welcome. It must be made clear to them that the traditional unchristian attitudes of antipathy and condemnation have been dispelled. Otherwise the homosexuals, understandably, will not come forward.

And so we come back to the opening of this essay: the need to reexamine and discard the ancient, outworn rejection of the homosexual by the churches, and the need to accept him as a homosexual and as an equal to the heterosexual.

A church whose faith is fulfilled in love of one's fellowman cannot, consistently and morally, perpetuate the traditional attitudes of hatred and rejection of the homosexual, but is bound, in consistency and morality, to make an affirmative, active effort to accept and welcome the homosexual, unreservedly and openly, as the whole, healthy human being that he is, and to assist him in his efforts to secure his rights as a human being to basic human dignity, to equality of opportunity, to equality before the law, to equality in the sight of his fellowmen—and to equality in the worship of his God.

Homosexuals justifiably feel aggrieved that they should need to remind the churches that "love is the fulfilling of the law"; that no man or group of men can properly claim to have the special insight and authority to prescribe to other men the form of love which is best, most fulfilling, highest, or most acceptable for them or for God; and that the churches have a fundamental moral responsibility both to practice love and to be advocates for love.

The churches have long denied the homosexual the right to be true to himself. Not only have the churches failed to meet the burden of justification for their denial: the justification cannot be shown because it does not exist. It is therefore time for the churches gracefully to admit their error, and to proceed meaningfully to rectify the damage caused by it. A truly Christian church can do no less.

ALA Speech, 1975

The following speech by Gittings, written by J. Lee Lehman and Gittings, is from the 4th Annual Gay Book Award for the ALA/SRRT Task Force on Gay Liberation, July 1, 1975, at the American Library Association conference in San Francisco.

The purpose of this year's Gay Book Award is slightly different from what it has been in the past. In this case we are saluting not one book, but a collection of books; not one author, but many authors.

As gay people move to create our own future, we must always remember that we have a past. Until recently very little of this past was known, since the topic of homosexuality was hardly a comfortable one for "polite" company or timid academia. As individuals we felt isolated in time as well as in space. Today we have begun to emerge, and our strength continues to grow. But we were not the first.

Many of us today are almost totally unaware of our past heritage. There are several reasons for this. One is the idea that The Gay Movement started in the 1950s, and that there was nothing before this. And that with the exception of a few notable individuals in literature, such as Sappho, Walt Whitman, Oscar Wilde, and Radclyffe Hall, there were no contributions to gay literature. And that with the exception of Freud and his school, there were no contributions to gay-anything-else. This viewpoint is not valid, but the reasons for its existence are understandable. Works on homosexuality have tended to remain obscure.

Sometimes writers would hesitate to offer writings on such a taboo subject and would have them published under a pseudonym or after death. Sometimes gay materials would be refused by publishers because the theme was too controversial or before its time. Sometimes gay books would be published but poorly distributed and scarcely noticed, and it was a challenge to learn about them, let alone find copies of them. Sometimes gay materials that found their way into libraries would be stolen by needy but fearful readers, or kept under lock and key which discouraged many people from asking for them. Years ago when I was trying to find out what it meant to be gay and was reading everything I could get my hands on, I had to go to the Rare Book Room to read John Addington Symonds, and I regularly browsed in the second-hand bookshops in hopes of turning up a copy of a hard-to-get novel like Gale Wilhelm's *Torchlight to Valhalla.* Sometimes gay materials have been hard to find simply because there were few topical bibliographies on this subject to steer readers to the scattered materials.

Presently we find our appreciation for past works hampered by the large numbers of books that are out of print. For instance, the winner of last year's Gay Book Award, Jeannette Foster's *Sex Variant Women in Literature,* was unavailable at the time, though it will be republished late this year by Diana Press of Baltimore. Another good example is Radclyffe Hall's classic novel *The Well of Loneliness,* which until recently was available only in libraries or second-hand bookstores. We welcome these books back into general availability, but there are far more books, which have stayed in obscurity; only the best-known of the out-of-print books have made it back.

But now there is a new approach: the printing of a collection specifically on the topic of homosexuality. This August a collection entitled *Homosexuality: Lesbians and Gay Men in Society, History, and Literature,* edited by Jonathan Ned Katz, will be published by Arno Press. The series contains 54 books which were out of print, and complete runs of *The Ladder* and *The Mattachine Review,* two of the longest-lived periodicals of the American gay movement. This collection marks the reentry into general availability of a number of important works. And for the first time, these works are gathered together under one subject headline: homosexuality. This collection can be of immense value to scholars as well as laypeople. Gay writings now are not only out, they're in demand!

This year's award is a deep-lavender commencement cap, to show that gay writing has graduated into the mainstream of academia as well as of serious public recognition of the value of gay experience and gay history.

Prayer Breakfast

Gittings spoke at a June 8, 1977, prayer breakfast in Norfolk, Virginia, sponsored by the city's Coalition for Human Rights.

The "Save Our Children" crusade [by Anita Bryant] is concerned about children. So are we. Who saved us when we were children growing up being taught that we were wrong and sick and sinful? Despite that cruel message from our parents and teachers and doctors and books and churches, we knew that our feelings were as natural and moral for us as left-handedness is natural and moral for people who are left-handed.

We owe it to ourselves, the gay children of yesterday, to make better conditions for gay people right now. We also owe it to the gay children of today and tomorrow, that hereafter every gay person can grow up feeling good and right and positive about being gay. Naturally, we need our own role models to look to—gay people as human beings who love and are loved—rather than distorted images of homosexuals as furtive and freakish.

Your presence here today is a clear message to those who would keep us hidden: we are here, we won't disappear, and we *will* be ourselves as God meant us to be!

The world needs more love. We want to contribute our share of love, openly and honestly. May your loving efforts toward this be blessed with success!

Human Rights Campaign Fund

This speech was given October 13, 1982, in Philadelphia, at a Human Rights Campaign Fund event.

When I joined the gay-rights movement 24 years ago, there were only half a dozen gay organizations in the entire U.S. The total number of us active in the movement was around 150: It was like a club, and we all knew each other even if we were 3,000 miles apart. Most people used false names to protect their jobs and their families. We were completely invisible on TV and we had just begun getting on radio talk shows—the ones late at night, after the kids were in bed.

It's very heartening for me to see so many people here tonight, for just one event for one of many, many organizations, because there's so much that still needs to be done, many bigotries and barriers to erase, and we need all hands and all hearts to help.

People often ask me, how come I haven't burned out, how come I'm still going strong after 24 years? I credit three factors.

One: sharing the work with me for the past 21 years is my nearest and dearest, Kay Lahusen. Among her own direct contributions to the cause, Kay was a founding member of Gay Activists Alliance in New York in 1970 and a co-founder of Gay Women's Alternative in New York in 1973. She is also co-author of the first book of biographies of activists in our movement, a book called *The Gay Crusaders,* published in 1972.

The second reason is the personal satisfaction I get. I'm a joiner by temperament, and it was a thrill to me to find groups of My Own People that I could join and work with. If it weren't for the gay movement, I'd probably be active in the wilderness conservation movement—but frankly the gay movement is a lot more fun!

The third key ingredient in the gasoline I run on is the response from gay people themselves. I'm lucky enough to get a lot of mail from gay people, because the gay group I head in the American Library Association has been listed in several books, and people pick up these books in libraries and bookstores and see us listed and reach out. Most of the letters are from people who are not part of the movement. There are thousands, hundreds of thousands, of them out there. They are, ultimately, the people we're doing all this for. Let me share with you messages from two of them.

From Lafayette, Indiana:

I don't want to subscribe to any magazines or newspapers because if I start receiving material on gay people in the mail, my mother would take me straight to the shrink. I just want to tell you: I read about a gay women's group in Boston and it made me want to die. You see, I live in a very small Indiana town and I go to a very small school. Believe me, at 17 in a hick town, with a bunch of super-prejudiced people, being gay can just about bring out the 'suicidal person' in anybody. So please, if you feel discouraged about a lot of shit you're seeing hit the fan, or if you think the articles published by Gay Lib aren't doing any good, feel or think again. If it wasn't for the fact that I know someone else out there has gone through the same battles I'm fighting now, I'd be dead by my own hand. Don't give up, PLEASE! Because when I get out of this town, I'm gonna be right out there fighting with you. I need you! Keep those articles and editorials and programs coming. They keep me alive.

A sister, Susie.

And this from a teacher in Massachusetts:

Thank you for keeping us singing in a society that would stop our song completely if it could.

If Susie had given her full name and an address, I could have written to her: Hang in there, Susie, because those of us who are out are oiling the closet door hinges just as fast as we can!

Whether you are gay or not, out or not, your support of the Human Rights Campaign Fund and other movement organizations is the necessary oil for those closet door hinges. Thanks for your help in the work.

And I hope you've had a gay time tonight, whether you are or not!

Gay Walk-A-Thon

This speech was given at the October 22, 1983, Philadelphia Lesbian and Gay Task Force Gay Walk-A-Thon.

For today, the West River Drive and East River Drive are Lavender Lane.

We're walking for gay rights. Oh, you thought we got gay rights with the passing of City Council Bill 1358 last year? Not by a long walk! That bill gives us a legal leg to stand on to challenge a few kinds of discrimination against us—but only a few, and the bill does not by itself do away with the prejudice behind discrimination.

Gay rights means much more than getting good laws and rules, and changing bad ones, though that is a key step. We have to change all the bad messages that still come from doctors and churches and books and public officials. Progress on paper is fine, but we can't stop there. The struggle for equal treatment has to be won in people's heads and hearts where it counts.

We want relief from the pain of wearing the mask. We want freedom from the big and small compromises that pinch the spirit. We want to be judged as individuals on our own merits. We want the right to live and love and work and play, without being penalized for being ourselves. …

Heterosexuals also need gay rights, because every non-gay person knows at least one gay person. It may be someone at the next desk, or the next counter, or the next pew in church, or the next chair at the family dinner table. When a gay person suffers discrimination for being gay, the non-gays who are close to her or him are bound to be affected.

So for all our sakes, we need to keep working for gay rights. There are still so many barriers to overcome, so many bigotries to erase. I think we have no energy shortage for our walk today. But if you do begin to feel a bit tired, just take 100 more steps for a lesbian or gay man friend who can't be here today. And then take another 100 steps for your favorite enemy of gay rights. And another 100 steps for gay pride—your pride.

If people along the way ask us who we are, tell them: We're an army of lovers! Join us and share the love!

So let's go. Naturally, not straight ahead—gayly forward!

Toasting Troy Perry

This speech was given by Gittings on June 15, 1990, at a Philadelphia Metropolitan Community Church dinner honoring the Reverend Troy Perry, founder of MCC, an LGBTQ-inclusive worldwide church.

My lover Kay Lahusen met Troy Perry before I did. She met him at the baths in New York City.

Kay at the baths? Troy at the baths?

You see, Kay was a co-founder of Gay Activists Alliance in New York in 1970, and GAA members sometimes did political leafleting in the baths. Troy happened to be in New York at one such time and he joined in the leafleting.

Then Kay and I both met Troy in Washington, D.C., in the spring of 1971. Troy and lots of us were there to help gay activist Frank Kameny in his campaign for Congress. The District of Columbia had been given a nonvoting seat in the House of Representatives, and Frank Kameny was running as the first openly gay candidate for Congress. He came in fourth among six candidates.

At some point I took Kay and Troy Perry to the Washington airport for a flight to Los Angeles. Troy was going home, and Kay was going along to interview him for a book she was writing about gay activists who had solid track records of accomplishment for the gay cause. At that time, almost 20 years ago, there were only a handful of such activists.

Kay interviewed Troy in the plane all the way across the country, and she interviewed him for a few days at his home while his mother and his lover treated her to Southern hospitality and home cooking.

Here's Kay's book *The Gay Crusaders,* published in 1972. Troy Perry's is the first interview and it opens quoting him, "When people call me the gay Billy Graham, I say—No, he's the straight Troy Perry."

A few years later, when Troy and I were both serving on the board of directors of the National Gay Task Force, several of us went to a meeting with top executives at NBC to complain about the lack of gay programming.

You know how such meetings go. We're polite, they're polite. We explain, they explain. We ask, they demur. We push, they postpone.

Then Troy spoke up. He said—and I'm sorry. I can't do the accent: "I've just come back from a trip to Australia, and one of their TV soaps has a gay male couple who are having problems in their relationship. And do you know, every afternoon 13 million Australians are on the edge of their chairs to see if Jack and Tom can work it out!"

You should have seen their eyes. Troy hit the NBC people right where it mattered—hooking an audience. In two sentences Troy got through to them after all our rational negotiation rolled off their backs.

I think most gay movement people outside MCC have been slow to appreciate the power of Troy's direct appeal.

For instance, there was the crisis in 1976 when Christian singer Anita Bryant launched her national crusade against gay rights. She called her campaign "Save Our Children" and hoped it would roll back job-protection laws and undo other gains we'd made toward equality. Anita Bryant and others who hopped on her bandwagon were vocal and fiery and Bible-thumping.

Sometimes you need fire to fight fire. But whom did top honchos in our gay movement send to Florida to lead the counter-campaign against Anita Bryant? They sent northern liberal ideologues who could explain a hundred reasons why gays were entitled to be teachers.

What we really needed was Troy Perry to pound the pulpit right back at our opponents and proclaim, "We're all God's children and I double-checked it with God just half an hour ago and He said, Yes, and keep spreading my love."

Now I come to my own moment of embarrassment with Troy Perry, I don't remember the date. The Philadelphia MCC was in trouble: It had been through three pastors in two years. Troy came here to mend the trouble. I recall that his viewpoint, his solution[s], weren't acceptable to the members of the congregation. But I don't remember what the exact issue was. Anyway, I found myself siding with my friends in the church here.

There was a meeting with Troy Perry at the Joseph Priestley Chapel here at First Unitarian. I attended to give support to my friends in the congregation. The atmosphere was very tense. In the middle of one heated exchange, I piped up and called Troy a Neanderthal.

You could have heard the hairpins drop.

The sequel is even more embarrassing. After [the] Rev. Joseph Gilbert came to this MCC church, he once asked me, "What's this I hear about your calling Troy Perry a Neanderthal?" I denied it. "Oh, I never said that," I claimed.

Later Joe came at me another way. "Say, Barbara, about that time you called Troy a Neanderthal. Was the meeting in this room or that one?"

"Oh, it was that one."

Back to that moment in the chapel. Troy is a real Christian. He forgave me, at least I think he forgave me. What's more, he converted me. I have had only good to say about him since.

What I think of Troy today is what I've known all these 20 years (except for that one mad moment): Troy is a national gay treasure who is underappreciated. And we're going to need him more than ever if Anita Bryant's comeback picks up any steam.

Memorial to A. Damien Martin

This text is from Gittings' remarks August 19, 1991, at the memorial service for A. Damien Martin, co-founder with his partner Dr. Emery Hetrick of the Hetrick-Martin Institute for the Protection of Lesbian and Gay Youth in New York City.

In the printed program for the 1989 Emery Awards sponsored by the Hetrick-Martin Institute, there's an unsigned ad with the simple message: "If only you'd been around when I was a kid."

If only Damien had been around when *I* was a kid! When I was in high school in the late 1940s, I was clearly showing my homosexual interests—I was too naïve to conceal them. Also I was confused and I desperately needed someone to talk to, someone who could tell me what it meant to be the way I was and how I could live as a homosexual.

Of course I know now that there must have been gay teachers in my school. But at that time, 45 years ago, none of them dared to reach out a friendly ear much less a helping hand to the likes of me. I'm sure Damien would have done so.

It's been great knowing Damien for 15 years, enjoying him as a friend—oh the bubbly warmth and the sense of humor!—and admiring his work.

With Emery, he built an organization that was meant to last and not just rise atop a wave of popular interest. They brought a new high level of professionalism to social services in our movement. And they attracted such wonderful talent.

Damien has also left us a body of fine writings that are outstanding for their lucidity, including articles in *ETC Journal* on homosexuals as a minority group and on anti-gay prejudice, and a carefully reasoned article on man/boy love in a New York City paper that's now defunct.

When I last talked with Damien, he was planning to work up some notes into a full article on horizontal hostility within the gay-rights movement. How badly we need his clear thinking and common sense and persuasiveness on such a messy topic!

Damien was generous-minded and always eager to honor others for their contributions—not forgetting Emery. Let me tell you of an incident which figures large in my memories of Damien.

In 1978, I prepared and ran a gay exhibit at the annual meeting of the American Psychiatric Association which was held in Atlanta that year. It was the third such exhibit I'd done for APA, the others being in 1976 and 1972. For 1978 I decided we had done enough to display "us" to "them." It was time to show that we are them and they are us.

I needed gay psychiatrists to come out in their own profession—and I began with Emery Hetrick. He thought about it, but not for long, and when he said yes, the dominoes began falling—four other gay psychiatrists also agreed. So the front part of that exhibit, the part that everyone passing in the aisle couldn't help seeing, featured Emery and the other four, with pictures and biographies with all their professional credentials. It was a marvelous breakthrough. It stirred up a lot of talk in the APA, and it spurred the efforts of the gay caucus which was formally established in the association.

Emery was thrilled with what he'd accomplished. But he was even more thrilled when Damien, on the spur of the moment, hopped a plane to Atlanta to share the triumph with him!

Incidentally, the title of that particular exhibit at the American Psychiatric Association was "Gay Love Is Good Medicine."

Damien, thank you. You were good medicine for me. I'll always love you!

Abraham Lincoln Award Acceptance Speech

This speech was given to the Log Cabin Club of Philadelphia on February 11, 1994. Gittings received the Abraham Lincoln Award that day. What follows is an excerpt.

Thank you for your recognition of my work. And thank you for your contributions of money and dedication and effort for our cause. I'm delighted that gay Republicans are shining out from the rich tapestry that is the gay and lesbian rights movement.

I'd like to pay tribute to a particular Republican gay activist who would thoroughly enjoy being here tonight if he could.

Before there was a Stonewall uprising, there were more orderly protests in Washington, New York, San Francisco, and Philadelphia. These were our early picket lines. As you may have heard, we had a dress code—women wore skirts, men wore suits and ties—according to the business dress standards of that time. And no matter how casually or unconventionally some of us dressed otherwise, when we got on the gay picket lines we put our egos in our hip pockets and put on our picketing drag.

But there was one picketer in the mid-1960s for whom the prescribed attire was natural and usual: Foster Gunnison Jr. Foster regularly wore Brooks Brothers suits—*rumpled* Brooks Brothers suits—and bow ties. He had a nondescript crew cut. He smoked good cigars. He had a master's degree in philosophy. He loved trains and especially loved riding in an elegant parlor car. He read *The Wall Street Journal.* And he lived, with exquisite symbolism, at #1 Gold Street in Hartford, Connecticut.

Foster was a bit of a puzzle even to those of us who liked him and worked well with him. At first some people thought he was an FBI plant inside our movement. But after watching him, the suspicious eventually decided that Foster was just another eccentric in our movement—a different sort of eccentric.

From the time he joined the cause 30 years ago, Foster did a lot of good work. He walked in our picket lines. He helped Craig Rodwell plan the first gay pride march in New York in 1970 on the first anniversary of Stonewall. He loved trying to bring order and discipline to our chaotic groups and he was active in our regional and national alliances that had begun in the early 1960s. He set up his own organization with a cryptic name, the Institute of Social Ethics, and under its cover did such things as sending me to spy on the psychiatrists' convention in 1968.

Eventually Foster threw up his hands over the unruly and chaotic nature of our movement. He spent more time on his other interests, including the national association of barbershop quartets. He remained a registered Republican but he hedged his bets and also supported the Conservative Party and the Libertarian Party.

Foster Gunnison died suddenly last month. I wanted to remember him in this setting especially. He would relish being in this gathering, at this unique establishment. Thanks, Foster, for being a pioneer.

And again my thanks to you who are here and to your friends for your support for gay and lesbian rights. We gay people need our rights because that is fair play, in the best American tradition.

Introduction to the 1995 Film *Stonewall*

This speech was given at the 1996 International Gay and Lesbian Film Festival in Philadelphia.
Welcome to our International Gay and Lesbian Film Festival.

I've been a gay-rights activist for 38 years. Tonight I've been plucked from the dustbin of history to introduce this film. But tonight's movie isn't meant to be a history lesson. It's a story, one person's story, with some engaging characters and imaginative play. After all, you did come here to be drawn into someone else's imagination.

Of course there are points of history in the movie story. For example, the police harassment and police brutality were real and were experienced by every one of us who ever entered any kind of gay bar or lesbian bar in the decades before Stonewall.

One of the plot lines is a gay picket march at Independence Hall. I was in the real Independence Hall picket line, not once but five times, every July Fourth from 1965 to 1969. These demonstrations were to tell the public that a large group of American citizens is not getting the benefit of "life, liberty and the pursuit of happiness" as promised in the Declaration of Independence we celebrate on July Fourth.

Yes, those pickets were sedate. And yes, we had a dress code. We had to reckon with the popular image of us at the time as perverted and sick and weird. We wanted the public to gawk not at us but at the messages on our signs and in our leaflets.

Remember, this was 30 years ago. Picketing was not a popular tactic then as it is now. Certainly our cause wasn't popular. Even many gay people thought our efforts were foolish and outlandish.

What we did was scary because we were cracking the cocoon of invisibility. Only a tiny handful of us could take the risk of being so publicly on view.

You might lose your job if your boss saw you on the 6 o' clock news. Your picture might appear in your parents' hometown newspaper and cause shock waves. Certainly your picture would go into government files. We were always surrounded by government agents filming and photographing and tape-recording us. Also there was the risk that some bystander would toss a brick instead of a brickbat.

The early gay pickets were protests. Stonewall was an uprising. It was a welcome flash point, and it sparked a great surge of activism.

Some people say that nothing really happened for us until the Stonewall riot. But as a pre-Stonewall activist friend of mine says, "We built the airplane, and the drag queens flew it away." Not only that— they managed to razz the police and to inject humor into even the most awful situations. Watch for this in tonight's story.

Humor as social protest has a long tradition. But I'm convinced we do it better than any other minority group. I love belonging to a special people. And I believe that even when all the bigotries and barriers are overcome, we will always have twice as much fun in each other's company. We'll continue to have gay and lesbian film festivals so we can show ourselves and see ourselves, our many selves. Enjoy!

Press Conference Remarks at New York Gay Pride March

Gittings spoke at a June 29, 1997, press conference for New York City's Gay Pride celebration. What follows is an excerpt.

Just five days from now, on July Fourth, we celebrate the Declaration of Independence, which proclaims the right to "life, liberty and the pursuit of happiness." And it doesn't say that it's for heterosexuals only. For too long our lives have been hidden, our liberty has been restricted, our pursuit of happiness has been tangled up in bigotries and barriers.

We want relief from the pain of wearing the mask. We want to be judged as individuals, on our merits. We want to be able to live and love and work and play, openly and safely, as ourselves.

Becoming visible is the key to our struggle for fair treatment and equal rights. We are everywhere, we are already part of every community—but we have to keep reminding others by our presence.

Today's march is one kind of presence. I'm thrilled to be part of this huge demonstration of gay pride and gay love, especially because this was unthinkable when I began working for gay rights almost 40 years ago. Being here today, I'm convinced it won't take another 40 years for us to have full equality.

Remembering Jim Kepner

Gittings spoke May 22, 1998, at the memorial celebration of the life of veteran gay activist, historian and archivist Jim Kepner. What follows is an excerpt.

My life partner Kay Lahusen and I were simply astonished when we first met Jim Kepner in 1963 at his home in Los Angeles. We saw books, *books,* BOOKS, and files, *files,* FILES, from floor to ceiling!

Jim and I clicked immediately. I too was a gay book buff, because in 1950 when I needed to learn about myself and what it meant to be gay, there was no one I could ask, so I instinctively turned to books.

Jim's library impressed us, but so did his dedication to activism, which we shared, and his passion for chronicling our movement.

The author George Eliot in her novel *Middlemarch* said, "The growing good of the world is partly dependent on unhistoric acts." I think of Jim's great legacy as those unhistoric acts, in the sense that his work wasn't headlined in the mainstream press, seldom even in gay/lesbian chronicles.

Jim was a sweet and low-key person who kept on plugging at his dream, never abandoning it, always tending it. The notion of burnout wasn't in his cosmos. And even when his health faltered, Jim didn't.

Jim put his time and energy and what little money he had into creating a better life for all of us, and he took the change he created as its own reward.

To Kay and me, Jim seemed self-effacing in many ways. In 1983, the gay group in the American Library Association put on a program at the annual librarians' conference called "Why Keep All Those Posters, Buttons and Papers?" Jim Kepner was one of our speakers.

I needed publicity photos on the flier to promote the event. Jim didn't have a publicity photo. The picture he sent was a tiny snapshot and in the picture Jim is, appropriately, submerged in papers.

The last time I saw Jim wasn't a gay movement event. I was visiting in Los Angeles, and Jim took me to the Huntington Library and Botanical Gardens. Naturally we ooohed and aaahed over the exotic rare books and manuscripts, but Jim also proved an enthusiastic guide to the specialty gardens around the library. A man of many interests and wide knowledge.

Introduction to the Documentary *Out of the Past*

Gittings spoke October 23, 1998, in Chicago at a screening of the documentary film Out of the Past *sponsored by GLSEN, the Gay, Lesbian and Straight Education Network.*

As a teenager in the late 1940s, I had to struggle all alone to learn about myself and what it means to be gay. Homosexuals then were completely invisible: Even the word "homosexual" was still in the closet. Back then, most homosexuals were isolated for years until we managed to find others and eventually build up a circle of friends. And it was hard to feel right about yourself when you had no others like yourself to look to, not even at the distance of history books.

So, opening up our history has been a favorite part of my 40 years of work in the gay-rights movement.

For example, in the early 1960s my partner Kay and I had the privilege of editing *The Ladder,* the first lesbian magazine with a national circulation. We published many articles about lesbians and maybe-lesbians throughout history.

In the 1970s when we worked with the gay group in the American Library Association, we searched for gay history materials to include in our gay reading lists. We also drew attention to gay and lesbian poets and artists. For example, at the ALA's conference in 1972 in Chicago, our gay group had a program of readings from Sappho, Walt Whitman, Gertrude Stein, and Constantin Cavafy, to remind our listeners that these writers whose works we value on our library shelves had this homosexual dimension to their lives and their art.

Also in the 1970s, I was on a committee trying to find a major library willing to collect and preserve the unique materials being produced by our civil-rights movement. This idea was ahead of its time. Of the 13 university and research libraries we contacted with our proposal, all of them with track records for having collections on minority and social change issues, only one even bothered to respond—and that response was a rejection.

The world has moved ahead since then. Still, two decades later, Kelli Peterson, the high school student whose battle against prejudice in Utah is the framework for this documentary, tells us she started the Gay-Straight Alliance at her school "to end the misery and isolation of being gay in high school." Unlike me in the 1940s, Kelli in the 1990s was in fact hearing some messages about homosexuality, but they were very negative.

Fortunately, help was on the way in the form of GLSEN, the Gay, Lesbian, and Straight Education Network. Kevin Jennings, founder and executive director of GLSEN, had reviewed high school curricula to see what, if anything, was being taught about us. He came up with a Big Blank. So he wrote a book called *Becoming Visible: A Reader in Gay and Lesbian History for High School and College,* and he prepared a gay history slide show and took it around to schools. The huge demand for this exciting fresh material sparked the making of the film we're about to see.

The section of the film on me is called Becoming Visible. Now you might think that because I've been visible all my 40 years in the gay rights movement, that's not an issue for me. Yes, I'm out—but I'm still dealing with the consequences.

For instance, I have an elderly aunt who lives in a retirement community near me in Wilmington, Delaware. She is 102. She grew up in a time when "one knew there were people like that, but one never talked about it." She does not like it that I'm so public. She understands that living a hidden life has a cost and is dishonest, but she still wants us to stay hidden because to her, being open amounts to being public about your private sex life.

Every time I'm due to appear in public such that I'm likely to be seen on TV, I have to tell her so she won't be surprised if a friend calls to comment. But she always gets upset about it. And at age 102, an upset could be serious. Still, she loves me and I love her, and we muddle through the distress every time.

How I deal with my aunt's cultural bias is my responsibility. But we all have a responsibility toward students in school, both gay and non-gay, to change the cultural bias that affects them.

I hope you enjoy the film. And I hope you'll find ways to use it to Teach Our Schools a Lesson.

Jacksonville, Florida, Gay Pride Rally Speech

Gittings was co-grand marshal of the Jacksonville, Florida, Gay Pride Rally on June 19, 1999. Here are some of her prepared remarks.

... We were completely invisible on television and we had just begun appearing on radio talk shows—the ones late at night, after children were in bed. The rare mentions of us in newspapers were under headlines like "Perverts Dismissed From State Department" or "Dozens Caught in Raid on Homosexual Bar."

We invited lawyers and clergy and psychotherapists who weren't gay to address our public meetings and conferences. Our own lawyers and clergy and psychotherapists were still deep in the closet. We were in the wake of the McCarthy witch hunts, when an accusation of being "commie-pinko-queer" could and did ruin the lives and careers of many decent people. In that climate of fear on top of the stigma of being gay, most people couldn't afford to be linked with anything concerning homosexuality.

We did have an occasional mad moment of triumph. For example, our longtime Washington gay activist Frank Kameny used to give a talk called "Tweaking the Lion's Tail, or, Constructive Fun and Games With Your Government." One of his stories was about how in 1963 the lone gay organization in the nation's capital stood up to FBI Director J. Edgar Hoover. Since the gay group often had to deal with the government's anti-gay policies, it wanted to keep top officials informed of its activities, so it routinely sent its newsletter, unasked, to everyone at the White House and in the Cabinet and in Congress.

J. Edgar Hoover didn't appreciate this. J. Edgar Hoover desperately wanted his name *off* that gay group's mailing list! He tried to bully, he tried to scare. But the group stood firm and made Hoover back down. The organization's newsletter continued to be sent to Hoover along with all the other federal bigwigs. It must be the only time in the career of that powerful man he didn't get his way—and *we* did it!

In 1965—yes, four years before Stonewall—we tore off the shroud of invisibility when a handful of us walked in the first gay picket lines at the White House and the Pentagon and the Civil Service Commission in Washington, and at Independence Hall in Philadelphia.

It was scary. Picketing was not a popular tactic 34 years ago. Certainly our cause wasn't popular. Even many gay people thought our efforts were outlandish and unseemly. Only a few of us could take the risk of being so public. …

What a great change this crowd today signals.

We're here to celebrate gay pride, gay love, and gay rights.

Do you think we'll have our rights once ENDA, the Employment Non-Discrimination Act, is passed by Congress and when gay marriage is finally legal? These *will* happen—after all, you are writing and calling your state and federal lawmakers, aren't you? Such laws give us a legal leg to stand on and to challenge the most blatant kinds of discrimination against us. But laws alone can't end the personal prejudice behind the discrimination. …

We also have to change the hurtful messages that still come from many religious leaders and many public officials, including school board members. Progress on paper is fine but we can't stop there. The struggle for equal treatment has to be won in people's hearts and minds, where it really counts.

We want relief from the pain of wearing the mask. We want freedom from those big and little compromises that pinch the spirit. We want to be judged as individuals, on our own merits. We want the right to live and love and work and play, without being denounced and penalized for being true to ourselves.

One way to secure that right is to live and love and work and play as ourselves when we can, to exercise our right openly, to let this city and the whole country know that we are here, we are everywhere.

We are everywhere—but lest they forget, keep reminding them. We're fortunate to have the visibility of Barney Frank in politics and Martina Navratilova in sports and Ellen DeGeneres in show business and the visibility of Ellen Hayes and Tony Suszczynski here at home. But we need also the everyday visibility of people like you, a constant presence, always reminding others that we're at the next desk at work and at school, we're in the next pew at church or temple, we're in the next chair at the family dinner table. We're already part of every community. We won't go away and we won't be converted, and more and more of us are refusing to hide and pretend.

Being visible takes courage and persistence. You're here today because you want to make a difference, to leave a legacy. …

Our goal is equality in society, but there's no one best way to achieve it. We advance thanks to a thousand different talents and interests. We are everywhere and everybody. You know, this is very frustrating for those who oppose us. It's like punching pillows; they squelch us here—and we just pop up somewhere else!

Sometimes I'm asked for advice on how to avoid burnout. I have a two-part prescription:

1) Don't be daunted. Over the long haul, for every setback and every stubborn problem, we've

made three or four giant strides forward. Be patient, be persistent, be persuasive. Remember that success comes in little moments as well as in grand events. Take care of minor issues along with the main job, and you'll have the satisfaction of seeing results every week, not just once in two or three years.

2) Keep and use your sense of humor. Gay rights is serious business, but it doesn't always have to be grim. And a light touch often helps to push our message. So let loose your sense of fun.

In a world in which we are often despised and rejected, in which we are put down, harassed, hounded and even killed for being who we are, we refuse to buckle. We believe in the rightness of our lives, our loves and our cause. Despite the bigotries and barriers we have to cope with, most of us lead wonderful lives useful to ourselves and to society.

In the face of the AIDS epidemic, we have been constructive, innovative, caring and heroic. We have not been defeated.

And we are loving. How well *we* know the power of love! The world needs more love, and we're contributing our share of love—without waiting for approval.

Just 15 days after this march, on July Fourth, we celebrate the Declaration of Independence which proclaims the right to "life, liberty and the pursuit of happiness." And it doesn't say that's for heterosexuals only. It's *your* life. It's *your* liberty. It's *your* pursuit of happiness. It's up to you—go get them!

Accepting the SPARC Lifetime Achievement Award

Gittings received the Statewide Pennsylvania Rights Coalition (SPARC) award September 16, 2000. Following are her remarks.

I'm thrilled to be receiving this award. For those of us who put our energy and time and money into creating a better life for gay people, a big pat on the back is always welcome, even if you believe that the change you bring about is its own reward. ...

A few years ago I was being introduced by someone who wanted to emphasize that I had the longest track record of all the gay activists in Philadelphia. But he got flustered and it came out as "Barbara is the oldest living lesbian."

Not quite! But I'm working on it. And I've been fighting the good gay fight for 42 years!

Our gay-rights movement got started in this country over 50 years ago, with a handful of people who met in someone's apartment in Los Angeles to discuss homosexuals' problems in society. They had the blinds drawn and the door locked and a lookout posted for the police, because they feared they might be arrested just for gathering to talk about the taboo topic of homosexuality.

But they persisted and gained courage, and soon there were three organizations: ONE, Inc., in Los Angeles, Mattachine Society which started in L.A. then moved to San Francisco, and the lesbian organization Daughters of Bilitis in San Francisco. For a while these three groups were the only ones, even though each group did have a few chapters elsewhere in the country. Each organization started publishing a magazine or newsletter.

When I joined the Daughters of Bilitis in 1958, 10 years after our movement started, there were only about eight organizations in the whole U.S. ... Most people in the movement at that time used false names to protect their jobs and their families. The word "gay" wasn't used even by us, let alone outside our groups.

The three gay publications in existence in 1958 couldn't be sold anywhere. There were few subscribers because people were afraid to have their names on any kind of gay list. ...

Our movement started with three objective problems to tackle:

— We were considered *sick,* so we had to labor under the albatross of the sickness label, which infected everything we said and did. They said you're sick, we said no we aren't, they said that's your sickness talking.

— We were considered *sinful,* so we had to start dialogue with the churches and make a presence in the churches.

— We were considered *criminal,* so we had to cope with the sodomy laws, which were still on the books in all the states—and by extension with any problems connected with the law or the courts.

One of our earliest legal victories was the case of *ONE Magazine,* which began publishing in 1951. In 1953 and 1954 the Los Angeles postmaster stopped issues from going out in the mails because he objected to the content. The organization ONE, with the help of an established law firm, challenged this censorship in the federal courts, all the way to the U.S. Supreme Court, which issued in 1958 a ruling that guarantees forever the right of gay periodicals to travel in the mail. ...

I've mentioned the early movement's three big objective problems: sin, sickness, criminality. (I call them objective because you could get a handle on them, there was something concrete you could go after.) But the overriding problem in our early days was invisibility. How can you organize people to do something about their problems if they're invisible?

Breaking out of invisibility was tough and it was scary.

For instance, in 1965, several years before Stonewall, a handful of us picketed at the White House and the Pentagon and the Civil Service Commission in Washington, to protest the government's anti-gay policies in employment, security clearances and the military. Also there were pickets at Independence Hall in Philadelphia every July Fourth from 1965 to 1969. ...

Becoming visible could sometimes be fun. For instance, I was involved in the first-ever gay kissing booth, held at a librarians' convention in Dallas in 1971. Our gay librarians group called it "Hug-a-Homosexual" and we offered free same-sex kisses and hugs. ...

Our greater visibility nowadays has really advanced our cause and helped many lesbians and gay men to come out of the closet. It also had brought a lot of heterosexual hostility out of the closet.

There are still plenty of people who heartily wish we would just disappear off the face of the earth. Or if not that, they want us to hide and pretend to protect their sensitivities. Even some of our non-gay friends and family who claim they support our rights find our visibility a stumbling block. They say, Why make such an issue of your lifestyle? Why can't you just live your lives without announcing it to the world? Why do you flaunt yourselves?

We have an old joke that if we had a nickel for every time we've been accused of flaunting, we'd be a rich movement, not a shoestring effort. For these people, a little homosexuality goes a l-o-o-o-n-g way!

Heterosexuals flaunt themselves all the time, only it isn't called flaunting, it's just the standard social scenery, it's taken for granted. They wear wedding rings. They proudly show pictures of their spouses or opposite-sex partners. They kiss and embrace in public. Why, they even announce their relationships in the newspapers for thousands of strangers to see. How much more public can you get about your sexual interests?

If we do hide and pretend, we're usually assumed to be heterosexual and treated as such. And we don't get our rights as gays. So we have to explain and show what's important to us—thus making an issue of our private lives. We are not yet part of the official picture of life, and we have to keep drawing attention to our situation until we're thoroughly woven into the fabric of life. We can't continue to live our lives under a rock.

While I believe that our visibility is the engine that drives us to secure our rights, I also believe high visibility isn't for everyone. Some of us have problem situations or other priorities. But there's no shortage of behind-the-scenes jobs for those who are willing. You should do what you can, and enlist others to do what they can, to support the cause. And no one should feel that her or his contributions count for less because it's less public.

A side note on visibility: Many of you may not know that SPARC has a sort of old-auntie ghost behind it. That was the Pennsylvania Council for Sexual Minorities, the first official government body in the country set up to deal with gay issues. It was launched in 1976 by Governor Milton Shapp, who also issued an executive order banning discrimination on the basis of sexual orientation. Gay men and lesbians and transgender persons were appointed to the council. It was not a high-profile group. Its members focused on working quietly with state agencies to make real changes in Pennsylvania's regulations and policies on everything from education to health to prisons to welfare to youth services to state police to employment. The council lasted only about three years—but it was a start and a good model. …

We want relief from the pain of wearing the mask. We want to be judged as individuals on our own merits. We want the right to live and love and work and play, openly and safely, as ourselves.

Does this seem an impossible dream? Just think how far we've come since the old days I've told you about. If you still feel daunted, here's a four-part prescription to give you fresh energy: Practicality, Perseverance, Presence, and Playfulness.

Practicality—This means, look ahead but keep your feet moving on the ground. And remember that success comes in small moments as well as grand events. Take care of minor issues along with the main job and you'll get the satisfaction of seeing results every month, not just once in two or three years.

Perseverance—If you expect our work to change the world overnight, you might get discouraged. One reason I haven't burned out is that I'm always happily surprised by each advance, each victory, each creation—and I want to be around for the next great turn. When I joined the movement I never dreamed we would soon have parents-of-gays groups, or gay caucuses in the professions, or full-scale gay community centers, or gay choruses and marching bands, or openly gay elected officials, or gay documentary films. Marvelous changes, unthinkable to me 42 years ago! Over the long haul, for every setback, we've made four or five giant strides forward. So whatever you set yourself to do, keep at it, be persistent, be persuasive.

Presence—This is closely tied to perseverance. We are everywhere—but lest they forget, keep reminding them. …

Our goal is equality in society, but there's no one best way to achieve it. We advance thanks to a thousand different talents, a thousand different interests. It's really a blessing that our movement is not centralized or like a disciplined army, that gay individuals can erupt into whatever they do best to make a presence. You know, this is very frustrating for those who oppose us. …

Playfulness—Gay rights is serious business, but it doesn't always have to be grim. Humor can cut through homophobia. And a light touch often helps to get our message across. And we can have fun doing good!

When we've achieved equality, when all the bigotries and barriers have been erased, we'll continue to enjoy being a special people. I'm glad to be with you. Thank you for your dedication and work, for SPARC and for our cause and our lives.

Bibliography

—*About Time: Exploring the Gay Past*, by Martin Duberman, Meridian (1991). Revised edition; first published in 1986. Revised edition also appeared in 1994.

—*American Psychiatry and Homosexuality: An Oral History*, edited by Jack Drescher and Joseph Merlino, introduction by Barbara Gittings, Harrington Park Press (2007).

—*An Annotated Bibliography of Homosexuality*, by Vern L. Bullough, Barrett W. Elcano, W. Dorr Legg and James Kepner, Garland Publishing (1976). Lists 308 titles.

—*Becoming Visible: A Reader in Gay and Lesbian History for High School and College,* by Kevin Jennings, Alyson Books (1994).

—*Before Stonewall: Activists for Gay and Lesbian Rights in Historical Context*, by Vern L. Bullough (editor), Judith M. Saunders and Sharon Valente (associate editors) and C. Todd White (assistant editor), Harrington Park Press (2002).

—*Celluloid Activist: The Life and Times of Vito Russo*, by Michael Schiavi, University of Wisconsin Press (2011).

—*Chloe Plus Olivia: An Anthology of Lesbian Literature from the 17th Century to the Present*, by Lillian Faderman, Viking/Penguin (1994).

—*City of Sisterly and Brotherly Loves: Lesbian and Gay Philadelphia, 1945–1972*, by Marc Stein, University of Chicago Press (2000).

—*Completely Queer: The Gay and Lesbian Encyclopedia*, by Steve Hogan and Lee Hudson, Henry Holt & Co. (1998).

—*Dancing the Gay Lib Blues: A Year in the Homosexual Liberation Movement*, by Arthur Bell, Simon and Schuster (1971).

—*Different Daughters: A History of the Daughters of Bilitis and the Rise of the Lesbian Rights Movement*, by Marcia M. Gallo, Seal Press (paperback, 2007). First published by Carroll & Graf (2006).

—*Encyclopedia of Homosexuality*, by Wayne R. Dynes (editor) and Warren Johansson and William A. Percy (associate editors), with the assistance of Stephen Donaldson, Garland Publishing (1990). Two volumes.

—*Encyclopedia of Lesbian, Gay, Bisexual and Transgender History in America*, 3 Volumes, edited by Marc Stein, Charles Scribner's Sons/Thomson/Gale (2004).

—*Encyclopedia of Lesbian and Gay Histories and Cultures*, Vol. 1 on lesbians edited by Bonnie Zimmerman, Vol. 2 on gay men edited by George E. Haggerty, Garland Publishing (2000).

—*From "Perverts" to "Fab Five": The Media's Changing Depiction of Gay Men and Lesbians*, by Rodger Streitmatter, Routledge (2008).

—*Gay American History: Lesbians and Gay Men in the U.S.A: A Documentary History*, by Jonathan Ned Katz, Meridian Books (1992). Revised edition; first published under name Jonathan Katz and with second subtitle *A Documentary* by Thomas Y. Crowell Co. (1976).

—*The Gay Crusaders*, by Kay Tobin and Randy Wicker, Paperback Library (1972). Reprinted by Arno Press (1975); Kay Tobin was pen name of Kay Tobin Lahusen.

—*Gay Is Good: The Life and Letters of Gay Rights Pioneer Franklin Kameny*, by Michael G. Long, Syracuse University Press (2014).

—*Gay, Lesbian, Bisexual, and Transgender Events, 1848–2006*, by editorial board including Lillian Faderman, Salem Press (2007). Two volumes.

—*The Gay Militants: How Gay Liberation Began in America, 1969–1971*, by Donn Teal, St. Martin's Press (1971).

—*Gay Press, Gay Power: The Growth of LGBT Community Newspapers in America*, by Tracy Baim (editor), Prairie Avenue Books (2012).

—*The Gay Report: Lesbians and Gay Men Speak Out About Sexual Experiences and Lifestyles*, by

Karla Jay and Allen Young, Summit Books (1979).

—*The Gay Revolution: The Story of the Struggle*, by Lillian Faderman, Simon & Schuster (2015).

—*Hidden From History: Reclaiming the Gay and Lesbian Past*, by Martin Duberman, Martha Vicinus and George Chauncey Jr. (editors), Meridian Books (1990). First published by New American Library (1989).

—*Historic Speeches and Rhetoric for Gay and Lesbian Rights (1892–2000)*, edited by Robert B. Ridinger, Routledge (2004).

—*Homosexuality and American Psychiatry: The Politics of Diagnosis*, by Ronald Bayer, Basic Books (1981).

—*The Homosexual in America: A Subjective Approach*, by Donald Webster Cory, Greenberg (1951).

—*Homosexuality: A History*, by Vern L. Bullough, New American Library (1979).

—*Homosexuality: A Research Guide*, by Wayne Dynes, Garland Publishing (1987).

—*Jack Nichols, Gay Pioneer: "Have You Heard My Message?"* by J. Louis Campbell III, Harrington Park Press (2007).

—*The Lavender Scare: The Cold War Persecution of Gays and Lesbians in the Federal Government*, by David K. Johnson, University of Chicago Press (2004).

—*Leading the Parade: Conversations with America's Most Influential Lesbians and Gay Men*, by Paul D. Cain, foreword by Jack Nichols, Scarecrow Press (paperback, 2007). First published 2002.

—*Lesbian/Woman*, by Del Martin and Phyllis Lyon, Volcano Press (1991). First published by Glide Publications and by Bantam Books (1972).

—*Making Gay History: The Half-Century Fight for Lesbian and Gay Equal Rights*, by Eric Marcus, Harper Perennial (2002). Revised paperback edition; first published as *Making History: The Struggle for Gay and Lesbian Equal Rights, 1945–1990: An Oral History*, HarperCollins (1992).

—*Odd Girls and Twilight Lovers: A History of Lesbian Life in Twentieth-Century America*, by Lillian Faderman, Penguin (paperback, 1992). First published by Columbia University Press (1991) and republished (2011).

—*On Being Different: What It Means to Be a Homosexual*, by Merle Miller, Random House (1971). Republished by Penguin (2012), with foreword by Dan Savage, afterword by Charles Kaiser, and fragments of a foreword by Franklin E. Kameny; originally published in *The New York Times Magazine* (January 17, 1971).

—*Out for Good: The Struggle to Build a Gay Rights Movement in America*, by Dudley Clendinen and Adam Nagourney, Simon & Schuster (paperback, 2001). First published 1999.

—*Out in All Directions: A Treasury of Gay and Lesbian America*, by Lynn Witt, Sherry Thomas and Eric Marcus (editors), Warner Books (paperback, 1997). First published, with subtitle *The Almanac of Gay and Lesbian America* and with Don Romesburg as assistant editor, 1995.

—*Out of the Closets: The Sociology of Homosexual Liberation*, by Laud Humphreys, Prentice-Hall (1972).

—*Out of the Closets: Voices of Gay Liberation*, by Karla Jay and Allen Young, Douglas Book Corp. (1972). Lists just more than a dozen publications. A 20th-anniversary edition with foreword by John D'Emilio was published in 1992 by New York University Press.

—*Out of the Past: Gay and Lesbian History From 1869 to the Present*, by Neil Miller, Alyson Publications (2006). Revised edition; first published by Vintage Books (1995).

—*The Politics of Homosexuality: How Lesbians and Gay Men Have Made Themselves a Political and Social Force in Modern America*, by Toby Marotta, Houghton Mifflin (1981).

—*Profiles in Gay & Lesbian Courage*, by the Reverend Troy Perry and Thomas L.P. Swicegood, St. Martin's Press (1991, paperback 1992).

—*Queer America: A GLBT History of the 20th Century*, by Vicki L. Eaklor, Greenwood Publishing Group (2008).

—*A Queer Capital: A History of Gay Life in Washington, D.C.*, by Genny Beemyn, Routledge (2014).

—*A Queer History of the United States*, by Michael Bronski, Beacon Press (paperback, 2012).

Originally published 2011.
— *Queers in Court: Gay Rights Law and Public Policy*, by Susan Gluck Mezey, Rowman & Littlefield (2007).
—*Queers in History: The Comprehensive Encyclopedia of Historical Gays, Lesbians, Bisexuals, and Transgenders*, by Keith Stern, BenBella Books (2009). Previously published with subtitle *Hundreds of Prominent People Who Were Gay, Lesbian, Bisexual, or Transgender*, Quistory Publishers (2007).
— *Rethinking the Gay and Lesbian Movement*, by Marc Stein, Routledge (2012).
—*The Same Sex: An Appraisal of Homosexuality*, edited by Ralph Weltge, United Church Press (1969).
—*Sappho was a Right-On Woman*, by Sidney Abbott, Stein & Day (1972).
—*Sex Variant Woman: The Life of Jeannette Howard Foster*, by Joanne Passet, Da Capo Press (2008).
—*Sexual Politics, Sexual Communities: The Making of a Homosexual Minority in the United States, 1940–1970*, by John D'Emilio, University of Chicago Press (1998). Second edition; first published in 1983.
—*Surpassing the Love of Men: Romantic Friendship and Love Between Women from the Renaissance to the Present*, by Lillian Faderman, William Morrow (1981).
— *To Believe in Women: What Lesbians Have Done for America—a History*, by Lillian Faderman, Houghton Mifflin (1999).
—*A Way of Love, a Way of Life: A Young Person's Introduction to What It Means to Be Gay*, by Frances Hanckel and John Cunningham, Lothrop, Lee & Shepard Books (1979).
—*We're Here, We're Queer*, by Owen Keehnen, Prairie Avenue Productions (2011).

Articles and Pamphlets
—"Can Young Gays Find Happiness in YA Books?" by Frances Hanckel and John Cunningham, *Wilson Library Bulletin*, Vol. 50, No. 7 (March 1976).
—"Gay Rights Pioneer Gittings Dies," by Tracy Baim, *Windy City Times* (February 21, 2007).
—"Gay Liberation: From Task Force to Round Table," by Leonard Kniffel, *American Libraries* (December 1999).
—"Gays in Library Land: The Gay and Lesbian Task Force of the American Library Association: The First Sixteen Years," by Barbara Gittings (1990).
—"Homophobia in Encyclopedias," by Dale C. Burke, *Interracial Books for Children Bulletin*, Vol. 14, Nos. 3 and 4 (1983).
—"John E. Fryer, MD, and the Dr. H. Anonymous Episode," by David Scasta, *Journal of Gay & Lesbian Psychotherapy* (2003).
—"LGBT History Month: Kay Lahusen—The Woman Behind the Lens," by Jen Colletta, *Philadelphia Gay News* (October 4, 2012).
—"Philadelphia Marks 40th Anniversary of Protests," by Tracy Baim, *Windy City Times* (May 4, 2005).
—"Sex and the Single Cataloger," in *Revolting Librarians,* edited by Celeste West, Elizabeth Katz, *et al.* (Booklegger Press, 1972).
—"They Sparked a Movement—Together," by Kevin Riordan, in *Visions Today* (Wilmington, Delaware, LGBT magazine) (Fall 2001).

Website resource
   The website www.OutHistory.org provides an extensive collection of articles and interviews, including Marc Stein's interviews with Barbara Gittings and Kay Lahusen, and with people who interacted with them in activism and movement politics.
   Also see http://www.glbtq.com.

Index

21979103R00133

Made in the USA
San Bernardino, CA
16 June 2015